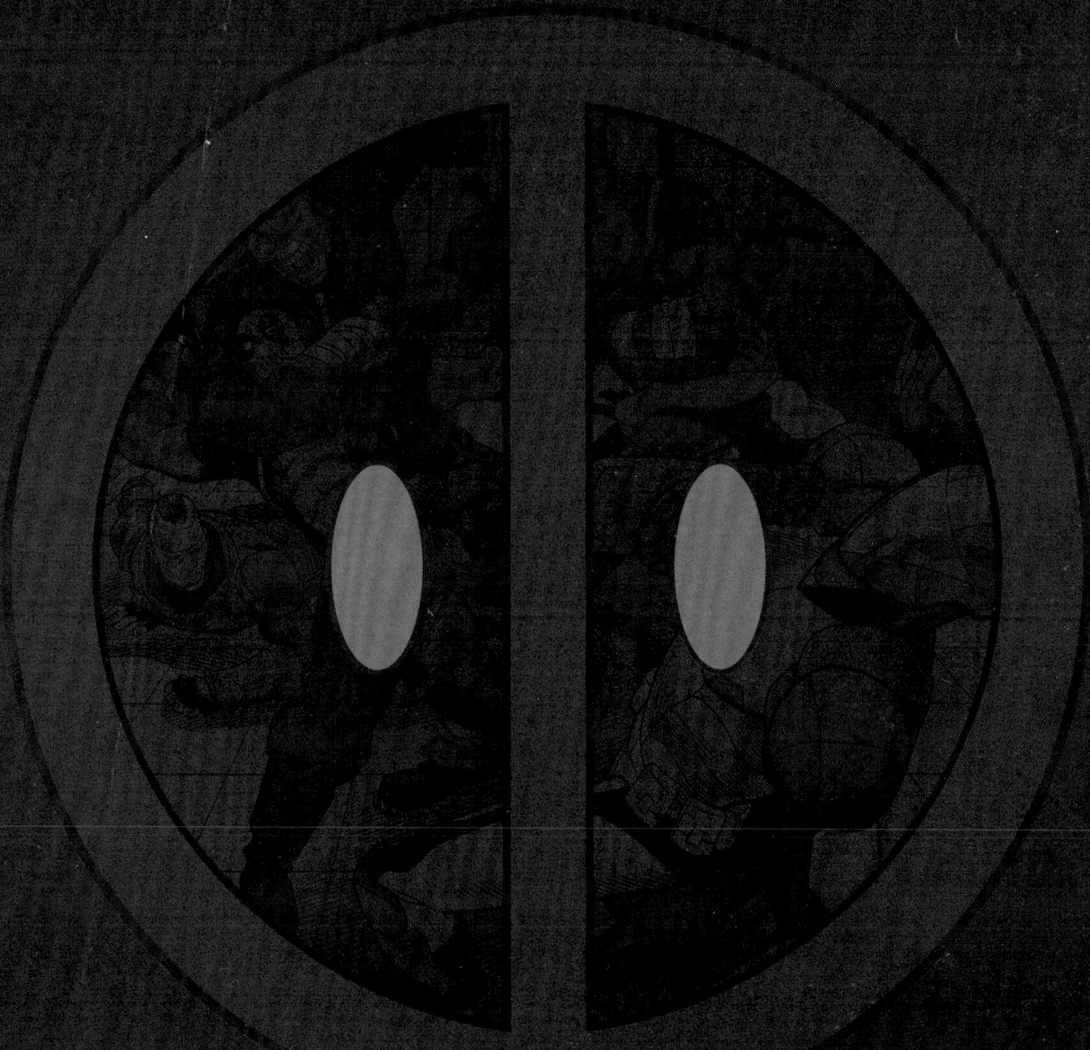

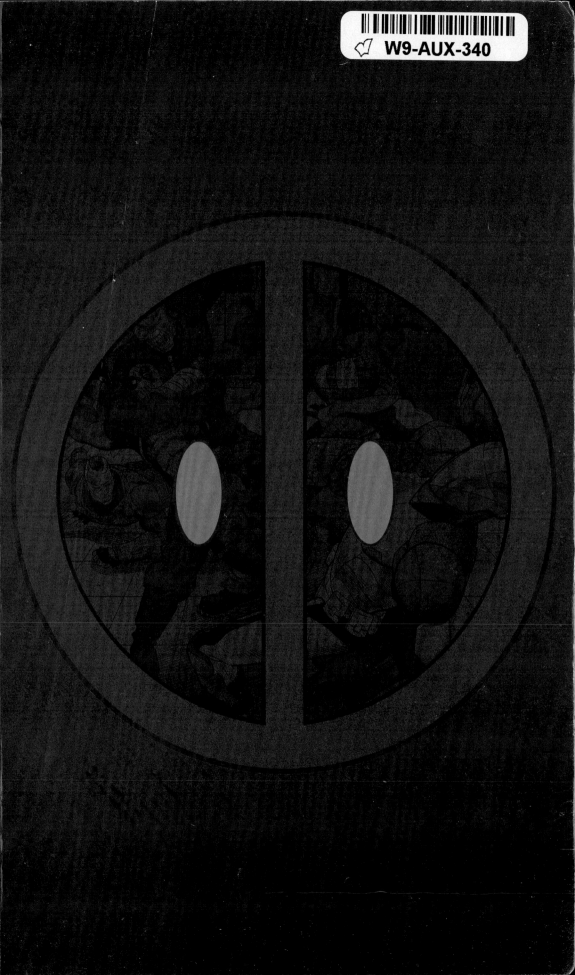

THE WORLD'S GREATEST COMIC MAGAZINE!

DEADPOOL

CIVIL WAR II

GERRY DUGGAN
writer

ISSUES #14-18

MIKE HAWTHORNE
WITH **BRIAN LEVEL** [#18]
pencilers

TERRY PALLOT
inker

JORDIE BELLAIRE WITH **RACHELLE ROSENBERG** [#18]
colorists

RAFAEL ALBUQUERQUE & DAVE McCAIG
cover art

ISSUE #19

SCOTT KOBLISH
artist

NICK FILARDI
color artist

**SCOTT KOBLISH &
NICK FILARDI**
cover art

VC's JOE SABINO   HEATHER ANTOS   JORDAN D. WHITE

Avenger...assassin...superstar...smelly person... possibly the world's most skilled mercenary, definitely the world's most annoying, **WADE WILSON** was chosen for a top-secret government program that gave him a healing factor allowing him to heal from any wound. Somehow, despite making his money as a gun for hire, Wade has become one of the most beloved "heroes" in the world.

Recently, Wade has put together a team called **"The Mercs for Money,"** ostensibly to take mercenary jobs for...money. Unfortunately, with Wade more and more concerned with his Avengers team, the money has not been too forthcoming for the mercs. And, oh my gosh, I am having a vision of the future... This might be a problem.

DEADPOOL created by ROB LIEFELD & FABIAN NICIEZA

collection editor JENNIFER GRÜNWALD
associate managing editor KATERI WOODY
associate editor SARAH BRUNSTAD
editor, special projects MARK D. BEAZLEY
vp production & special projects JEFF YOUNGQUIST
svp print, sales & marketing DAVID GABRIEL
book designer ADAM DEL RE

editor in chief AXEL ALONSO
chief creative officer JOE QUESADA
publisher DAN BUCKLEY
executive producer ALAN FINE

DEADPOOL: WORLD'S GREATEST VOL. 6 - CIVIL WAR II. Contains material originally published in magazine form as DEADPOOL #14-19. First printing 2016. ISBN# 978-1-302-90148-6. Published by MARVEL WORLDWIDE, INC., a subsidiary of MARVEL ENTERTAINMENT, LLC. OFFICE OF PUBLICATION: 135 West 50th Street, New York, NY 10020. Copyright © 2016 MARVEL. No similarity between any of the names, characters, persons, and/or institutions in this magazine with those of any living or dead person or institution is intended, and any such similarity which may exist is purely coincidental. **Printed in Canada.** ALAN FINE, President, Marvel Entertainment; DAN BUCKLEY, President, TV, Publishing & Brand Management; JOE QUESADA, Chief Creative Officer; TOM BREVOORT, SVP of Publishing; DAVID BOGART, SVP of Business Affairs & Operations, Publishing & Partnership; C.B. CEBULSKI, VP of Brand Management & Development, Asia; DAVID GABRIEL, SVP of Sales & Marketing, Publishing; JEFF YOUNGQUIST, VP of Production & Special Projects; DAN CARR, Executive Director of Publishing Technology; ALEX MORALES, Director of Publishing Operations; SUSAN CRESPI, Production Manager; STAN LEE, Chairman Emeritus. For information regarding advertising in Marvel Comics or on Marvel.com, please contact Vit DeBellis, Integrated Sales Manager, at vdebellis@marvel.com. For Marvel subscription inquiries, please call 888-511-5480. **Manufactured between 10/28/2016 and 12/5/2016 by SOLISCO PRINTERS, SCOTT, QC, CANADA.**

10 9 8 7 6 5 4 3 2 1

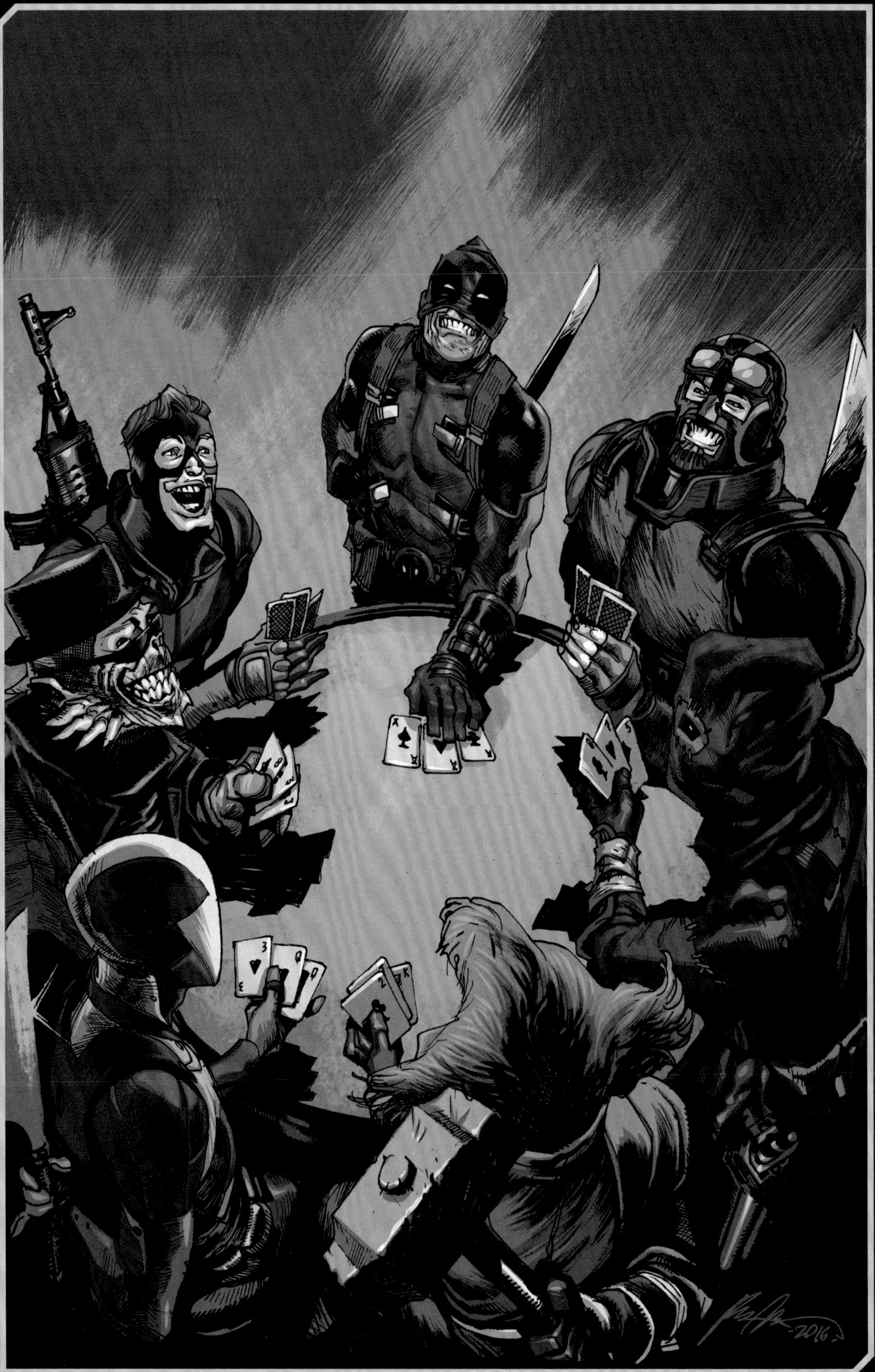

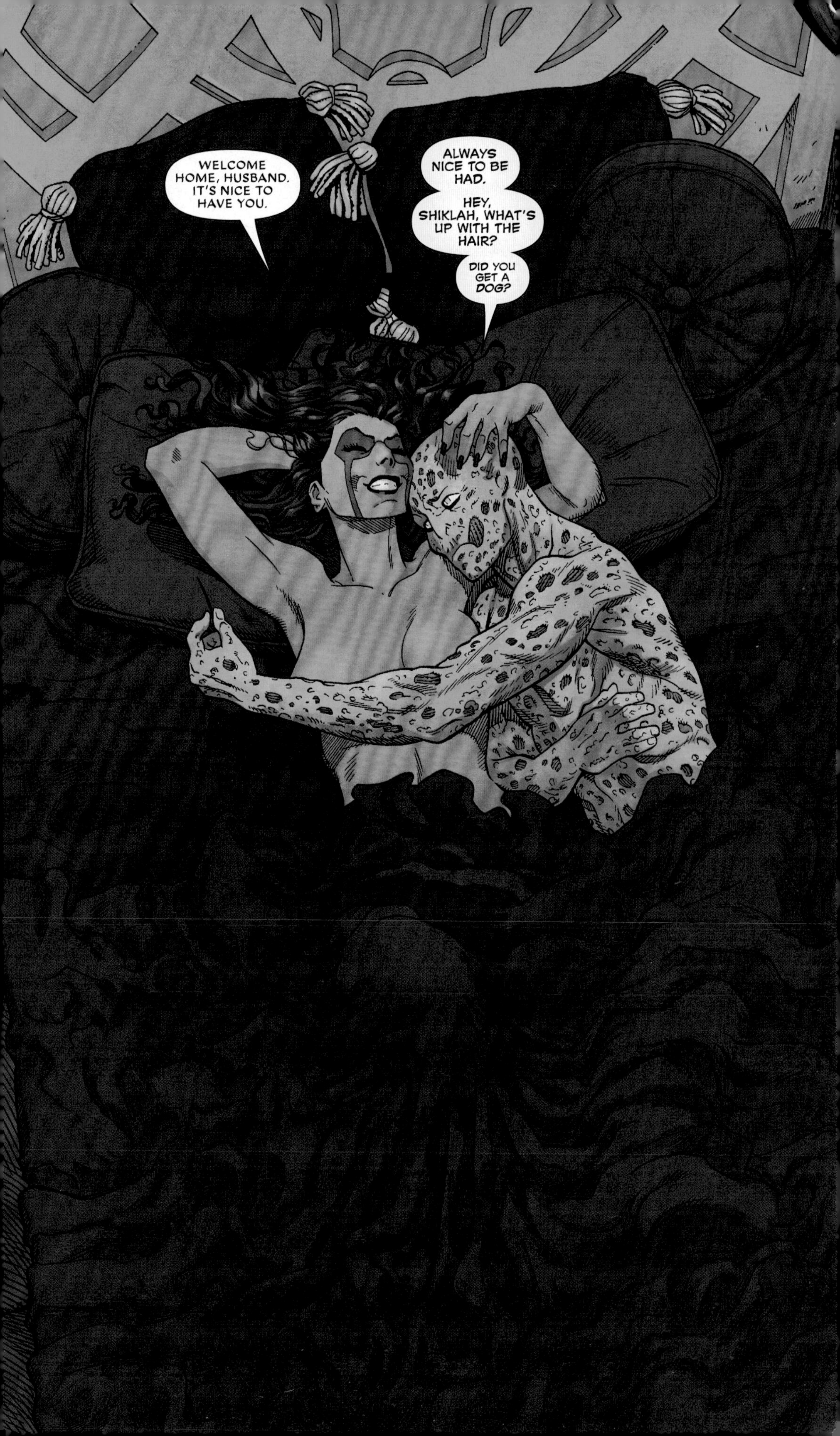
WELCOME HOME, HUSBAND. IT'S NICE TO HAVE YOU.
ALWAYS NICE TO BE HAD.
HEY, SHIKLAH, WHAT'S UP WITH THE HAIR?
DID YOU GET A *DOG?*

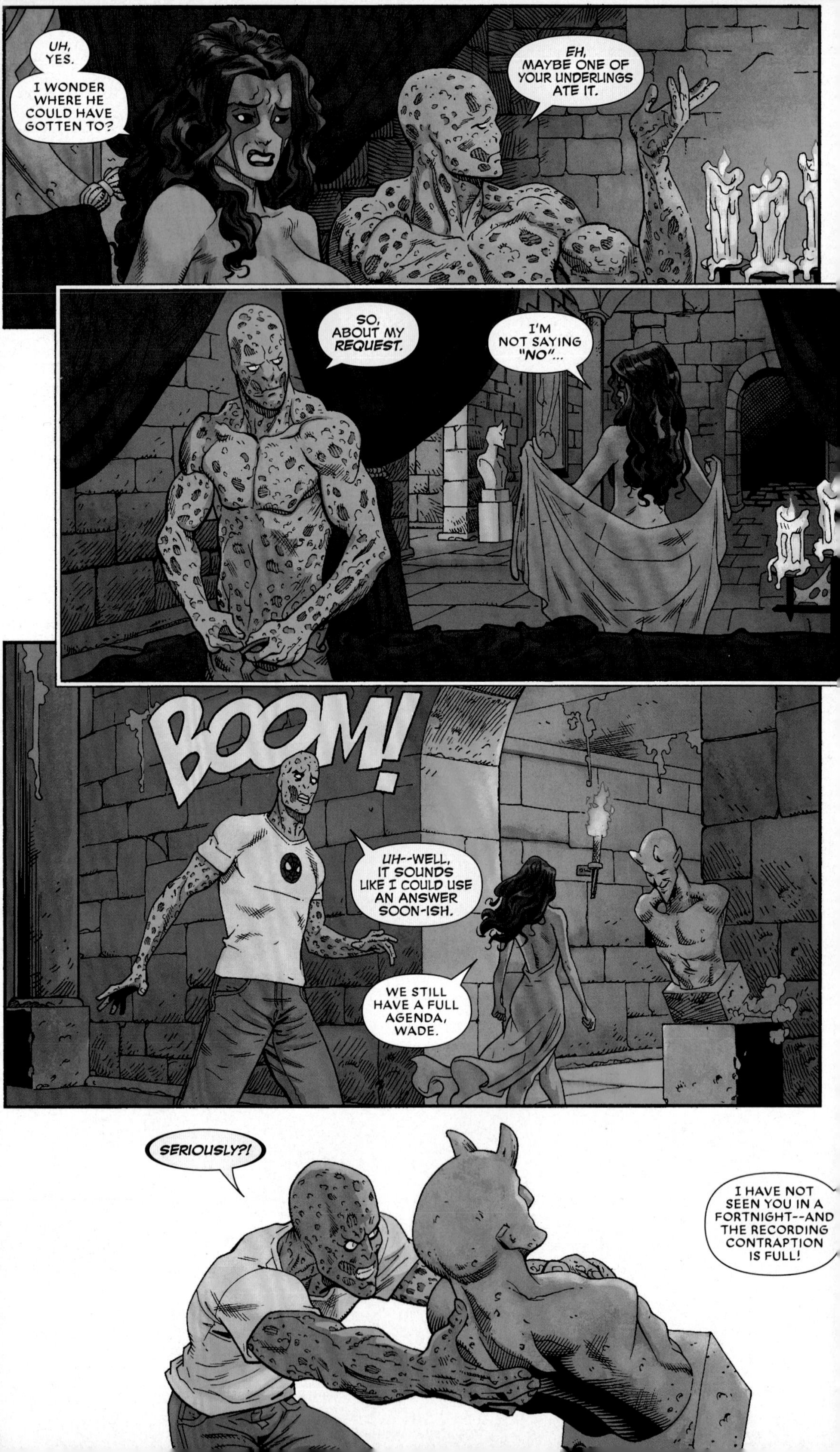
UH, YES.
I WONDER WHERE HE COULD HAVE GOTTEN TO?
EH, MAYBE ONE OF YOUR UNDERLINGS ATE IT.
SO, ABOUT MY REQUEST.
I'M NOT SAYING "NO"...
BOOM!
UH--WELL, IT SOUNDS LIKE I COULD USE AN ANSWER SOON-ISH.
WE STILL HAVE A FULL AGENDA, WADE.
SERIOUSLY?!
I HAVE NOT SEEN YOU IN A FORTNIGHT--AND THE RECORDING CONTRAPTION IS FULL!

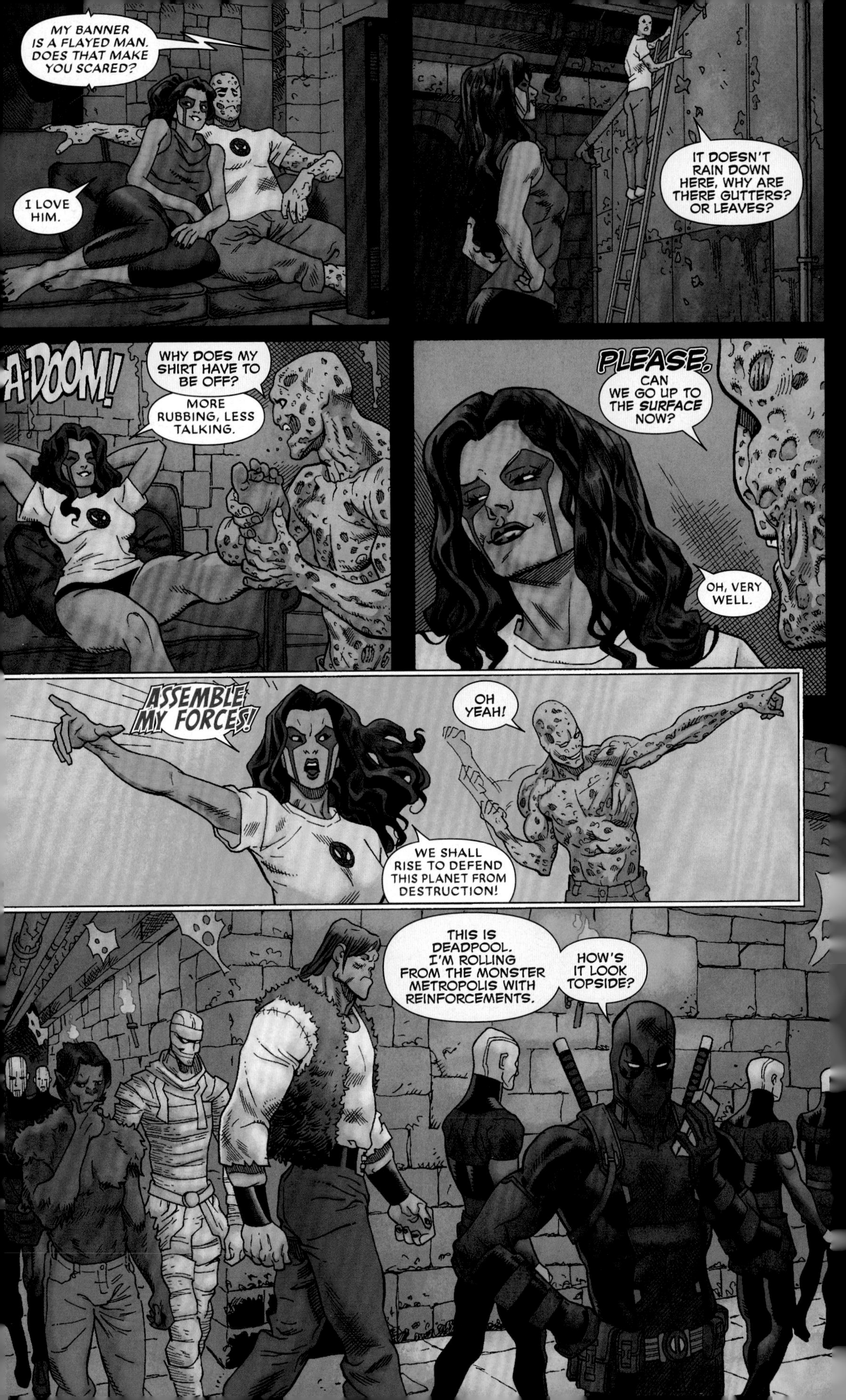

MY BANNER IS A FLAYED MAN. DOES THAT MAKE YOU SCARED?
I LOVE HIM.
IT DOESN'T RAIN DOWN HERE, WHY ARE THERE GUTTERS? OR LEAVES?
A-DOOM!
WHY DOES MY SHIRT HAVE TO BE OFF?
MORE RUBBING, LESS TALKING.
PLEASE. CAN WE GO UP TO THE SURFACE NOW?
OH, VERY WELL.
ASSEMBLE MY FORCES!
OH YEAH!
WE SHALL RISE TO DEFEND THIS PLANET FROM DESTRUCTION!
THIS IS DEADPOOL. I'M ROLLING FROM THE MONSTER METROPOLIS WITH REINFORCEMENTS.
HOW'S IT LOOK TOPSIDE?

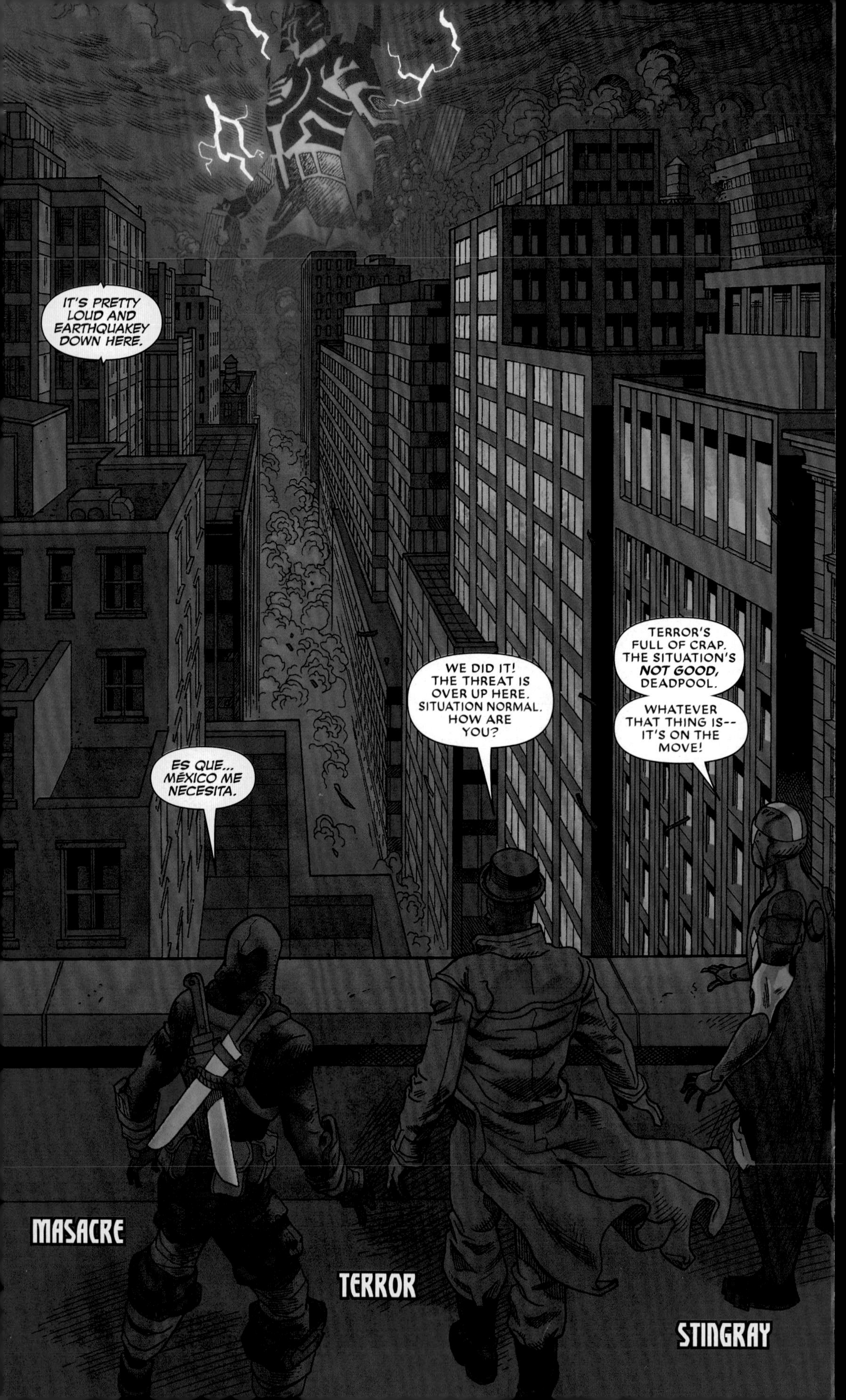
IT'S PRETTY LOUD AND EARTHQUAKEY DOWN HERE.
ES QUE... MÉXICO ME NECESITA.
WE DID IT! THE THREAT IS OVER UP HERE. SITUATION NORMAL. HOW ARE YOU?
TERROR'S FULL OF CRAP. THE SITUATION'S NOT GOOD, DEADPOOL.
WHATEVER THAT THING IS-- IT'S ON THE MOVE!
MASACRE
TERROR
STINGRAY

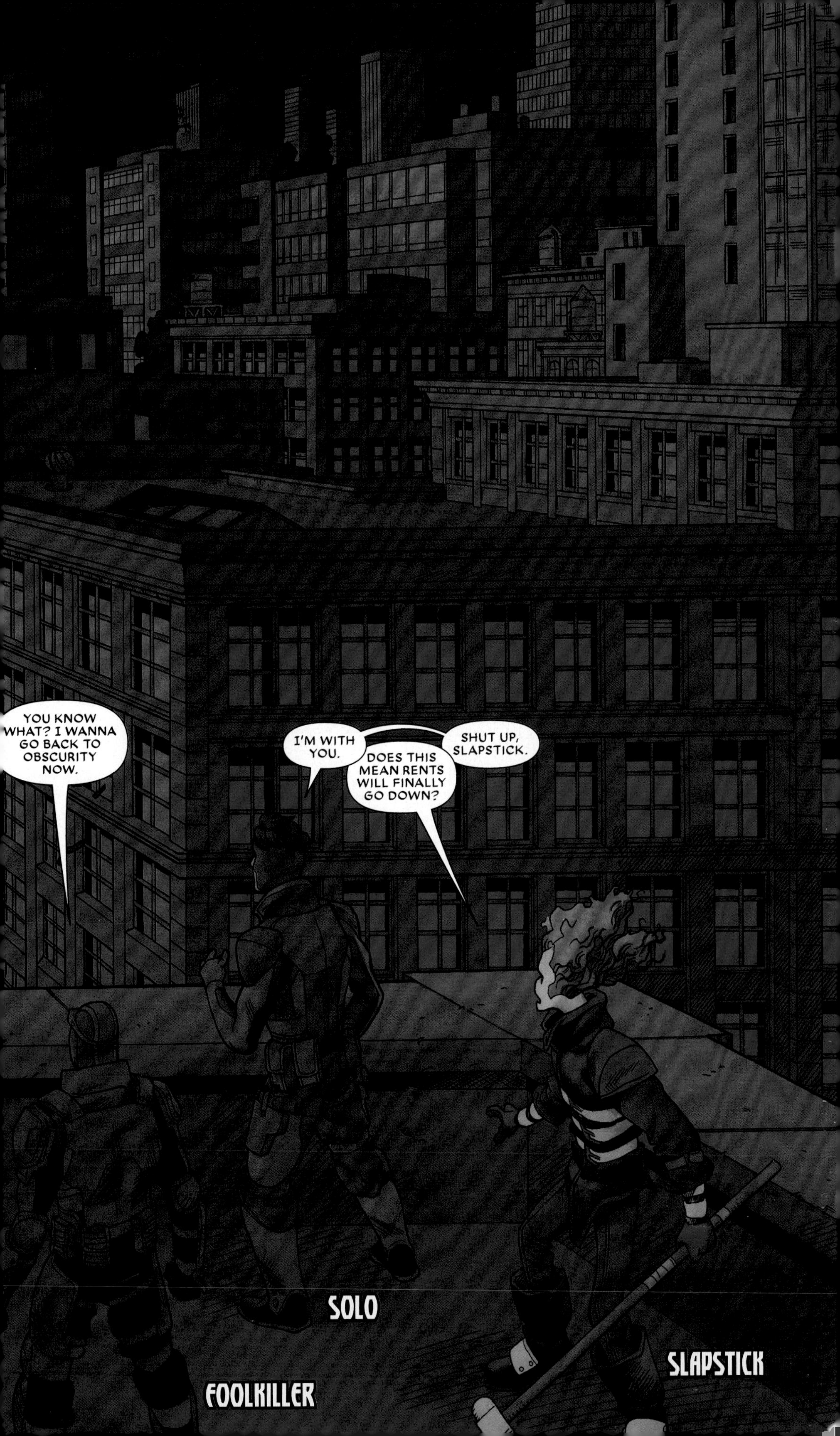
YOU KNOW WHAT? I WANNA GO BACK TO OBSCURITY NOW.
I'M WITH YOU.
SHUT UP, SLAPSTICK.
DOES THIS MEAN RENTS WILL FINALLY GO DOWN?
SOLO
FOOLKILLER
SLAPSTICK

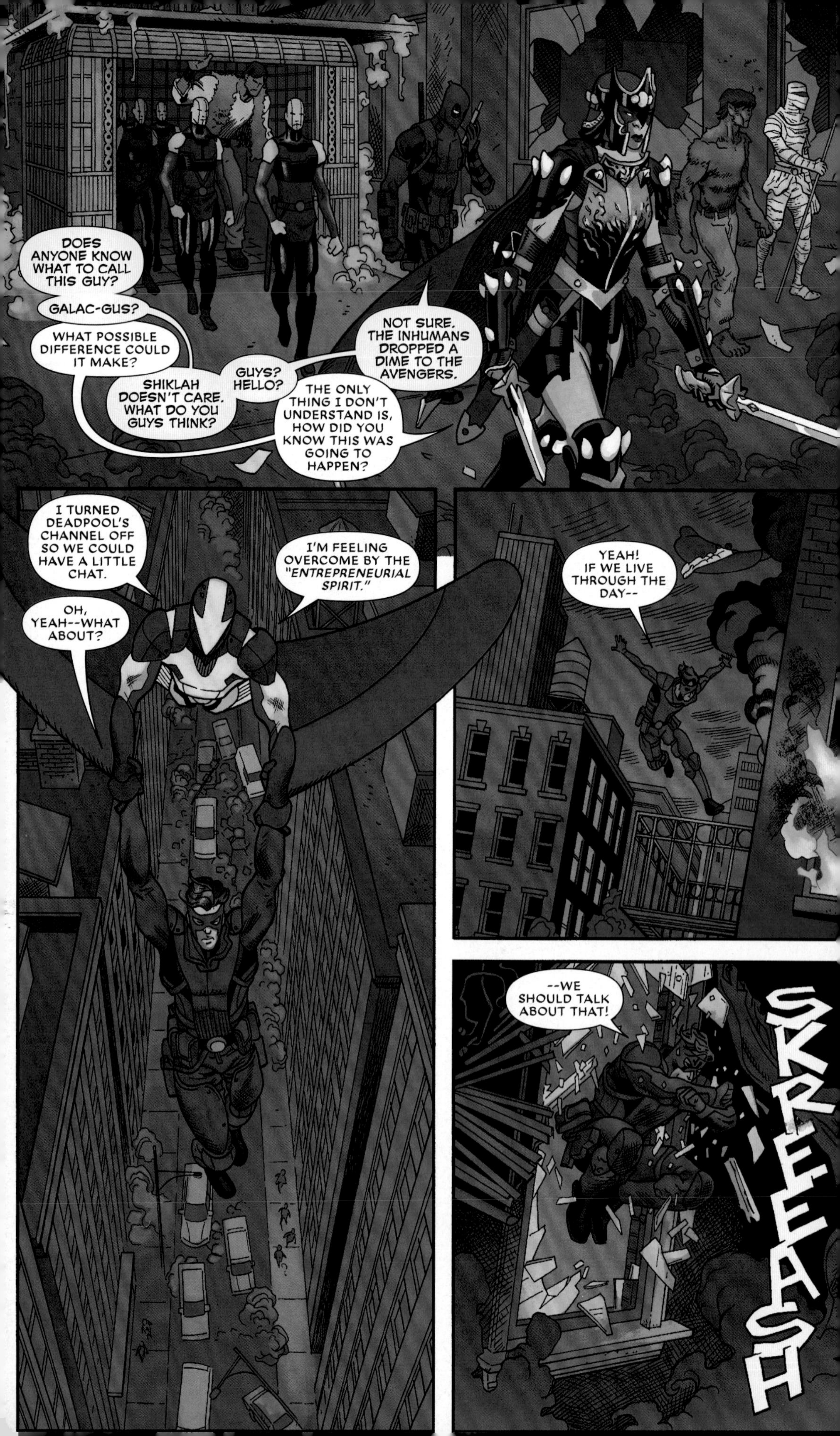
DOES ANYONE KNOW WHAT TO CALL THIS GUY?
GALAC-GUS?
WHAT POSSIBLE DIFFERENCE COULD IT MAKE?
SHIKLAH DOESN'T CARE. WHAT DO YOU GUYS THINK?
GUYS? HELLO?
NOT SURE. THE INHUMANS DROPPED A DIME TO THE AVENGERS.
THE ONLY THING I DON'T UNDERSTAND IS, HOW DID YOU KNOW THIS WAS GOING TO HAPPEN?
I TURNED DEADPOOL'S CHANNEL OFF SO WE COULD HAVE A LITTLE CHAT.
OH, YEAH--WHAT ABOUT?
I'M FEELING OVERCOME BY THE *"ENTREPRENEURIAL SPIRIT."*
YEAH! IF WE LIVE THROUGH THE DAY--
--WE SHOULD TALK ABOUT THAT!
SKREEEASH

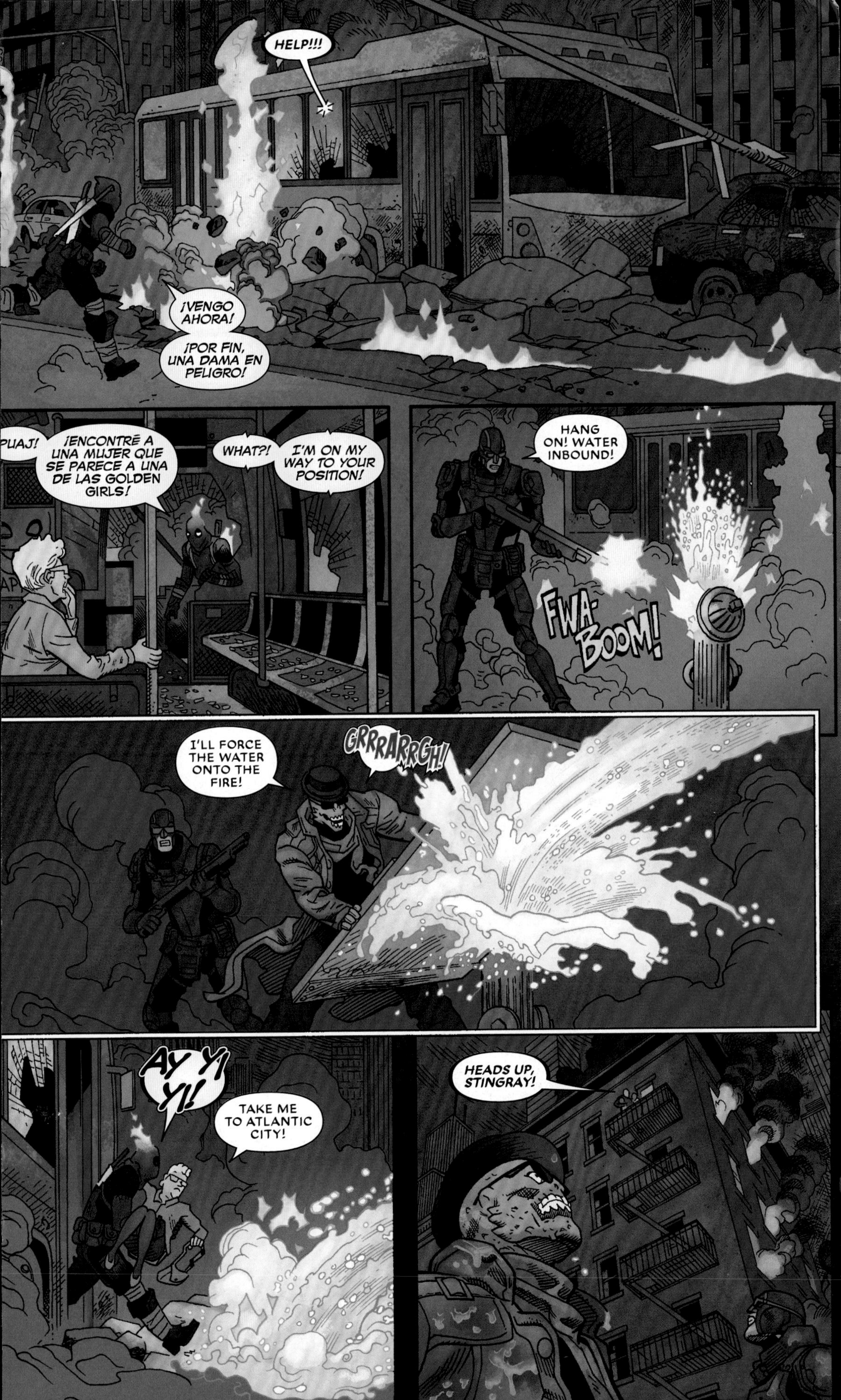
HELP!!!
¡VENGO AHORA!
¡POR FIN, UNA DAMA EN PELIGRO!
PUAJ!
¡ENCONTRÉ A UNA MUJER QUE SE PARECE A UNA DE LAS GOLDEN GIRLS!
WHAT?!
I'M ON MY WAY TO YOUR POSITION!
HANG ON! WATER INBOUND!
FWA-BOOM!
I'LL FORCE THE WATER ONTO THE FIRE!
GRRRARRGH!
AY YI YI!
TAKE ME TO ATLANTIC CITY!
HEADS UP, STINGRAY!

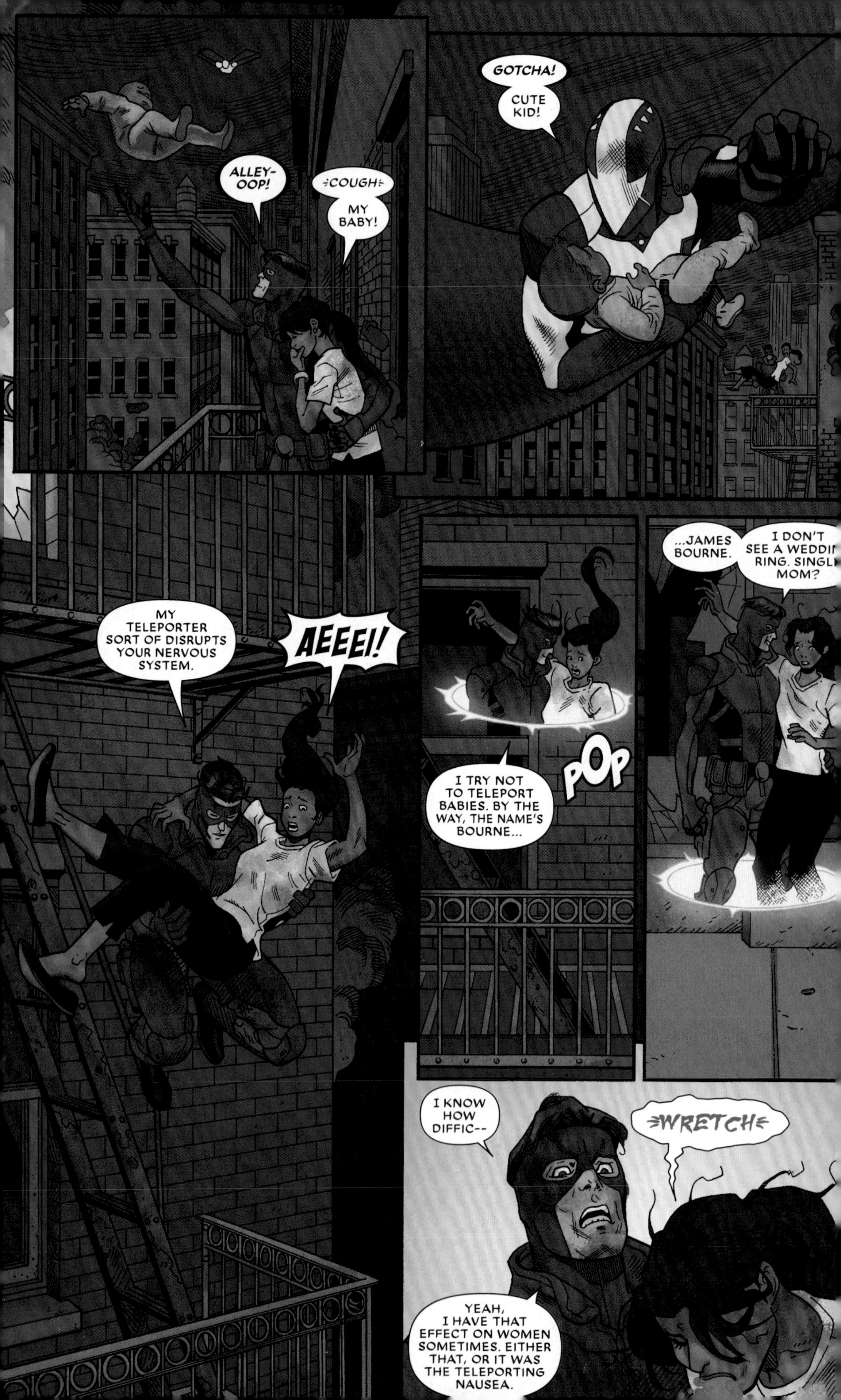

ALLEY-OOP!
COUGH
MY BABY!
GOTCHA!
CUTE KID!
MY TELEPORTER SORT OF DISRUPTS YOUR NERVOUS SYSTEM.
AEEEI!
I TRY NOT TO TELEPORT BABIES. BY THE WAY, THE NAME'S BOURNE...
POP
...JAMES BOURNE.
I DON'T SEE A WEDDI RING. SINGL MOM?
I KNOW HOW DIFFIC--
WRETCH
YEAH, I HAVE THAT EFFECT ON WOMEN SOMETIMES. EITHER THAT, OR IT WAS THE TELEPORTING NAUSEA.

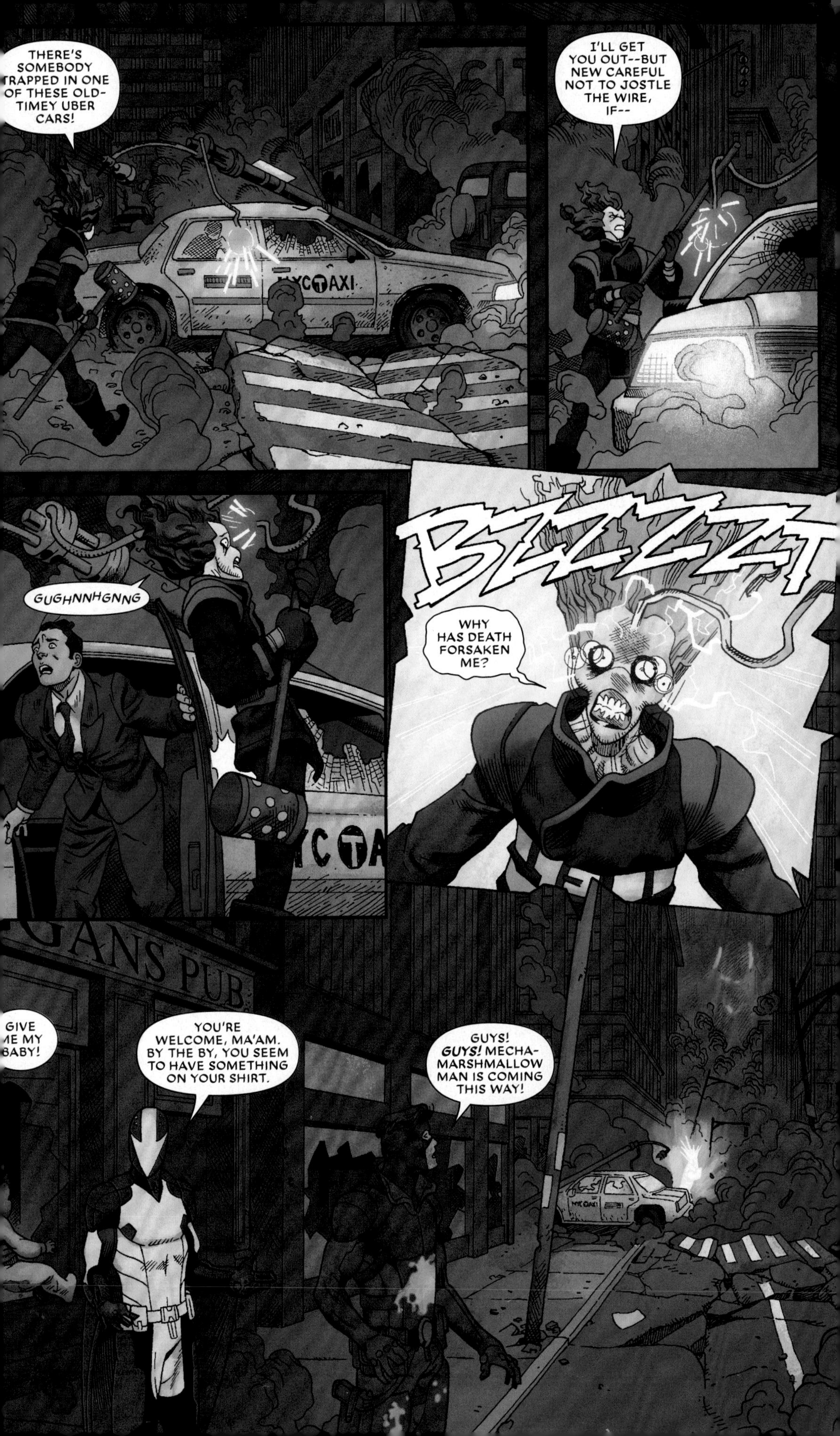

THERE'S SOMEBODY TRAPPED IN ONE OF THESE OLD-TIMEY UBER CARS!
NYC TAXI
I'LL GET YOU OUT--BUT NEW CAREFUL NOT TO JOSTLE THE WIRE, IF--
GUGHNNHGNNG
BZZZZT
WHY HAS DEATH FORSAKEN ME?
NYC TA
GANS PUB
GIVE ME MY BABY!
YOU'RE WELCOME, MA'AM. BY THE BY, YOU SEEM TO HAVE SOMETHING ON YOUR SHIRT.
GUYS! *GUYS!* MECHA-MARSHMALLOW MAN IS COMING THIS WAY!

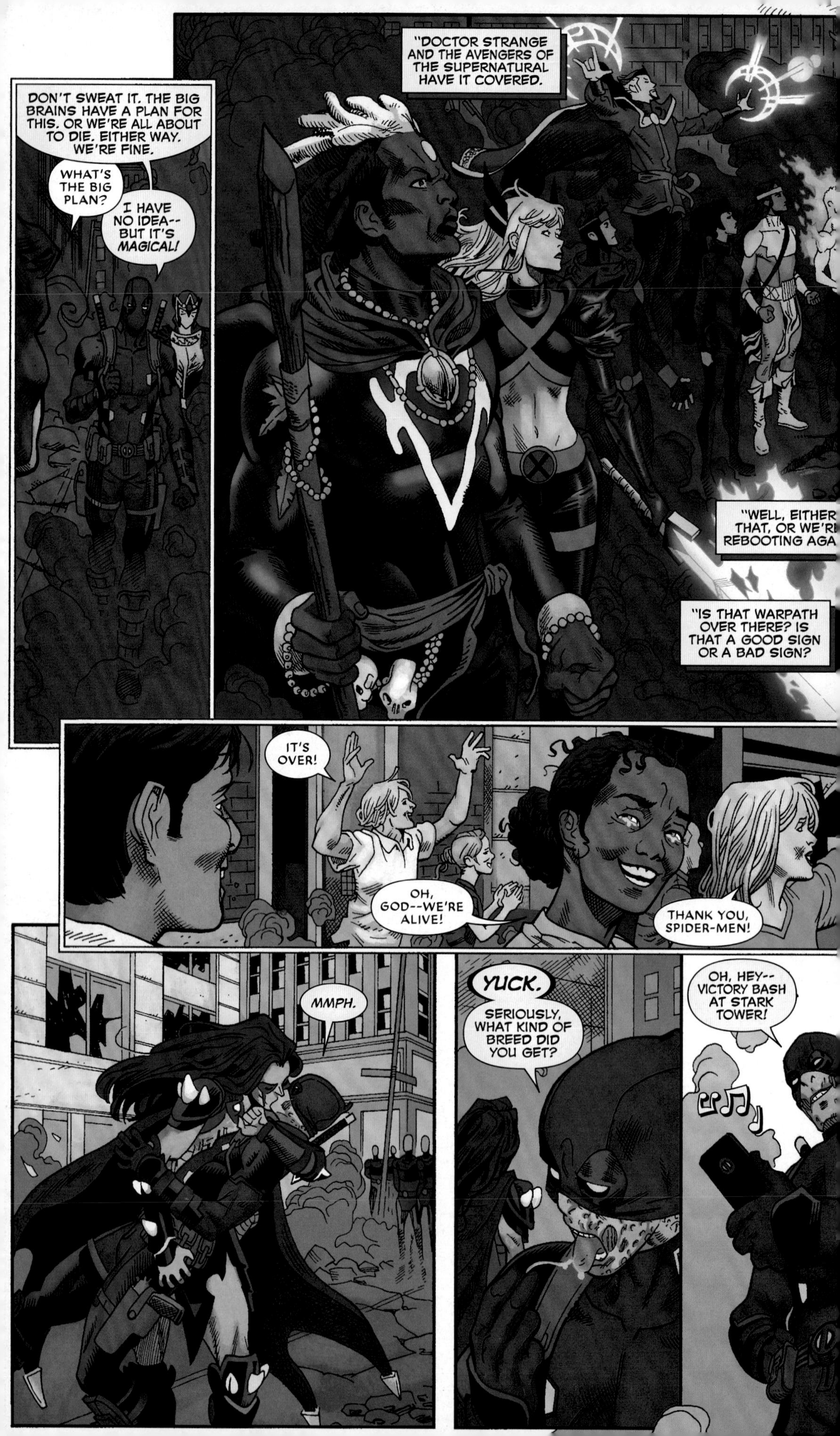
DON'T SWEAT IT. THE BIG BRAINS HAVE A PLAN FOR THIS. OR WE'RE ALL ABOUT TO DIE. EITHER WAY. WE'RE FINE.
WHAT'S THE BIG PLAN?
I HAVE NO IDEA--BUT IT'S *MAGICAL!*
"DOCTOR STRANGE AND THE AVENGERS OF THE SUPERNATURAL HAVE IT COVERED.
"WELL, EITHER THAT, OR WE'R
REBOOTING AGA
"IS THAT WARPATH OVER THERE? IS THAT A GOOD SIGN OR A BAD SIGN?
IT'S OVER!
OH, GOD--WE'RE ALIVE!
THANK YOU, SPIDER-MEN!
MMPH.
YUCK.
SERIOUSLY, WHAT KIND OF BREED DID YOU GET?
OH, HEY--VICTORY BASH AT STARK TOWER!

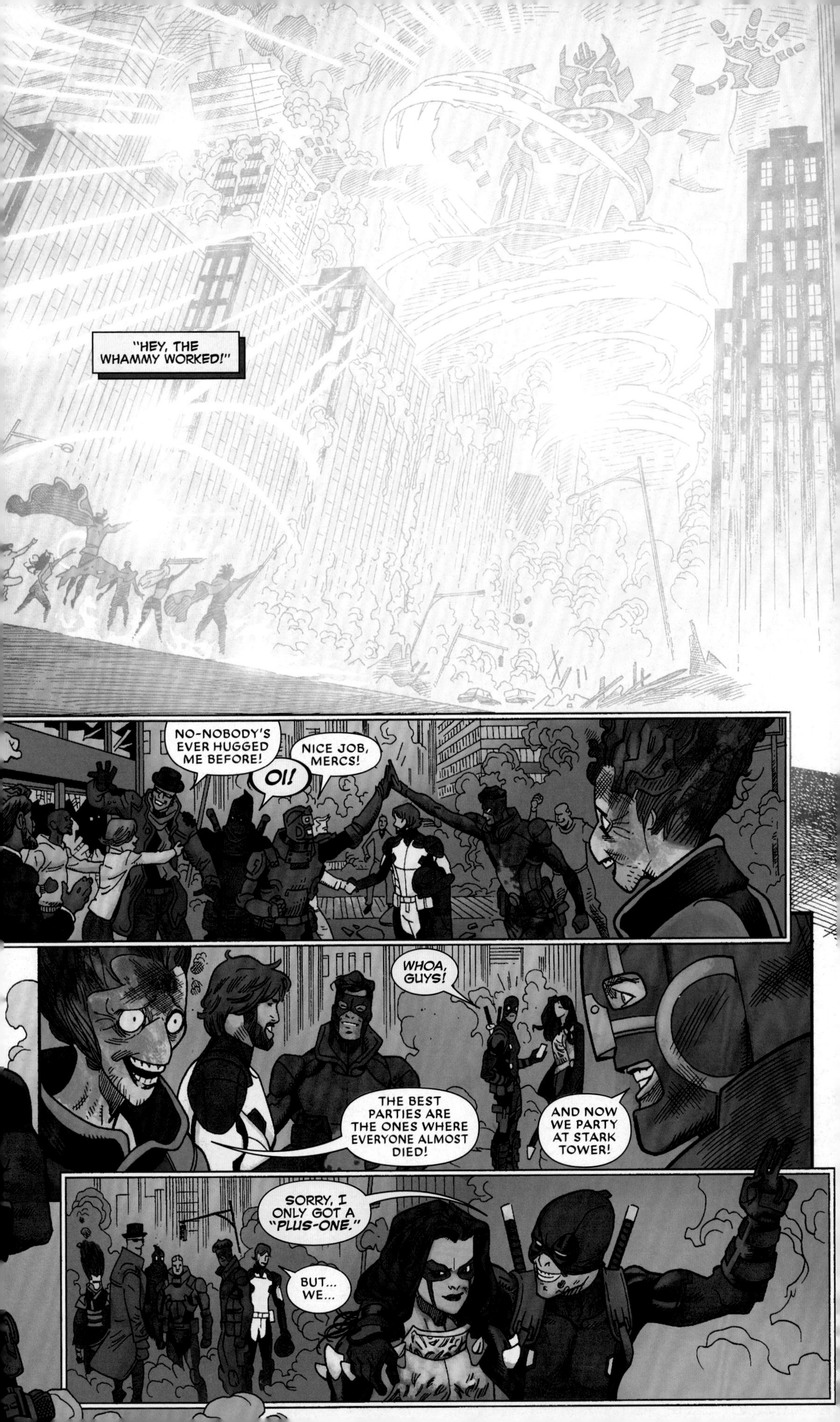
"HEY, THE WHAMMY WORKED!"
NO-NOBODY'S EVER HUGGED ME BEFORE!
OI!
NICE JOB, MERCS!
WHOA, GUYS!
THE BEST PARTIES ARE THE ONES WHERE EVERYONE ALMOST DIED!
AND NOW WE PARTY AT STARK TOWER!
SORRY, I ONLY GOT A "PLUS-ONE."
BUT... WE...

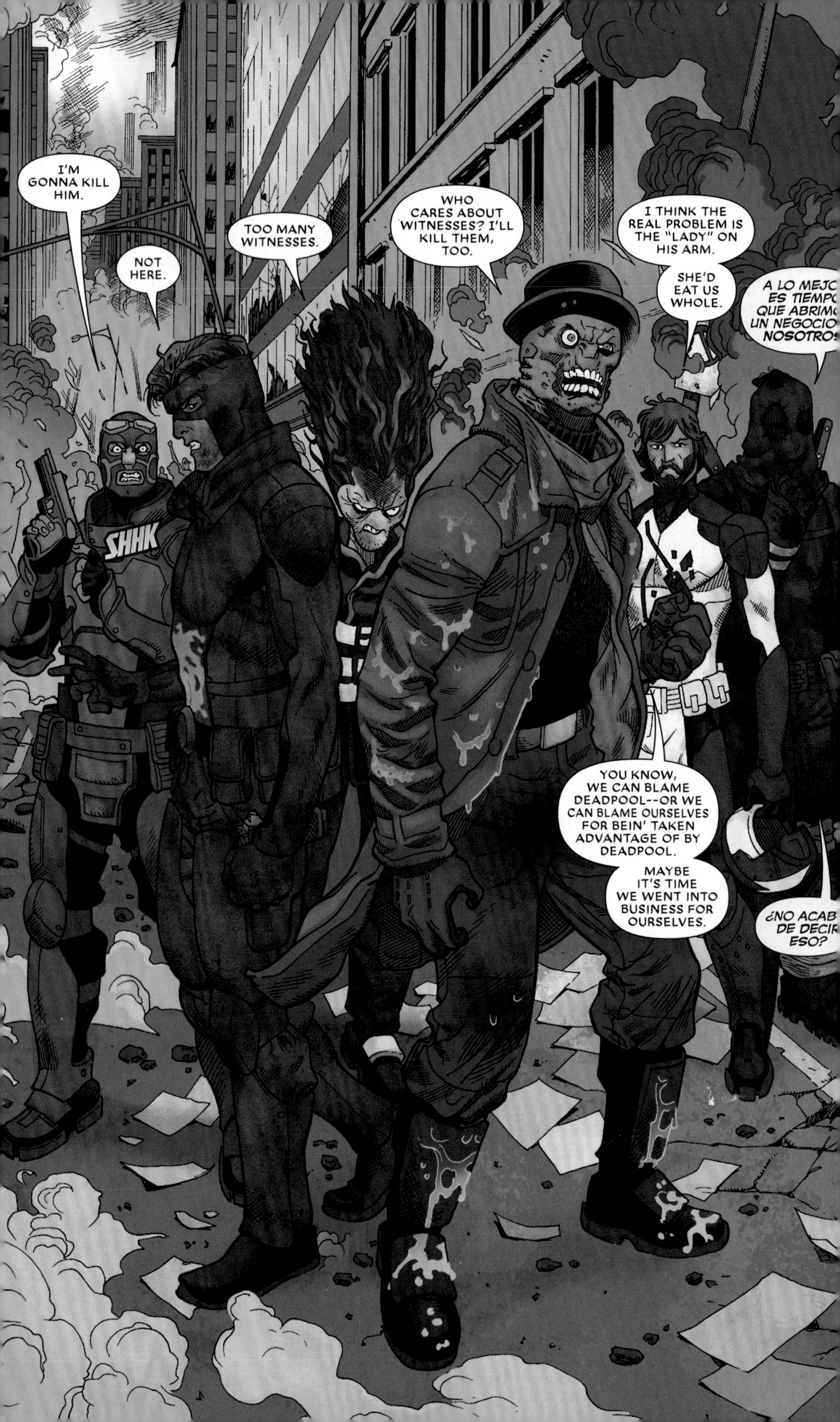
I'M GONNA KILL HIM.
NOT HERE.
TOO MANY WITNESSES.
WHO CARES ABOUT WITNESSES? I'LL KILL THEM, TOO.
I THINK THE REAL PROBLEM IS THE "LADY" ON HIS ARM.
SHE'D EAT US WHOLE.
A LO MEJO ES TIEMPO QUE ABRIMO UN NEGOCIO NOSOTRO
YOU KNOW, WE CAN BLAME DEADPOOL--OR WE CAN BLAME OURSELVES FOR BEIN' TAKEN ADVANTAGE OF BY DEADPOOL.
MAYBE IT'S TIME WE WENT INTO BUSINESS FOR OURSELVES.
¿NO ACAB DE DECIR ESO?

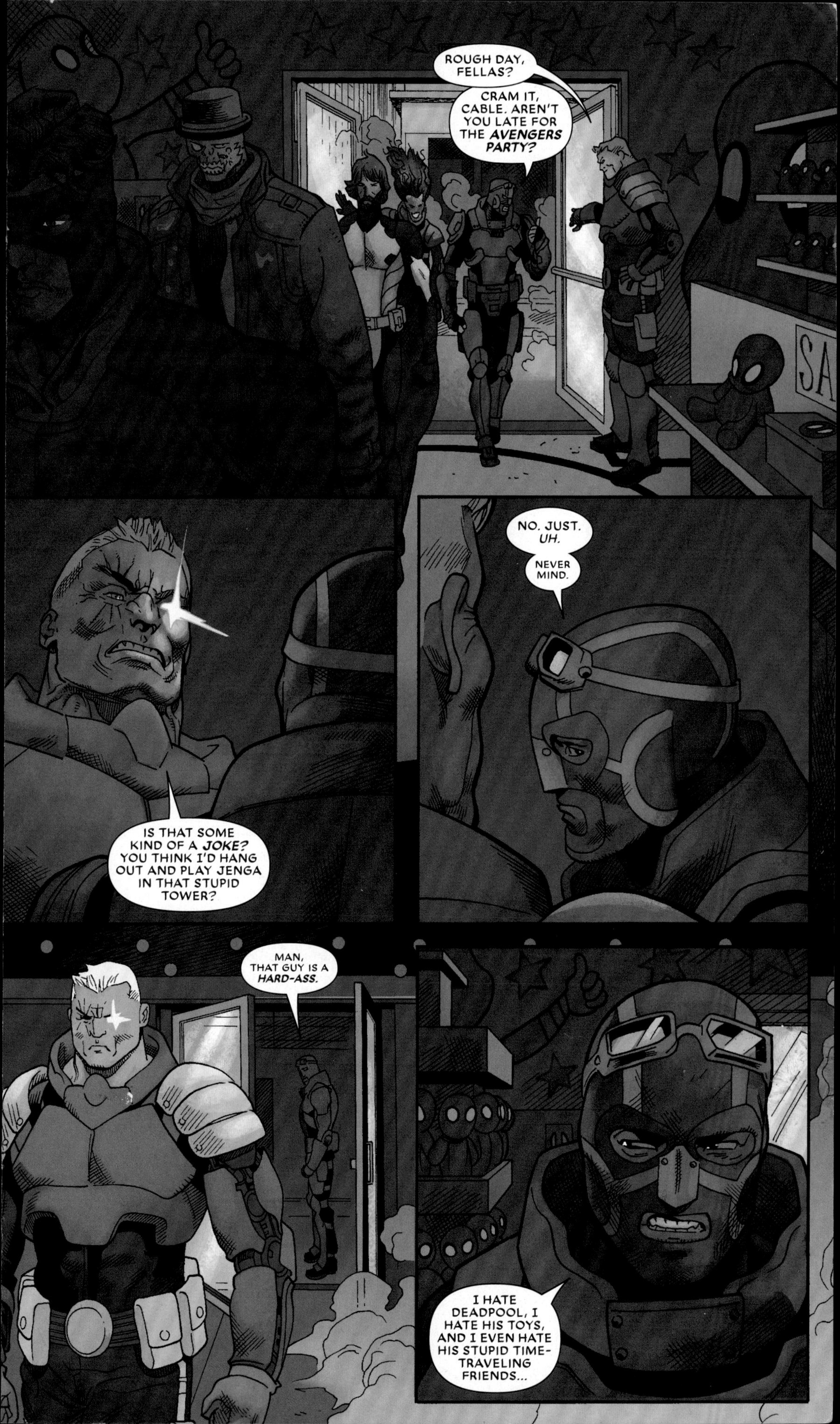
ROUGH DAY, FELLAS?
CRAM IT, CABLE. AREN'T YOU LATE FOR THE *AVENGERS PARTY?*
NO. JUST. *UH.*
NEVER MIND.
IS THAT SOME KIND OF A *JOKE?* YOU THINK I'D HANG OUT AND PLAY JENGA IN THAT STUPID TOWER?
MAN, THAT GUY IS A *HARD-ASS.*
I HATE DEADPOOL, I HATE HIS TOYS, AND I EVEN HATE HIS STUPID TIME-TRAVELING FRIENDS...

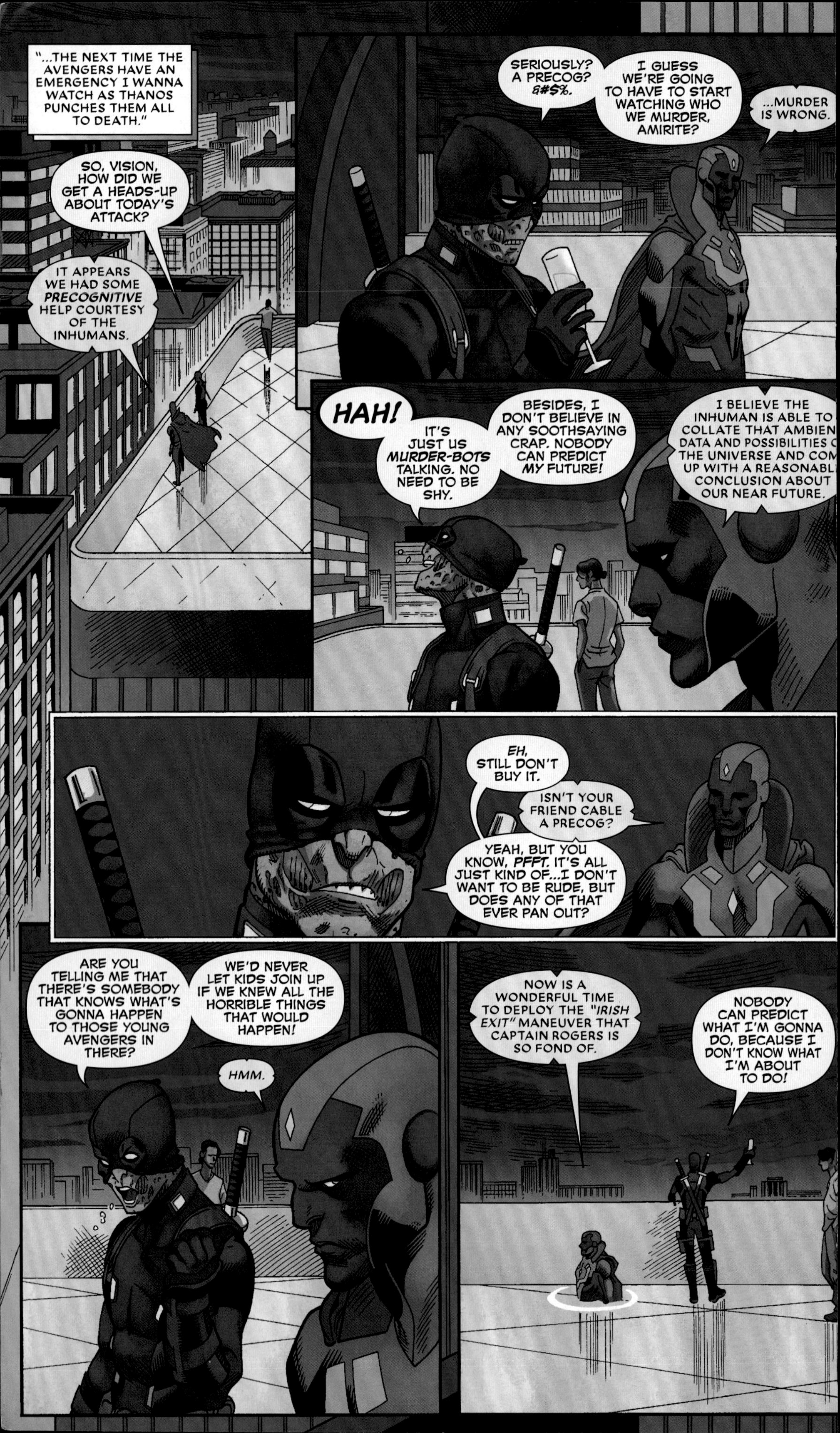
"...THE NEXT TIME THE AVENGERS HAVE AN EMERGENCY I WANNA WATCH AS THANOS PUNCHES THEM ALL TO DEATH."
SO, VISION, HOW DID WE GET A HEADS-UP ABOUT TODAY'S ATTACK?
IT APPEARS WE HAD SOME PRECOGNITIVE HELP COURTESY OF THE INHUMANS.
SERIOUSLY? A PRECOG? &#$%.
I GUESS WE'RE GOING TO HAVE TO START WATCHING WHO WE MURDER, AMIRITE?
...MURDER IS WRONG.
HAH!
IT'S JUST US MURDER-BOTS TALKING. NO NEED TO BE SHY.
BESIDES, I DON'T BELIEVE IN ANY SOOTHSAYING CRAP. NOBODY CAN PREDICT MY FUTURE!
I BELIEVE THE INHUMAN IS ABLE TO COLLATE THAT AMBIEN DATA AND POSSIBILITIES O THE UNIVERSE AND COM UP WITH A REASONABL CONCLUSION ABOUT OUR NEAR FUTURE.
EH, STILL DON'T BUY IT.
ISN'T YOUR FRIEND CABLE A PRECOG?
YEAH, BUT YOU KNOW, PFFT. IT'S ALL JUST KIND OF...I DON'T WANT TO BE RUDE, BUT DOES ANY OF THAT EVER PAN OUT?
ARE YOU TELLING ME THAT THERE'S SOMEBODY THAT KNOWS WHAT'S GONNA HAPPEN TO THOSE YOUNG AVENGERS IN THERE?
WE'D NEVER LET KIDS JOIN UP IF WE KNEW ALL THE HORRIBLE THINGS THAT WOULD HAPPEN!
HMM.
NOW IS A WONDERFUL TIME TO DEPLOY THE "IRISH EXIT" MANEUVER THAT CAPTAIN ROGERS IS SO FOND OF.
NOBODY CAN PREDICT WHAT I'M GONNA DO, BECAUSE I DON'T KNOW WHAT I'M ABOUT TO DO!

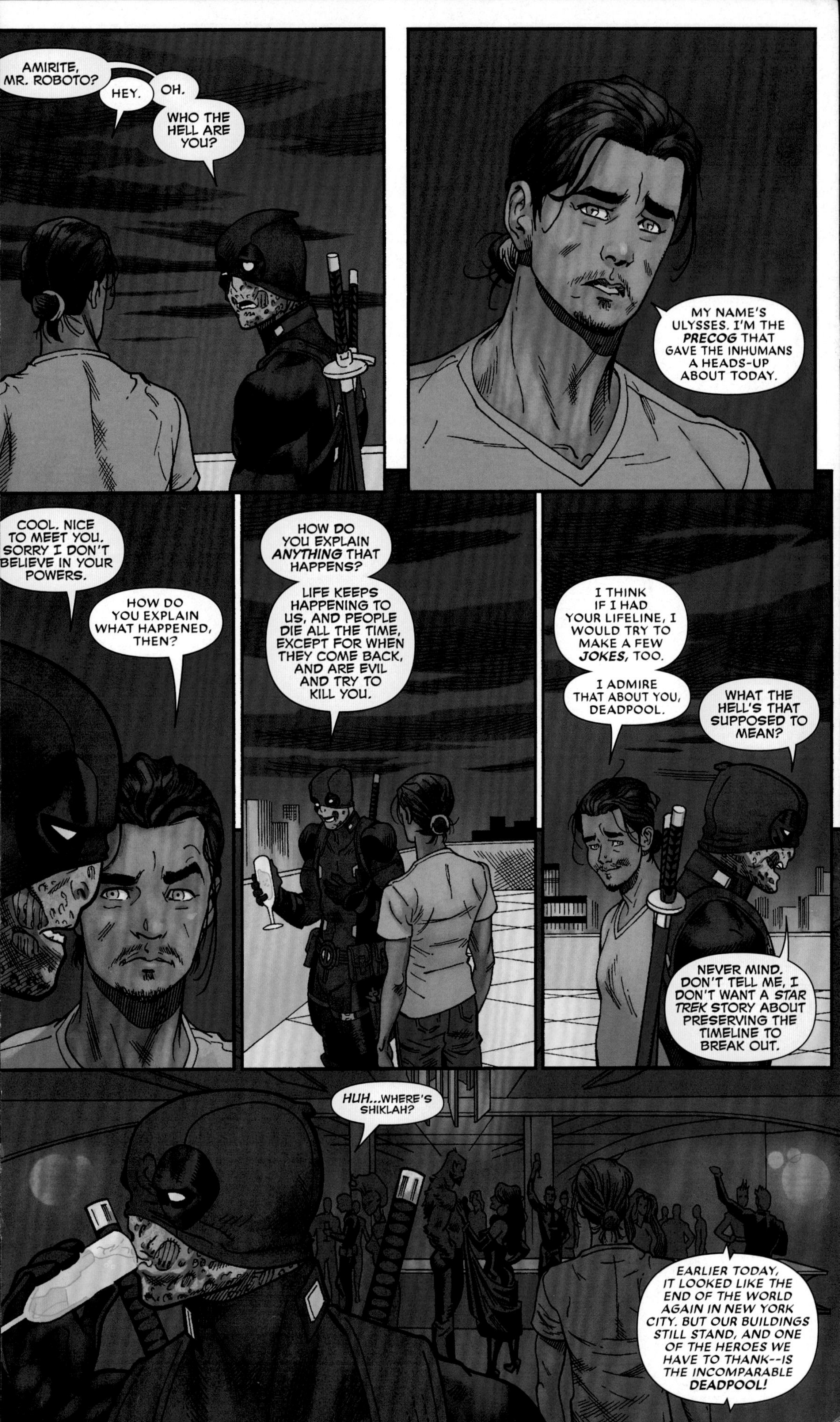
AMIRITE, MR. ROBOTO?
HEY.
OH.
WHO THE HELL ARE YOU?
MY NAME'S ULYSSES. I'M THE PRECOG THAT GAVE THE INHUMANS A HEADS-UP ABOUT TODAY.
COOL. NICE TO MEET YOU. SORRY I DON'T BELIEVE IN YOUR POWERS.
HOW DO YOU EXPLAIN WHAT HAPPENED, THEN?
HOW DO YOU EXPLAIN ANYTHING THAT HAPPENS?
LIFE KEEPS HAPPENING TO US, AND PEOPLE DIE ALL THE TIME, EXCEPT FOR WHEN THEY COME BACK, AND ARE EVIL AND TRY TO KILL YOU.
I THINK IF I HAD YOUR LIFELINE, I WOULD TRY TO MAKE A FEW JOKES, TOO.
I ADMIRE THAT ABOUT YOU, DEADPOOL.
WHAT THE HELL'S THAT SUPPOSED TO MEAN?
NEVER MIND. DON'T TELL ME, I DON'T WANT A STAR TREK STORY ABOUT PRESERVING THE TIMELINE TO BREAK OUT.
HUH...WHERE'S SHIKLAH?
EARLIER TODAY, IT LOOKED LIKE THE END OF THE WORLD AGAIN IN NEW YORK CITY. BUT OUR BUILDINGS STILL STAND, AND ONE OF THE HEROES WE HAVE TO THANK--IS THE INCOMPARABLE DEADPOOL!

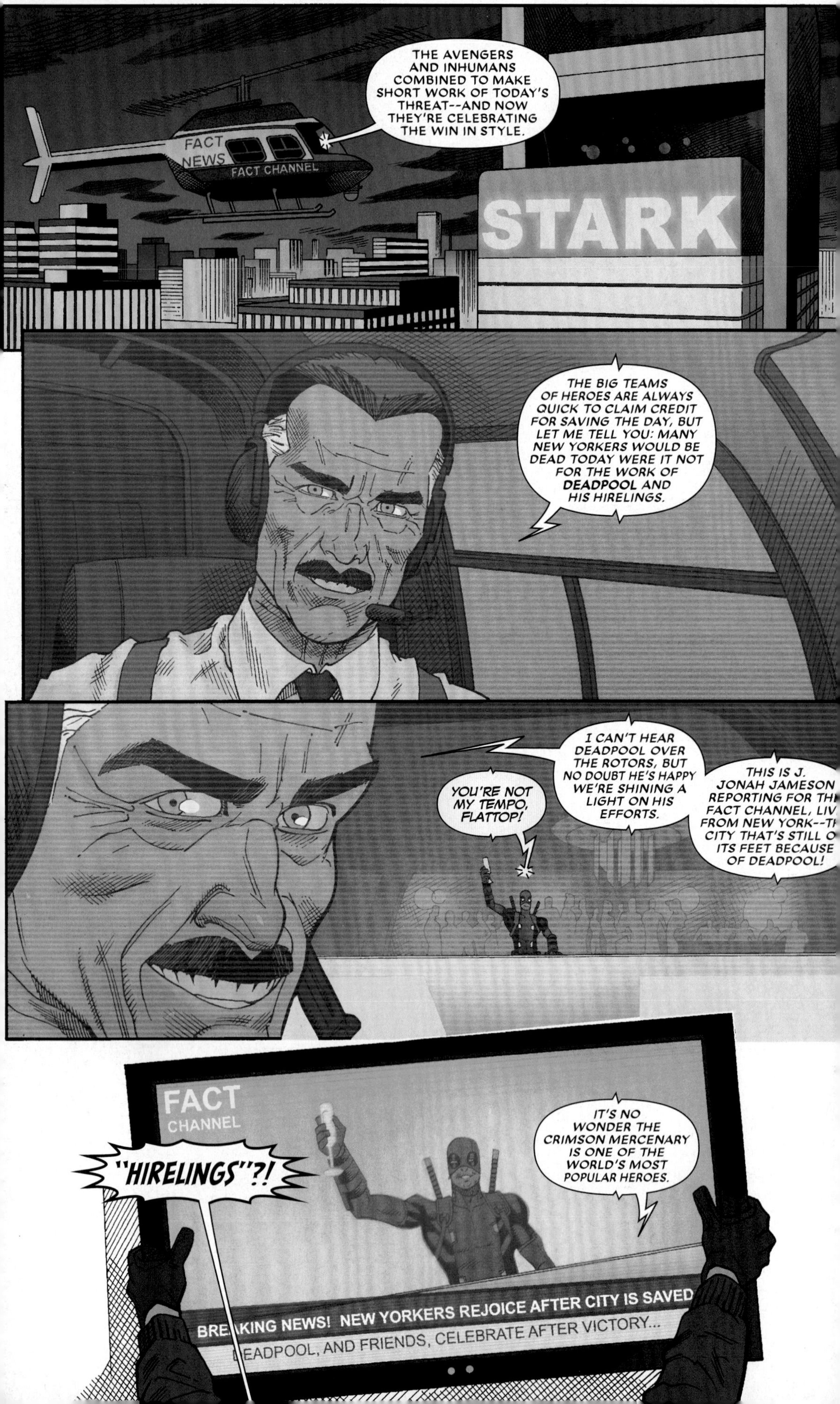
FACT NEWS
FACT CHANNEL
THE AVENGERS AND INHUMANS COMBINED TO MAKE SHORT WORK OF TODAY'S THREAT--AND NOW THEY'RE CELEBRATING THE WIN IN STYLE.
STARK
THE BIG TEAMS OF HEROES ARE ALWAYS QUICK TO CLAIM CREDIT FOR SAVING THE DAY, BUT LET ME TELL YOU: MANY NEW YORKERS WOULD BE DEAD TODAY WERE IT NOT FOR THE WORK OF DEADPOOL AND HIS HIRELINGS.
I CAN'T HEAR DEADPOOL OVER THE ROTORS, BUT NO DOUBT HE'S HAPPY WE'RE SHINING A LIGHT ON HIS EFFORTS.
YOU'RE NOT MY TEMPO, FLATTOP!
THIS IS J. JONAH JAMESON REPORTING FOR TH FACT CHANNEL, LIV FROM NEW YORK--T CITY THAT'S STILL O ITS FEET BECAUSE OF DEADPOOL!
FACT CHANNEL
IT'S NO WONDER THE CRIMSON MERCENARY IS ONE OF THE WORLD'S MOST POPULAR HEROES.
"HIRELINGS"?!
BRE KING NEWS! NEW YORKERS REJOICE AFTER CITY IS SAVED
EADPOOL, AND FRIENDS, CELEBRATE AFTER VICTORY...

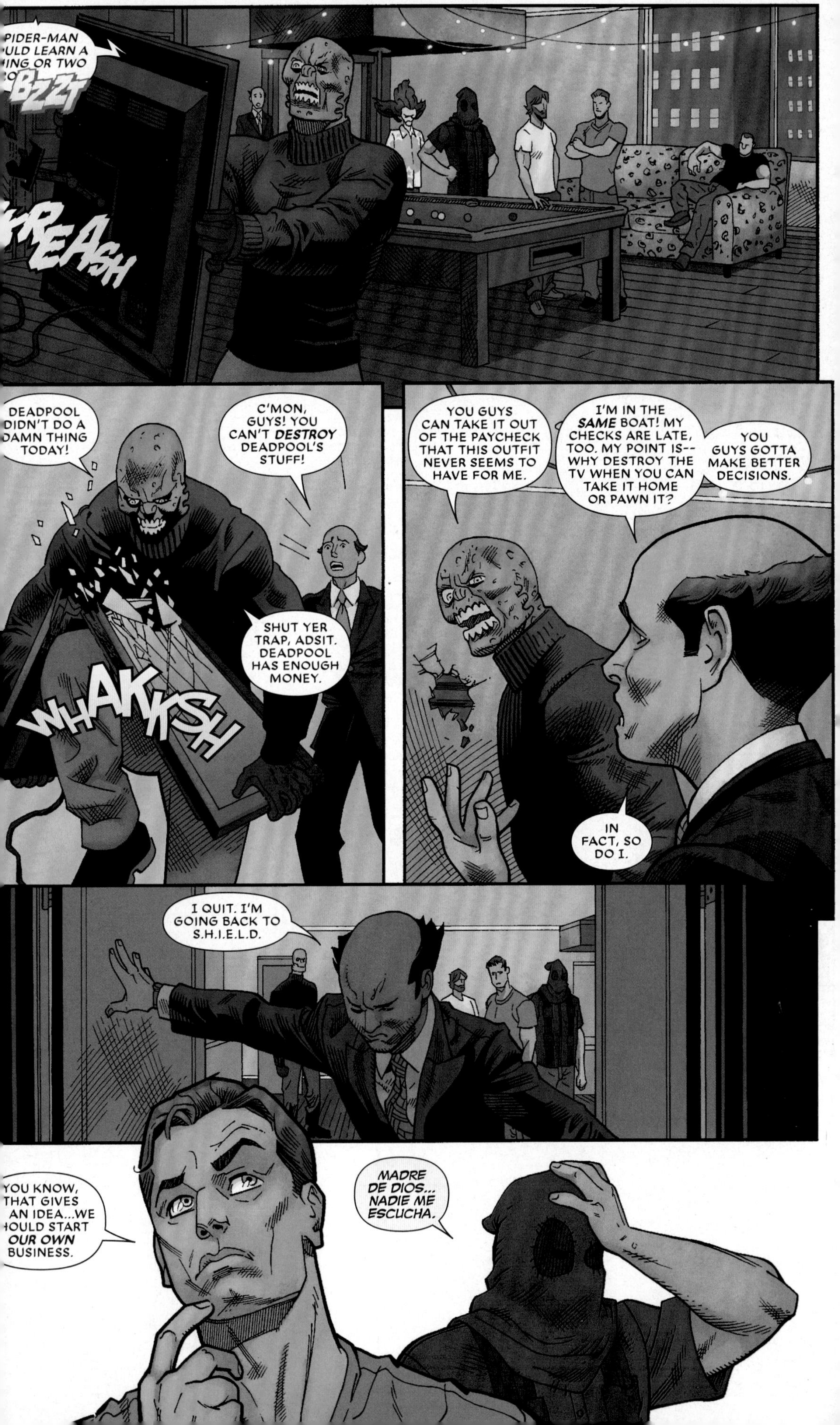
PIDER-MAN
ULD LEARN A
ING OR TWO
BZZT
KREASH
DEADPOOL
DIDN'T DO A
DAMN THING
TODAY!
C'MON, GUYS! YOU CAN'T DESTROY DEADPOOL'S STUFF!
SHUT YER TRAP, ADSIT. DEADPOOL HAS ENOUGH MONEY.
WHAKKSH
YOU GUYS CAN TAKE IT OUT OF THE PAYCHECK THAT THIS OUTFIT NEVER SEEMS TO HAVE FOR ME.
I'M IN THE SAME BOAT! MY CHECKS ARE LATE, TOO. MY POINT IS-- WHY DESTROY THE TV WHEN YOU CAN TAKE IT HOME OR PAWN IT?
YOU GUYS GOTTA MAKE BETTER DECISIONS.
IN FACT, SO DO I.
I QUIT. I'M GOING BACK TO S.H.I.E.L.D.
YOU KNOW,
THAT GIVES
AN IDEA...WE
HOULD START
OUR OWN
BUSINESS.
MADRE DE DIOS... NADIE ME ESCUCHA.

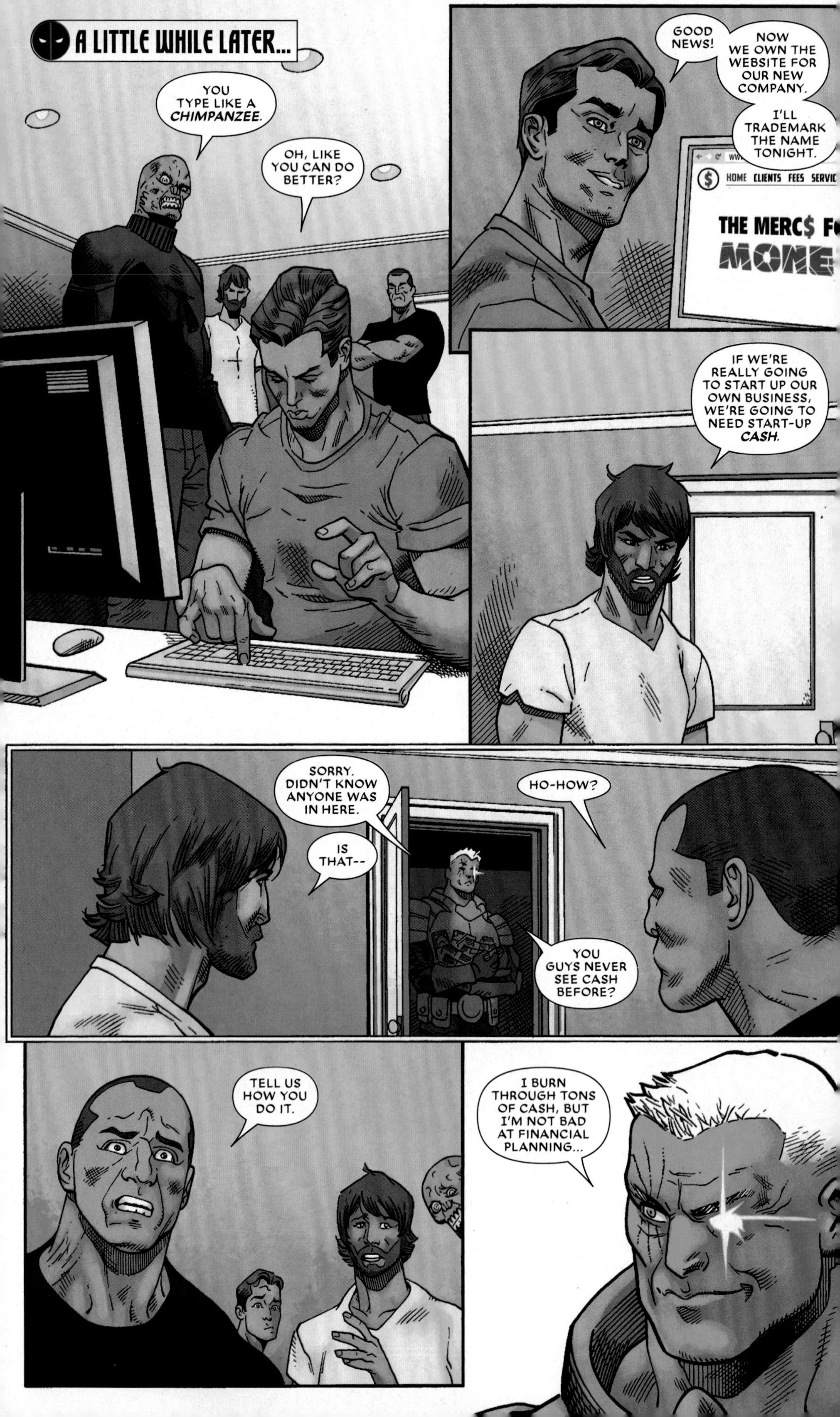
A LITTLE WHILE LATER...
YOU TYPE LIKE A CHIMPANZEE.
OH, LIKE YOU CAN DO BETTER?
GOOD NEWS!
NOW WE OWN THE WEBSITE FOR OUR NEW COMPANY.
I'LL TRADEMARK THE NAME TONIGHT.
HOME CLIENTS FEES SERVIC
THE MERC$ F
MONE
IF WE'RE REALLY GOING TO START UP OUR OWN BUSINESS, WE'RE GOING TO NEED START-UP CASH.
SORRY. DIDN'T KNOW ANYONE WAS IN HERE.
IS THAT--
HO-HOW?
YOU GUYS NEVER SEE CASH BEFORE?
TELL US HOW YOU DO IT.
I BURN THROUGH TONS OF CASH, BUT I'M NOT BAD AT FINANCIAL PLANNING...

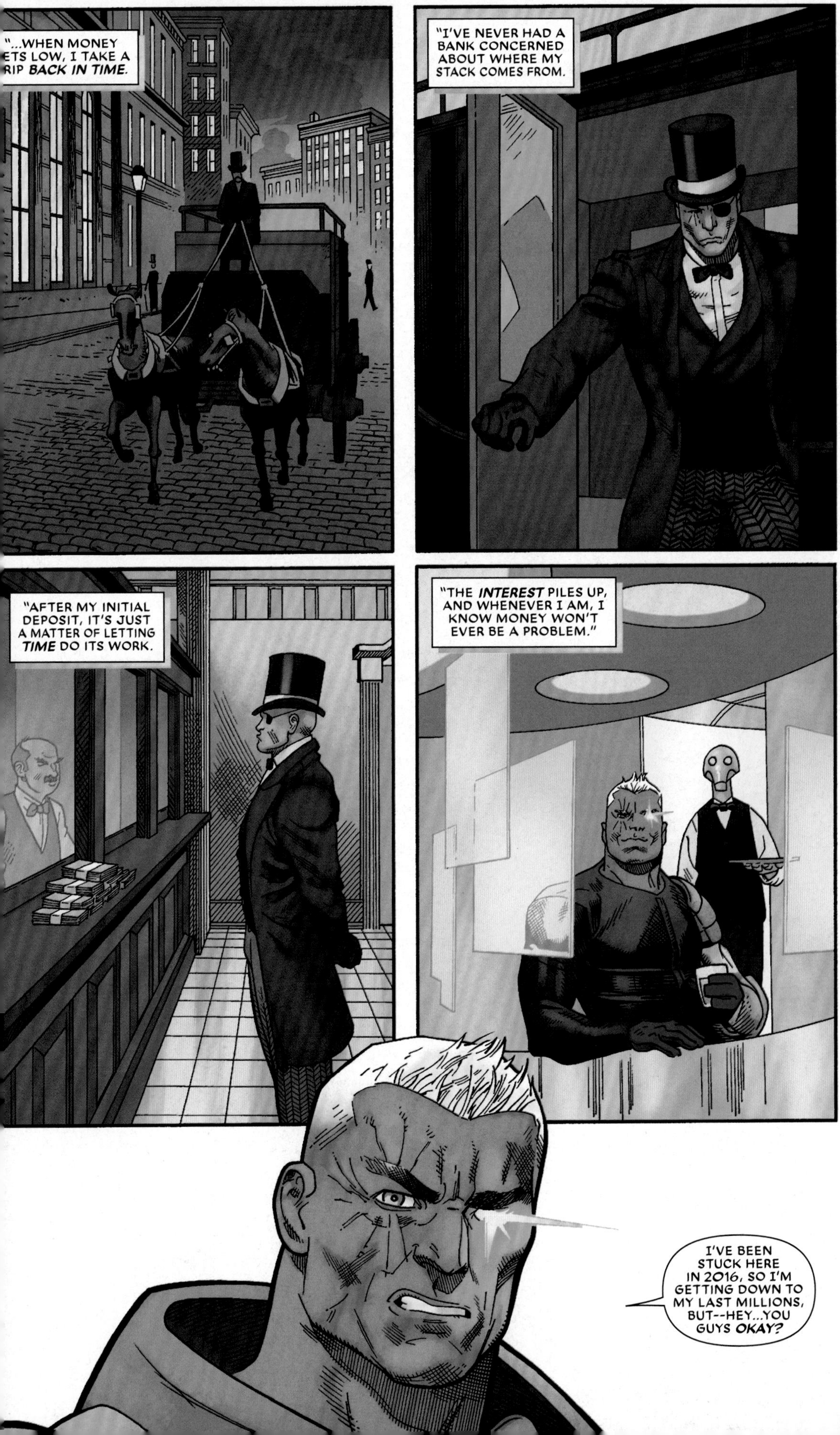
"...WHEN MONEY ETS LOW, I TAKE A RIP BACK IN TIME.
"I'VE NEVER HAD A BANK CONCERNED ABOUT WHERE MY STACK COMES FROM.
"AFTER MY INITIAL DEPOSIT, IT'S JUST A MATTER OF LETTING TIME DO ITS WORK.
"THE INTEREST PILES UP, AND WHENEVER I AM, I KNOW MONEY WON'T EVER BE A PROBLEM."
I'VE BEEN STUCK HERE IN 2016, SO I'M GETTING DOWN TO MY LAST MILLIONS, BUT--HEY...YOU GUYS OKAY?

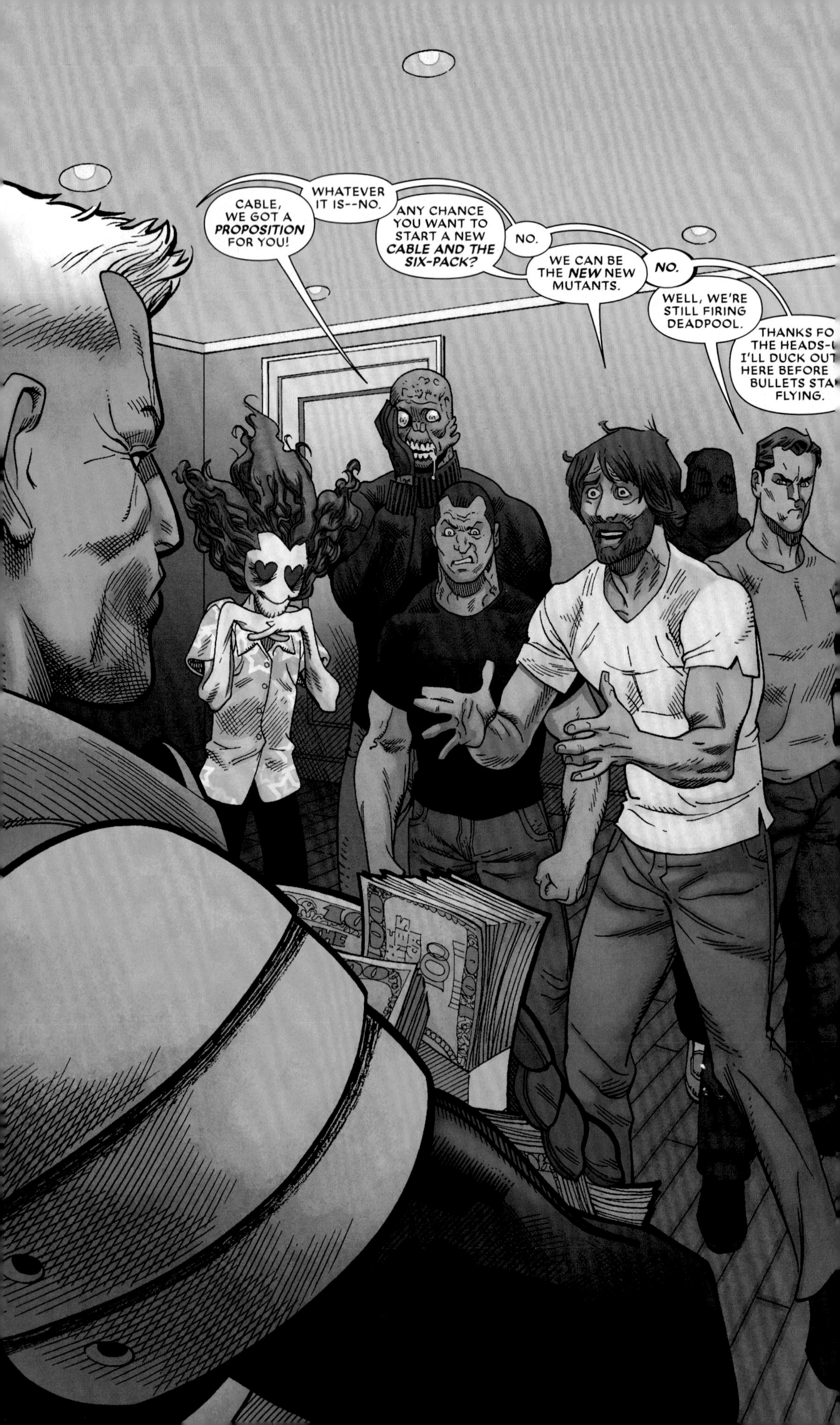

CABLE, WE GOT A *PROPOSITION* FOR YOU!
WHATEVER IT IS--NO.
ANY CHANCE YOU WANT TO START A NEW *CABLE AND THE SIX-PACK?*
NO.
WE CAN BE THE *NEW* NEW MUTANTS.
NO.
WELL, WE'RE STILL FIRING DEADPOOL.
THANKS FO THE HEADS- I'LL DUCK OUT HERE BEFORE BULLETS STA FLYING.

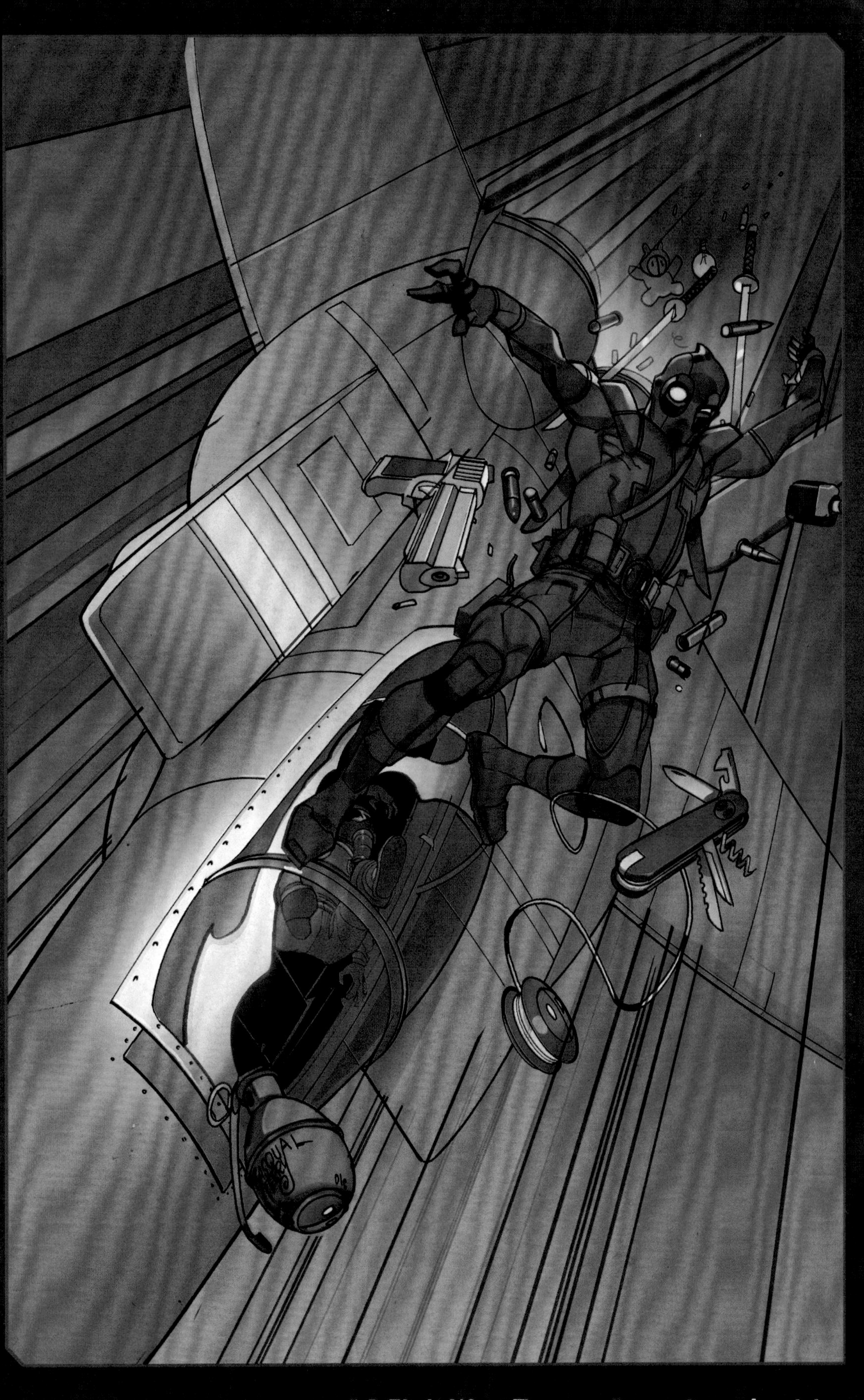

#14 Civil War Reenactment variant by
PASQUAL FERRY & FRANK D'ARMATA

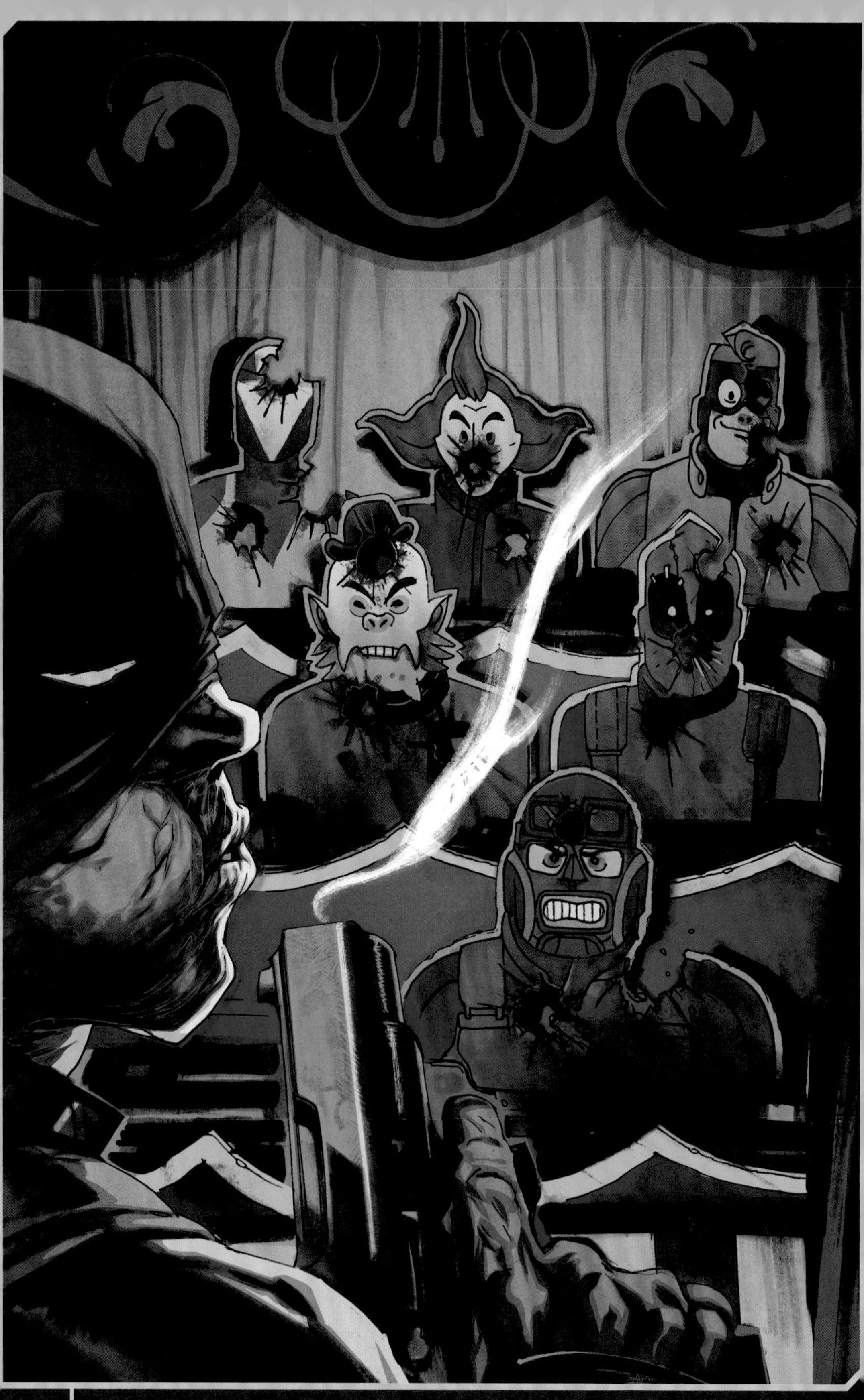

15 DEADPOOL'S UNCIVIL WAR - PART TWO

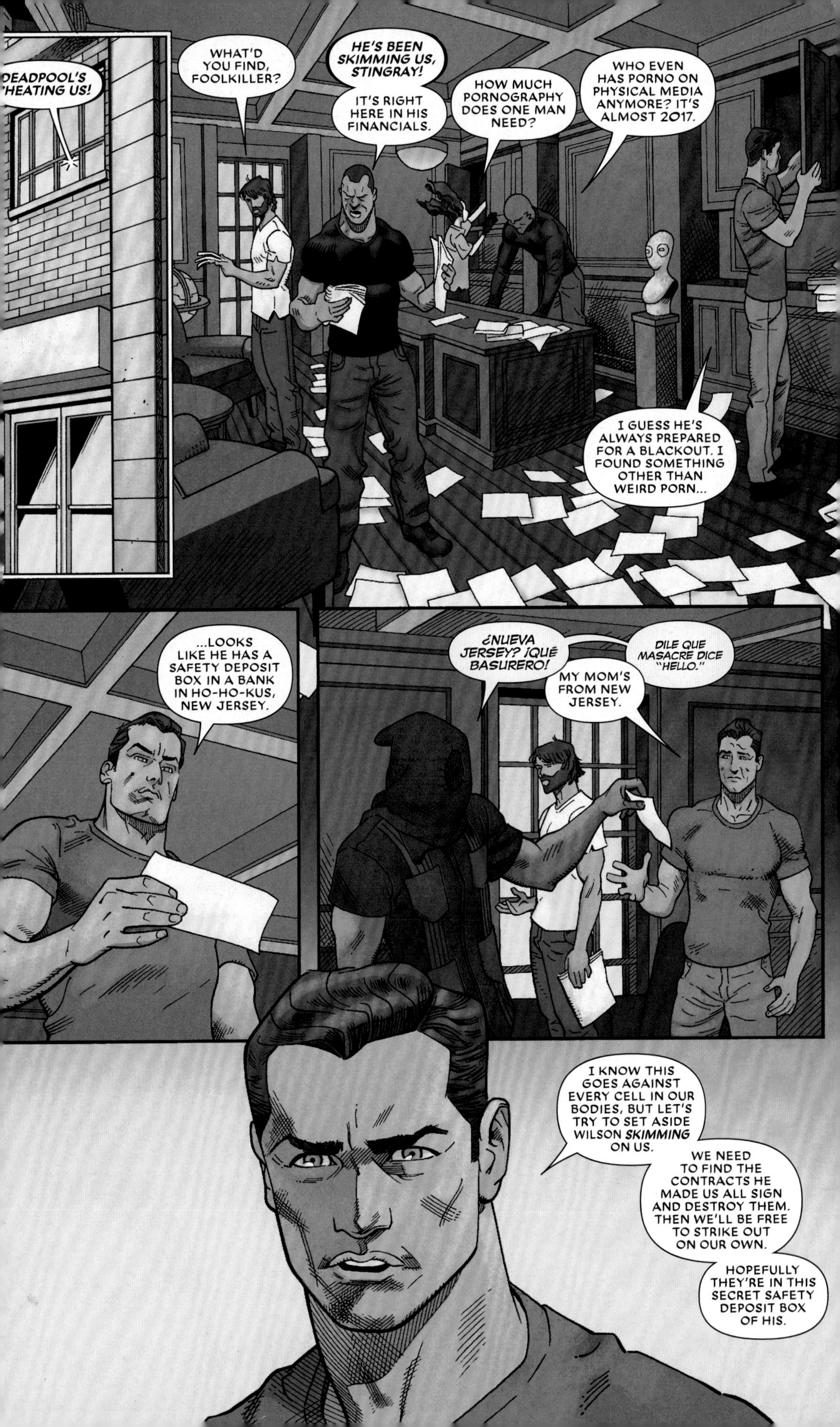

DEADPOOL'S CHEATING US!
WHAT'D YOU FIND, FOOLKILLER?
HE'S BEEN SKIMMING US, STINGRAY!
IT'S RIGHT HERE IN HIS FINANCIALS.
HOW MUCH PORNOGRAPHY DOES ONE MAN NEED?
WHO EVEN HAS PORNO ON PHYSICAL MEDIA ANYMORE? IT'S ALMOST 2017.
I GUESS HE'S ALWAYS PREPARED FOR A BLACKOUT. I FOUND SOMETHING OTHER THAN WEIRD PORN...
...LOOKS LIKE HE HAS A SAFETY DEPOSIT BOX IN A BANK IN HO-HO-KUS, NEW JERSEY.
¿NUEVA JERSEY? ¡QUÉ BASURERO!
DILE QUE MASACRE DICE "HELLO."
MY MOM'S FROM NEW JERSEY.
I KNOW THIS GOES AGAINST EVERY CELL IN OUR BODIES, BUT LET'S TRY TO SET ASIDE WILSON SKIMMING ON US.
WE NEED TO FIND THE CONTRACTS HE MADE US ALL SIGN AND DESTROY THEM. THEN WE'LL BE FREE TO STRIKE OUT ON OUR OWN.
HOPEFULLY THEY'RE IN THIS SECRET SAFETY DEPOSIT BOX OF HIS.

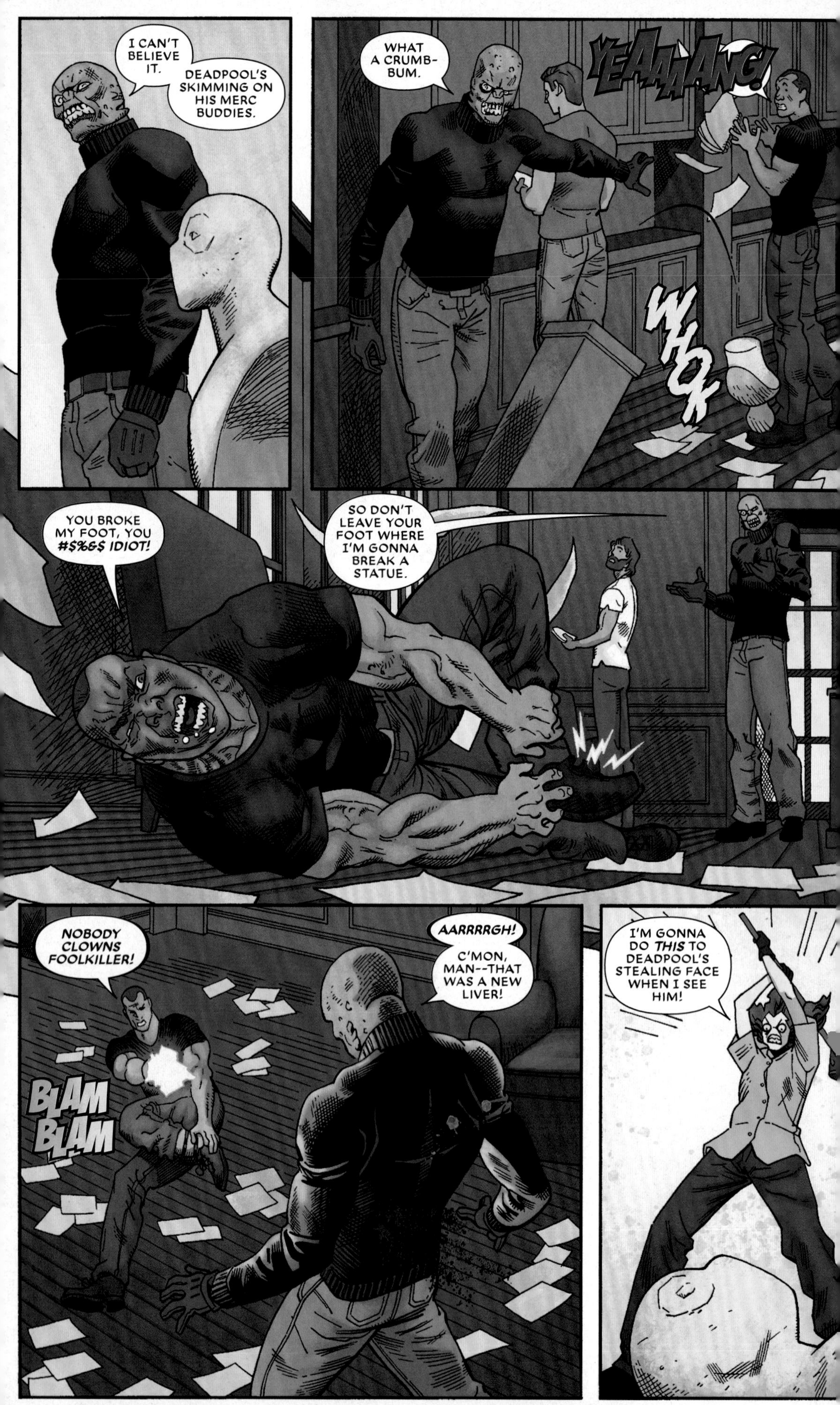
I CAN'T BELIEVE IT.
DEADPOOL'S SKIMMING ON HIS MERC BUDDIES.
WHAT A CRUMB-BUM.
YEAAAAANG!
WHOK
YOU BROKE MY FOOT, YOU #$%&$ IDIOT!
SO DON'T LEAVE YOUR FOOT WHERE I'M GONNA BREAK A STATUE.
NOBODY CLOWNS FOOLKILLER!
BLAM BLAM
AARRRRGH!
C'MON, MAN--THAT WAS A NEW LIVER!
I'M GONNA DO THIS TO DEADPOOL'S STEALING FACE WHEN I SEE HIM!

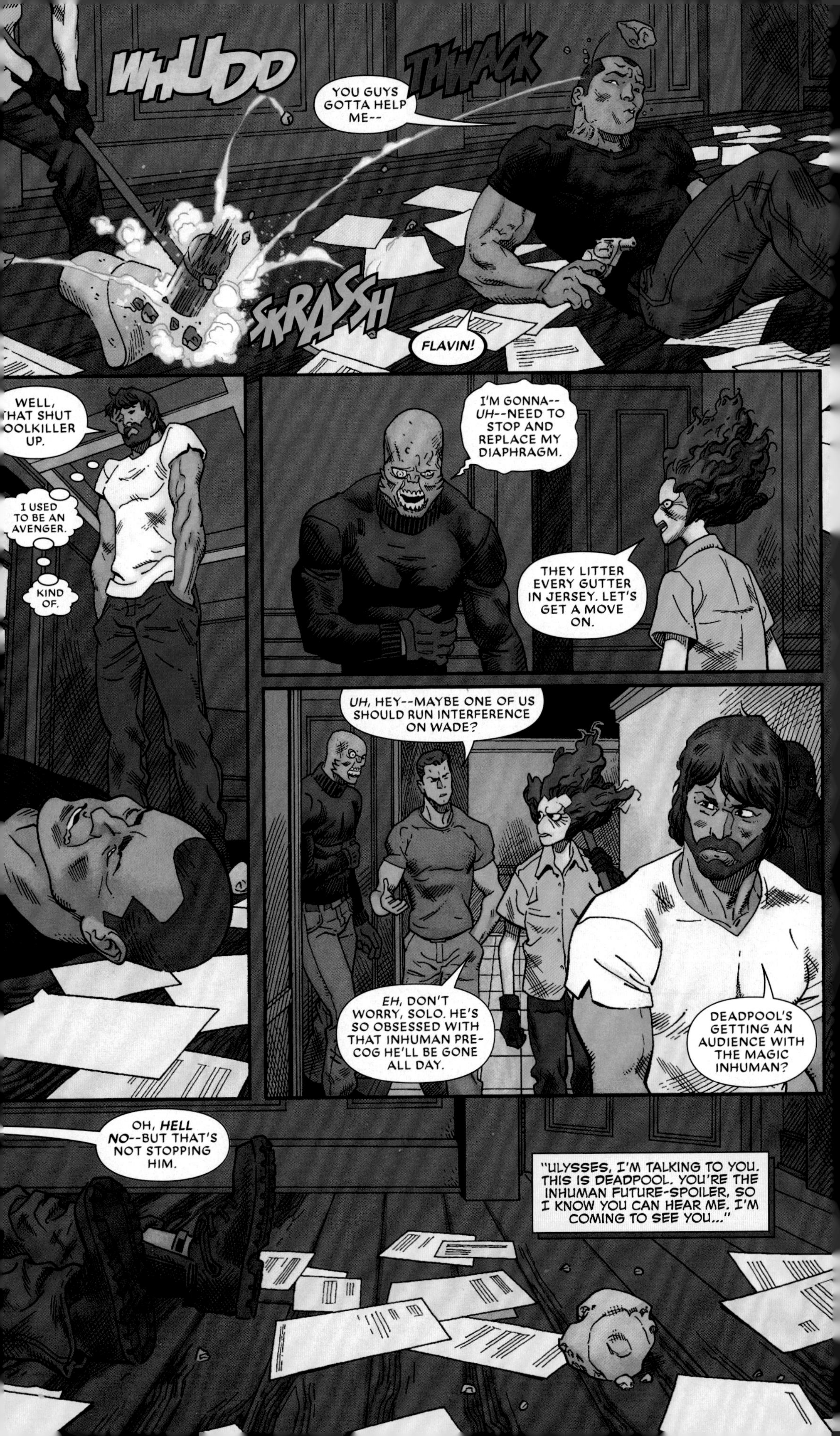
WHUDD
THWACK
YOU GUYS GOTTA HELP ME--
SKRASSH
FLAVIN!
WELL, THAT SHUT OOLKILLER UP.
I USED TO BE AN AVENGER.
KIND OF.
I'M GONNA-- UH--NEED TO STOP AND REPLACE MY DIAPHRAGM.
THEY LITTER EVERY GUTTER IN JERSEY. LET'S GET A MOVE ON.
UH, HEY--MAYBE ONE OF US SHOULD RUN INTERFERENCE ON WADE?
DEADPOOL'S GETTING AN AUDIENCE WITH THE MAGIC INHUMAN?
EH, DON'T WORRY, SOLO. HE'S SO OBSESSED WITH THAT INHUMAN PRE-COG HE'LL BE GONE ALL DAY.
OH, HELL NO--BUT THAT'S NOT STOPPING HIM.
"ULYSSES, I'M TALKING TO YOU. THIS IS DEADPOOL. YOU'RE THE INHUMAN FUTURE-SPOILER, SO I KNOW YOU CAN HEAR ME. I'M COMING TO SEE YOU..."

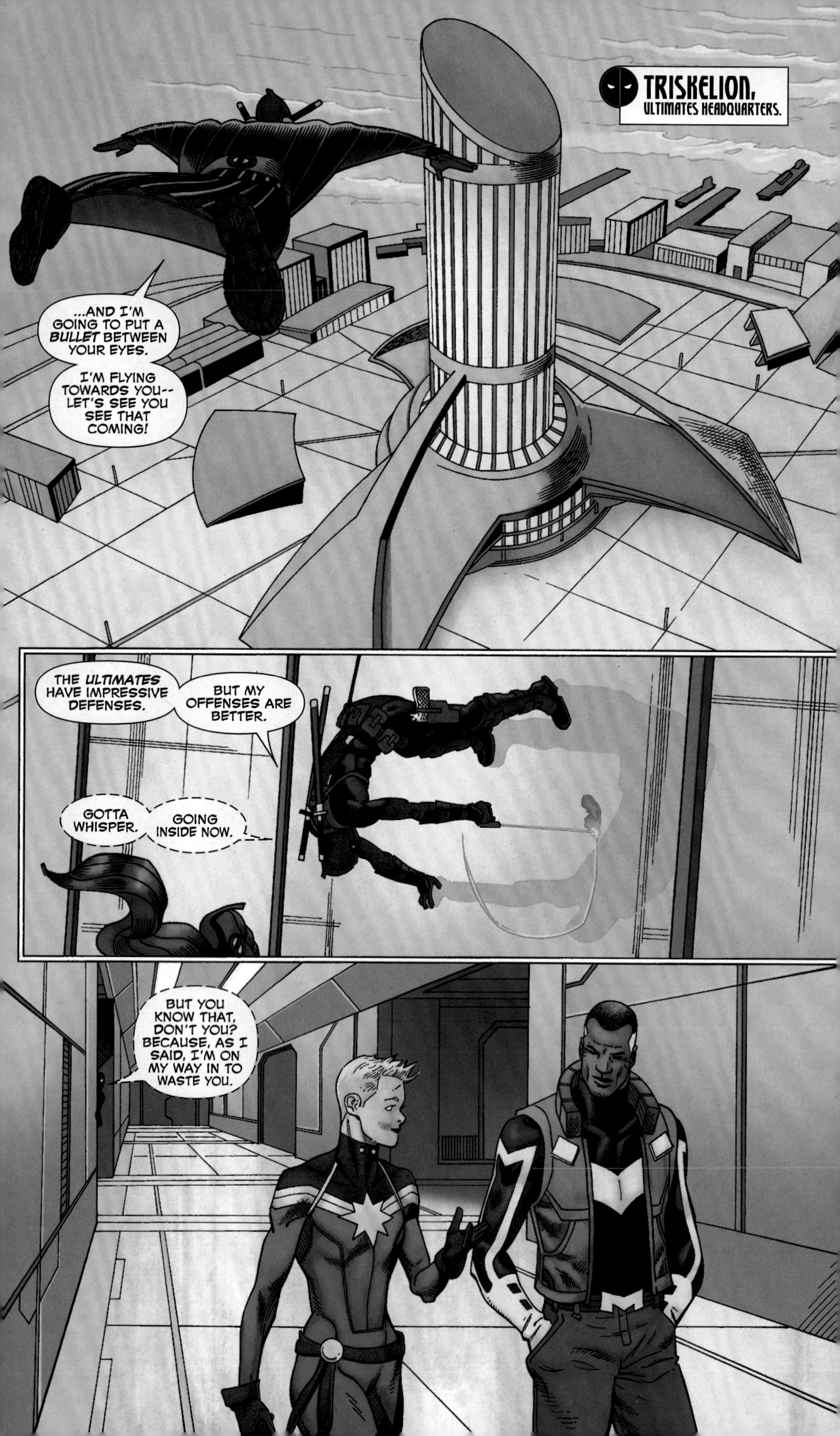
TRISKELION, ULTIMATES HEADQUARTERS.
...AND I'M GOING TO PUT A BULLET BETWEEN YOUR EYES.
I'M FLYING TOWARDS YOU-- LET'S SEE YOU SEE THAT COMING!
THE ULTIMATES HAVE IMPRESSIVE DEFENSES.
BUT MY OFFENSES ARE BETTER.
GOTTA WHISPER.
GOING INSIDE NOW.
BUT YOU KNOW THAT, DON'T YOU? BECAUSE, AS I SAID, I'M ON MY WAY IN TO WASTE YOU.

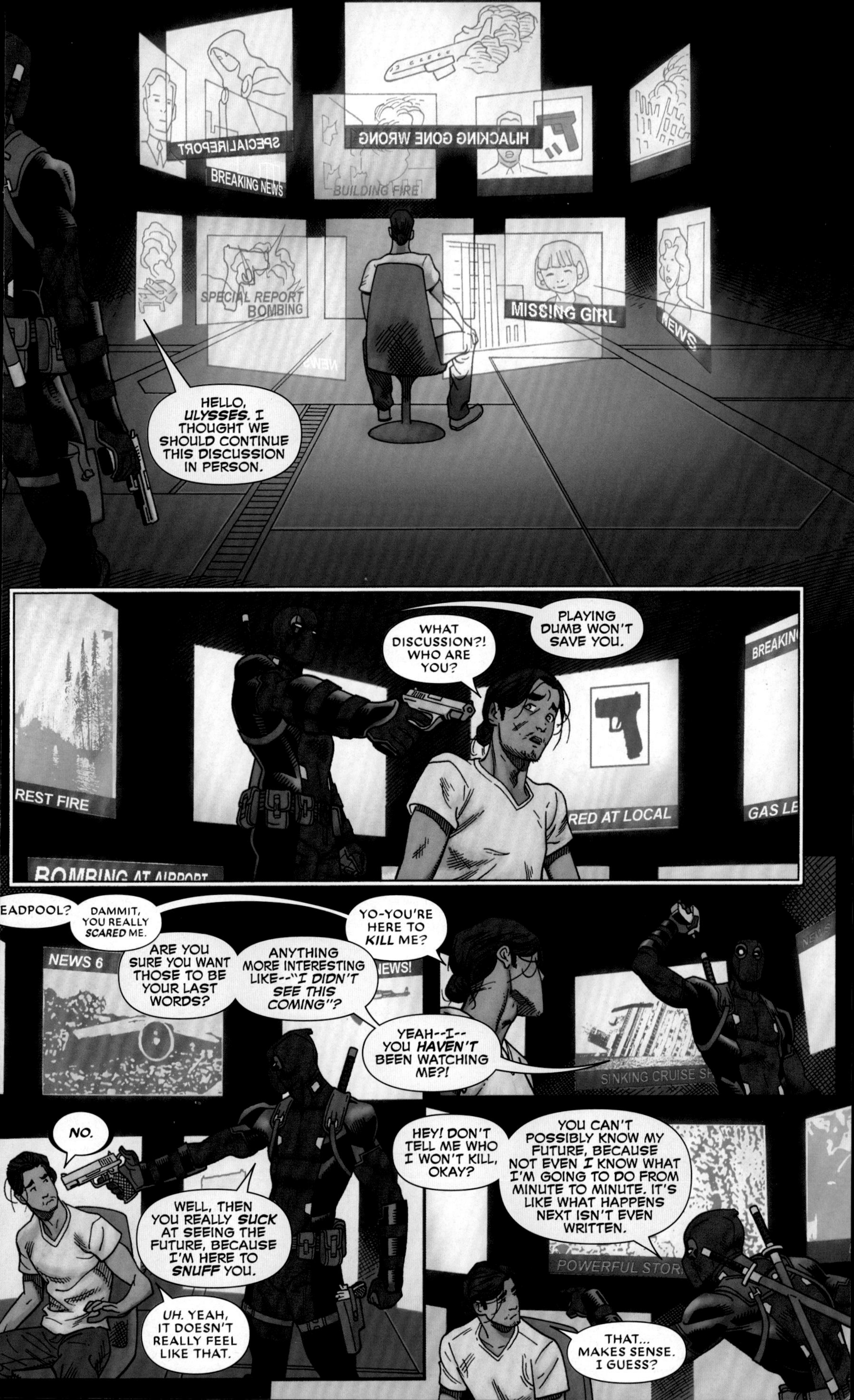

SPECIAL REPORT
BREAKING NEWS
BUILDING FIRE
HIJACKING GONE WRONG
SPECIAL REPORT BOMBING
MISSING GIRL
NEWS
HELLO, *ULYSSES.* I THOUGHT WE SHOULD CONTINUE THIS DISCUSSION IN PERSON.
REST FIRE
BOMBING AT AIRPORT
WHAT DISCUSSION?! WHO ARE YOU?
PLAYING DUMB WON'T SAVE YOU.
RED AT LOCAL
BREAKIN
GAS LE
EADPOOL?
DAMMIT, YOU REALLY *SCARED* ME.
YO-YOU'RE HERE TO *KILL* ME?
NEWS 6
ARE YOU SURE YOU WANT THOSE TO BE YOUR LAST WORDS?
ANYTHING MORE INTERESTING LIKE--"*I DIDN'T SEE THIS COMING*"?
YEAH--I-- YOU *HAVEN'T* BEEN WATCHING ME?!
SINKING CRUISE SH
NO.
WELL, THEN YOU REALLY *SUCK* AT SEEING THE FUTURE, BECAUSE I'M HERE TO *SNUFF* YOU.
UH. YEAH, IT DOESN'T REALLY FEEL LIKE THAT.
HEY! DON'T TELL ME WHO I WON'T KILL, OKAY?
YOU CAN'T POSSIBLY KNOW MY FUTURE, BECAUSE NOT EVEN *I* KNOW WHAT I'M GOING TO DO FROM MINUTE TO MINUTE. IT'S LIKE WHAT HAPPENS NEXT ISN'T EVEN WRITTEN.
POWERFUL STOR
THAT... MAKES SENSE. I GUESS?

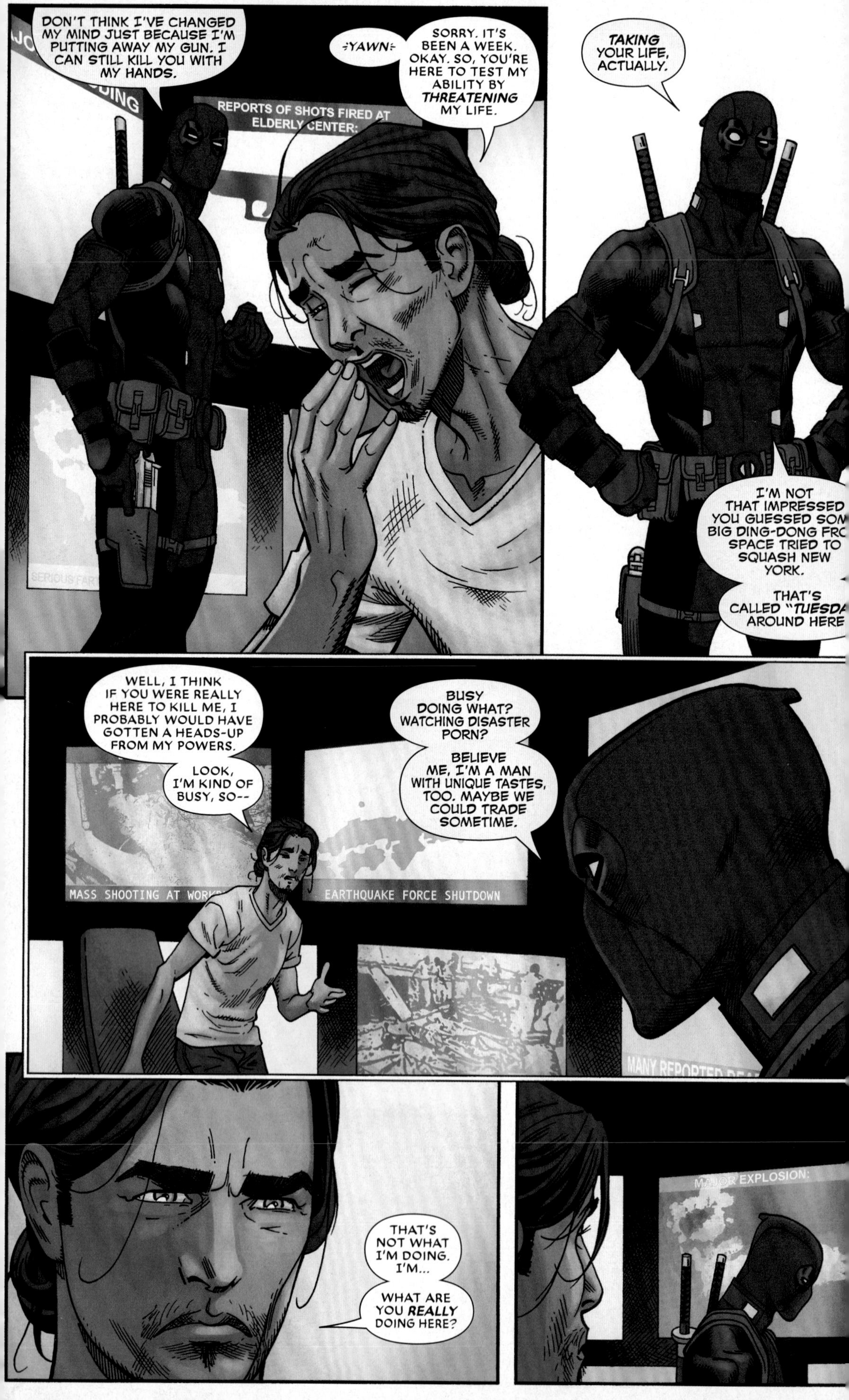
DON'T THINK I'VE CHANGED MY MIND JUST BECAUSE I'M PUTTING AWAY MY GUN. I CAN STILL KILL YOU WITH MY HANDS.
REPORTS OF SHOTS FIRED AT ELDERLY CENTER:
=YAWN=
SORRY. IT'S BEEN A WEEK. OKAY. SO, YOU'RE HERE TO TEST MY ABILITY BY THREATENING MY LIFE.
TAKING YOUR LIFE, ACTUALLY.
I'M NOT THAT IMPRESSED YOU GUESSED SOM BIG DING-DONG FRO SPACE TRIED TO SQUASH NEW YORK.
THAT'S CALLED "TUESDA AROUND HERE
WELL, I THINK IF YOU WERE REALLY HERE TO KILL ME, I PROBABLY WOULD HAVE GOTTEN A HEADS-UP FROM MY POWERS.
LOOK, I'M KIND OF BUSY, SO--
BUSY DOING WHAT? WATCHING DISASTER PORN?
BELIEVE ME, I'M A MAN WITH UNIQUE TASTES, TOO. MAYBE WE COULD TRADE SOMETIME.
EARTHQUAKE FORCE SHUTDOWN
THAT'S NOT WHAT I'M DOING. I'M...
WHAT ARE YOU REALLY DOING HERE?
MAJOR EXPLOSION:

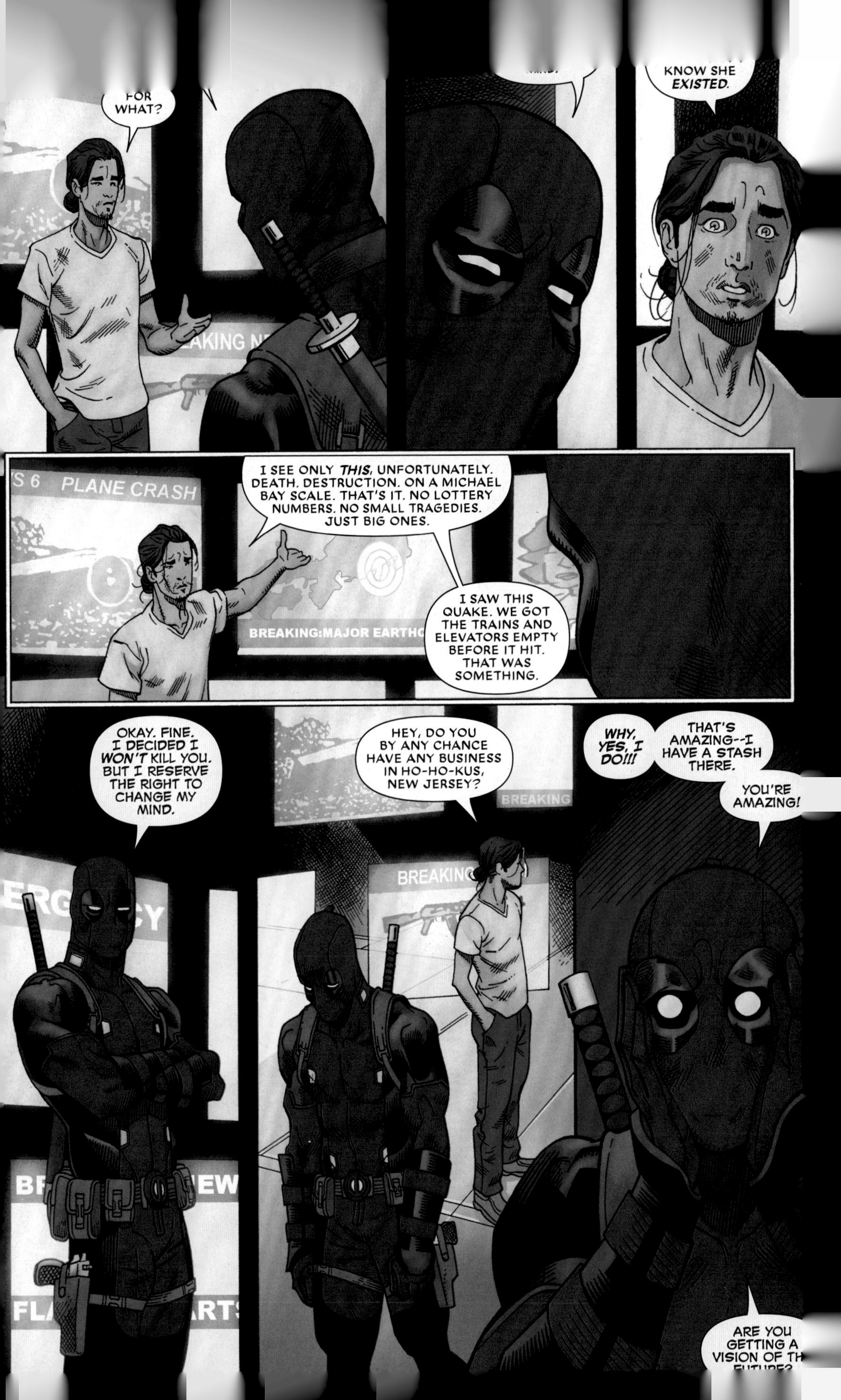
FOR WHAT?
KNOW SHE EXISTED.
PLANE CRASH
I SEE ONLY THIS, UNFORTUNATELY. DEATH. DESTRUCTION. ON A MICHAEL BAY SCALE. THAT'S IT. NO LOTTERY NUMBERS. NO SMALL TRAGEDIES. JUST BIG ONES.
I SAW THIS QUAKE. WE GOT THE TRAINS AND ELEVATORS EMPTY BEFORE IT HIT. THAT WAS SOMETHING.
OKAY. FINE. I DECIDED I WON'T KILL YOU. BUT I RESERVE THE RIGHT TO CHANGE MY MIND.
HEY, DO YOU BY ANY CHANCE HAVE ANY BUSINESS IN HO-HO-KUS, NEW JERSEY?
WHY, YES, I DO!!!
THAT'S AMAZING--I HAVE A STASH THERE.
YOU'RE AMAZING!
ARE YOU GETTING A VISION OF TH

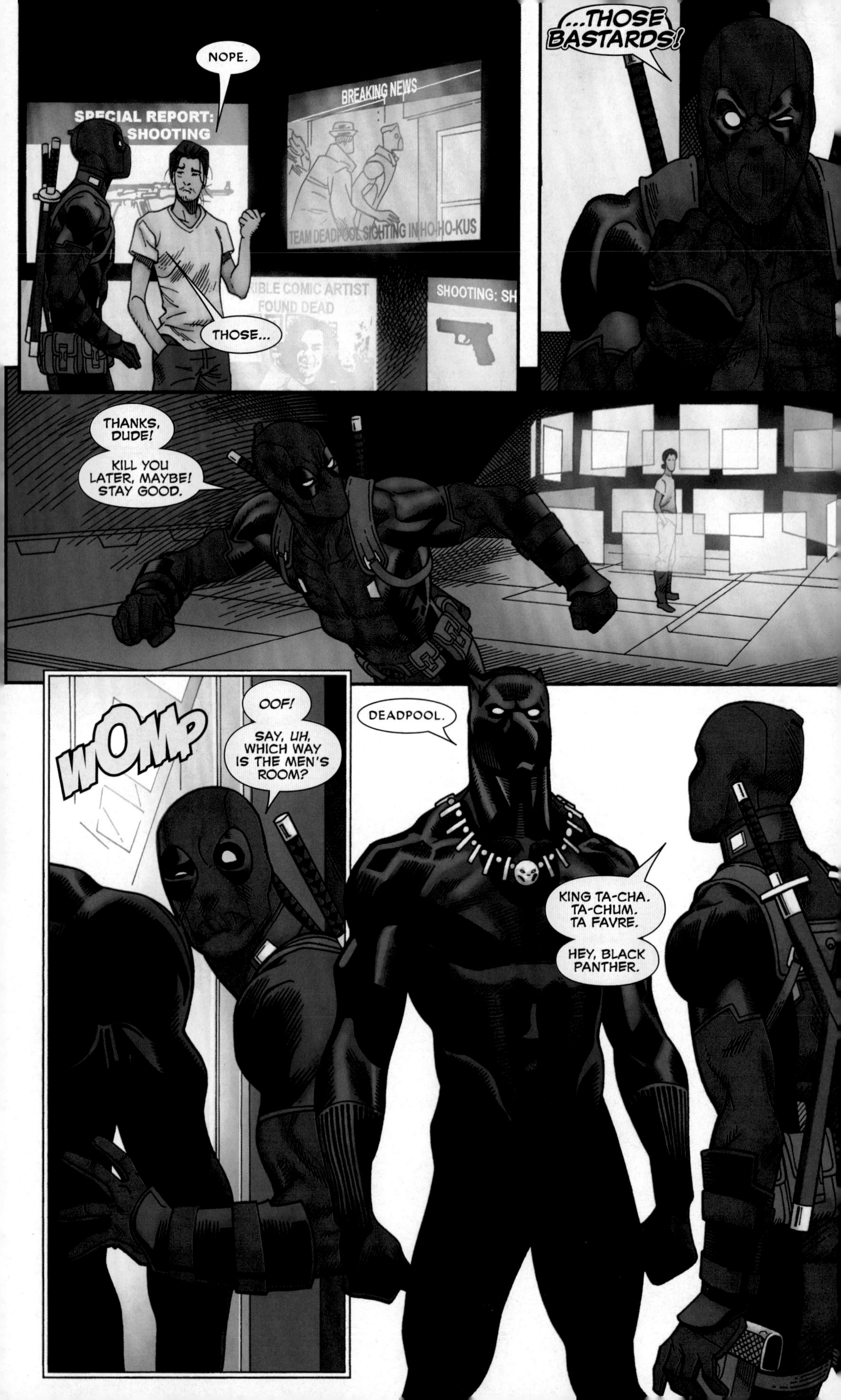
SPECIAL REPORT: SHOOTING
NOPE.
BREAKING NEWS
TEAM DEADPOOL SIGHTING IN HO-HO-KUS
IBLE COMIC ARTIST FOUND DEAD
SHOOTING: SH
THOSE...
...THOSE BASTARDS!
THANKS, DUDE!
KILL YOU LATER, MAYBE! STAY GOOD.
WOMP
OOF!
SAY, UH, WHICH WAY IS THE MEN'S ROOM?
DEADPOOL.
KING TA-CHA. TA-CHUM. TA FAVRE.
HEY, BLACK PANTHER.

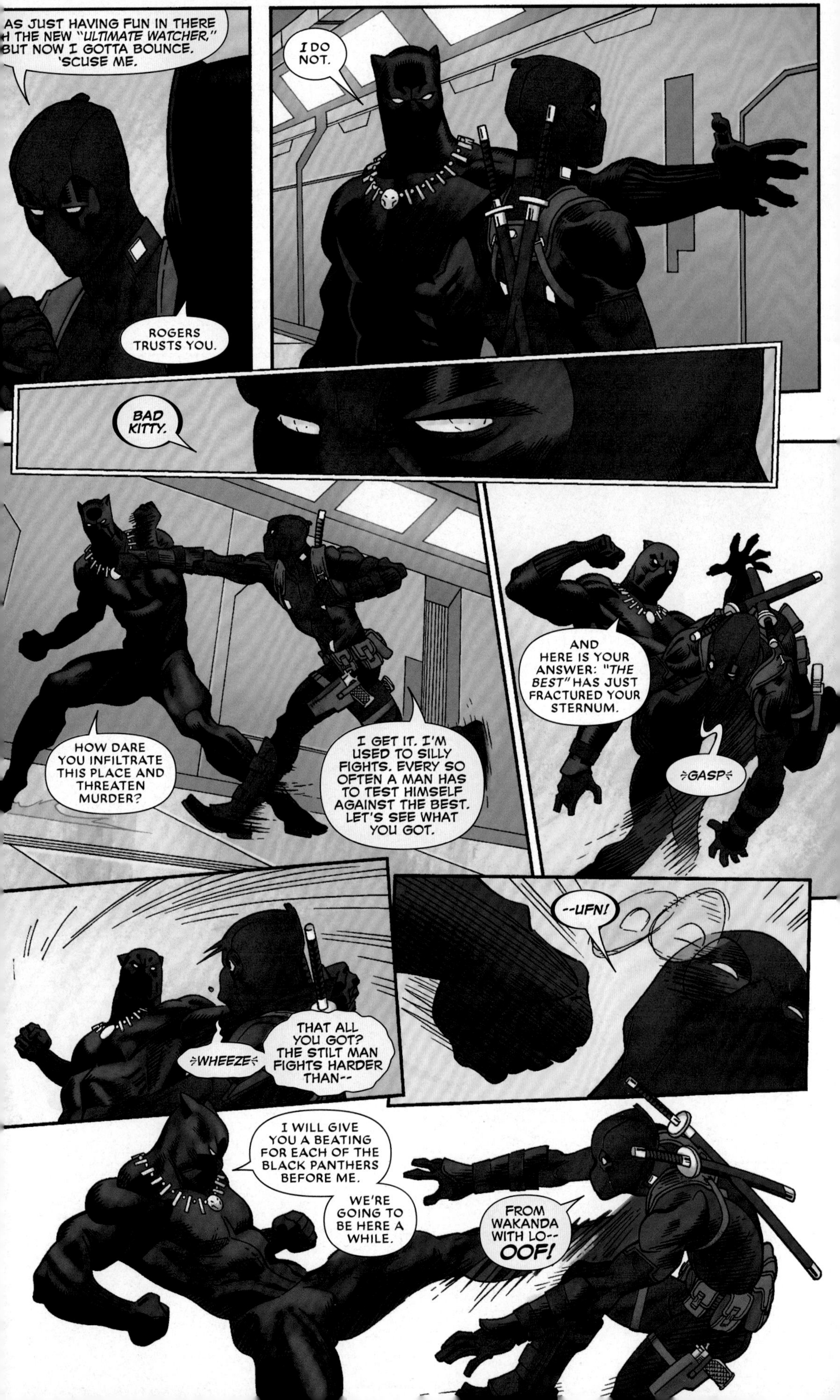

AS JUST HAVING FUN IN THERE
H THE NEW "ULTIMATE WATCHER,"
BUT NOW I GOTTA BOUNCE.
'SCUSE ME.
ROGERS TRUSTS YOU.
I DO NOT.
BAD KITTY.
HOW DARE YOU INFILTRATE THIS PLACE AND THREATEN MURDER?
I GET IT. I'M USED TO SILLY FIGHTS. EVERY SO OFTEN A MAN HAS TO TEST HIMSELF AGAINST THE BEST. LET'S SEE WHAT YOU GOT.
AND HERE IS YOUR ANSWER: "THE BEST" HAS JUST FRACTURED YOUR STERNUM.
GASP
WHEEZE
THAT ALL YOU GOT? THE STILT MAN FIGHTS HARDER THAN--
--UFN!
I WILL GIVE YOU A BEATING FOR EACH OF THE BLACK PANTHERS BEFORE ME.
WE'RE GOING TO BE HERE A WHILE.
FROM WAKANDA WITH LO-- OOF!

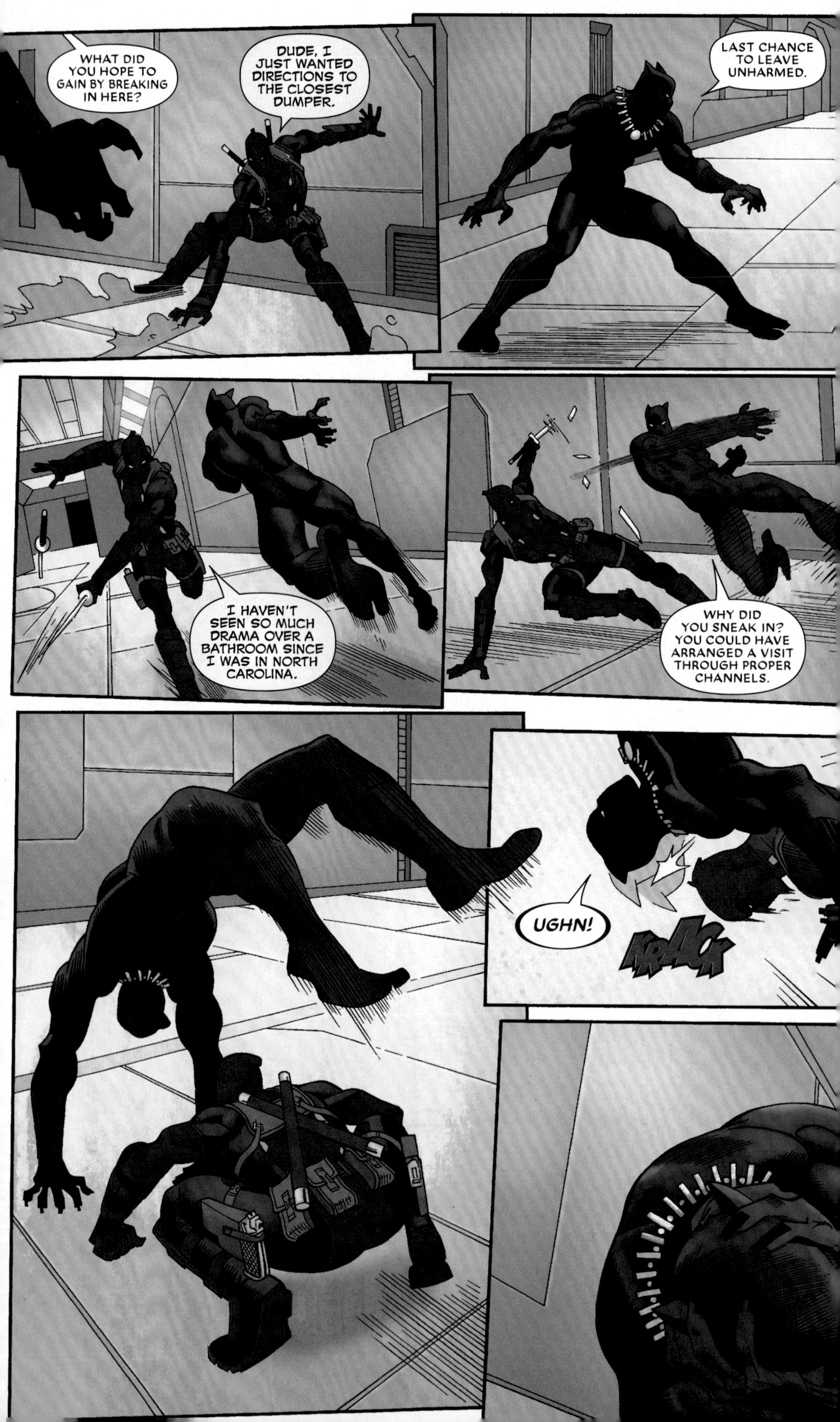

WHAT DID YOU HOPE TO GAIN BY BREAKING IN HERE?
DUDE, I JUST WANTED DIRECTIONS TO THE CLOSEST DUMPER.
LAST CHANCE TO LEAVE UNHARMED.
I HAVEN'T SEEN SO MUCH DRAMA OVER A BATHROOM SINCE I WAS IN NORTH CAROLINA.
WHY DID YOU SNEAK IN? YOU COULD HAVE ARRANGED A VISIT THROUGH PROPER CHANNELS.
UGHN!
KRACK

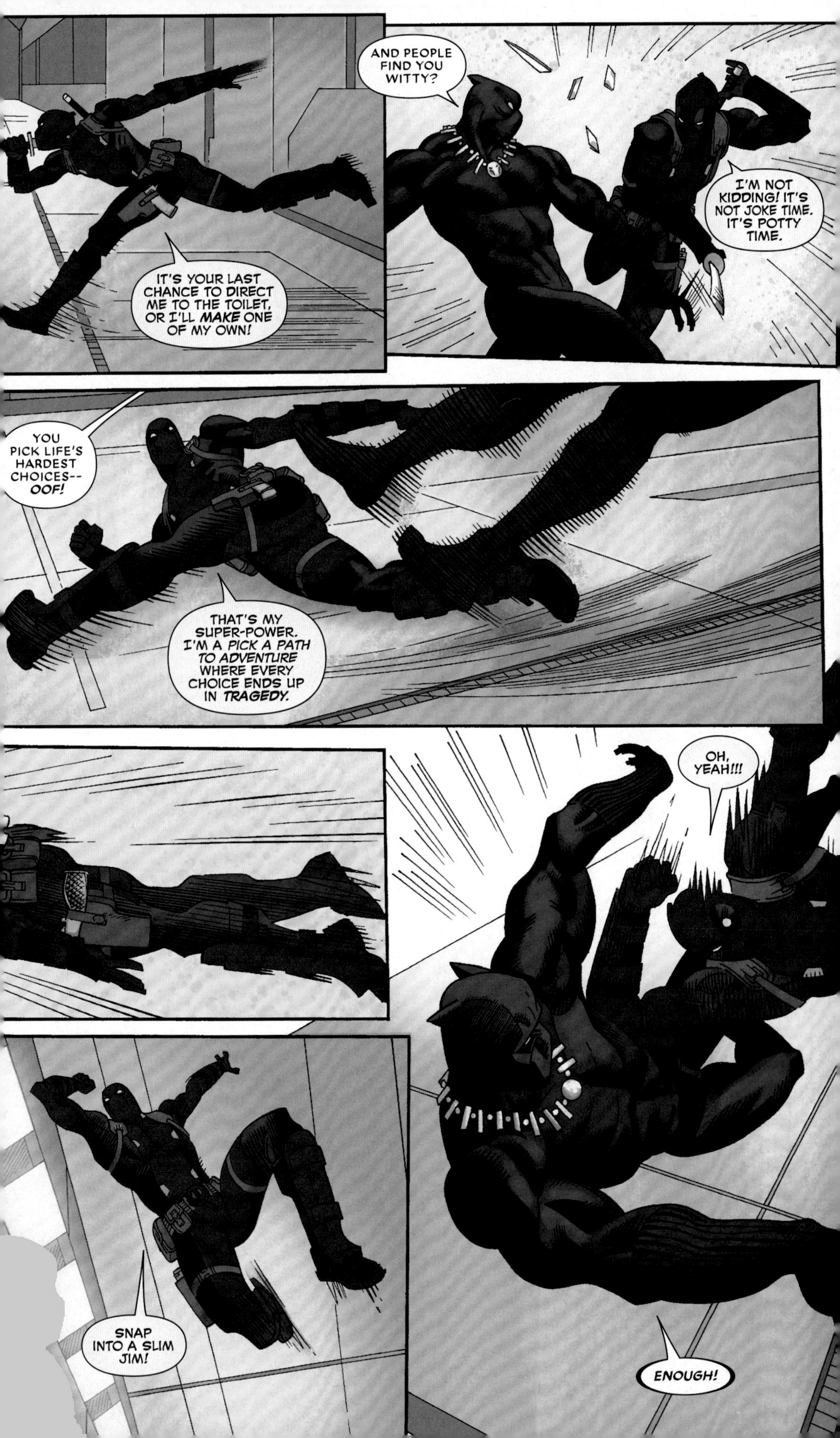
IT'S YOUR LAST CHANCE TO DIRECT ME TO THE TOILET, OR I'LL MAKE ONE OF MY OWN!
AND PEOPLE FIND YOU WITTY?
I'M NOT KIDDING! IT'S NOT JOKE TIME. IT'S POTTY TIME.
YOU PICK LIFE'S HARDEST CHOICES-- OOF!
THAT'S MY SUPER-POWER. I'M A PICK A PATH TO ADVENTURE WHERE EVERY CHOICE ENDS UP IN TRAGEDY.
OH, YEAH!!!
SNAP INTO A SLIM JIM!
ENOUGH!

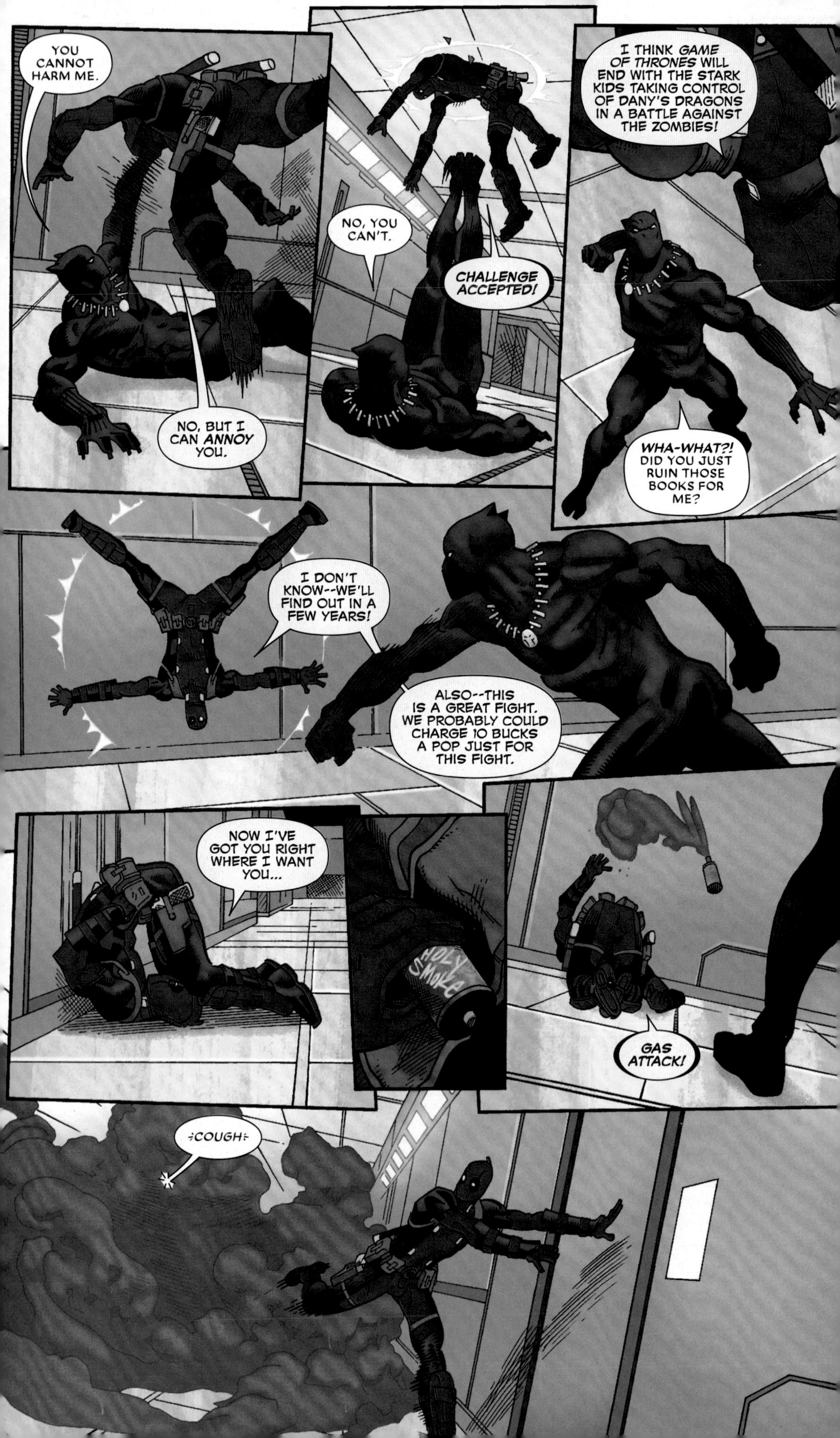
YOU CANNOT HARM ME.
NO, BUT I CAN ANNOY YOU.
NO, YOU CAN'T.
CHALLENGE ACCEPTED!
I THINK GAME OF THRONES WILL END WITH THE STARK KIDS TAKING CONTROL OF DANY'S DRAGONS IN A BATTLE AGAINST THE ZOMBIES!
WHA-WHAT?! DID YOU JUST RUIN THOSE BOOKS FOR ME?
I DON'T KNOW--WE'LL FIND OUT IN A FEW YEARS!
ALSO--THIS IS A GREAT FIGHT. WE PROBABLY COULD CHARGE 10 BUCKS A POP JUST FOR THIS FIGHT.
NOW I'VE GOT YOU RIGHT WHERE I WANT YOU...
HOLY SMOKE
GAS ATTACK!
COUGH

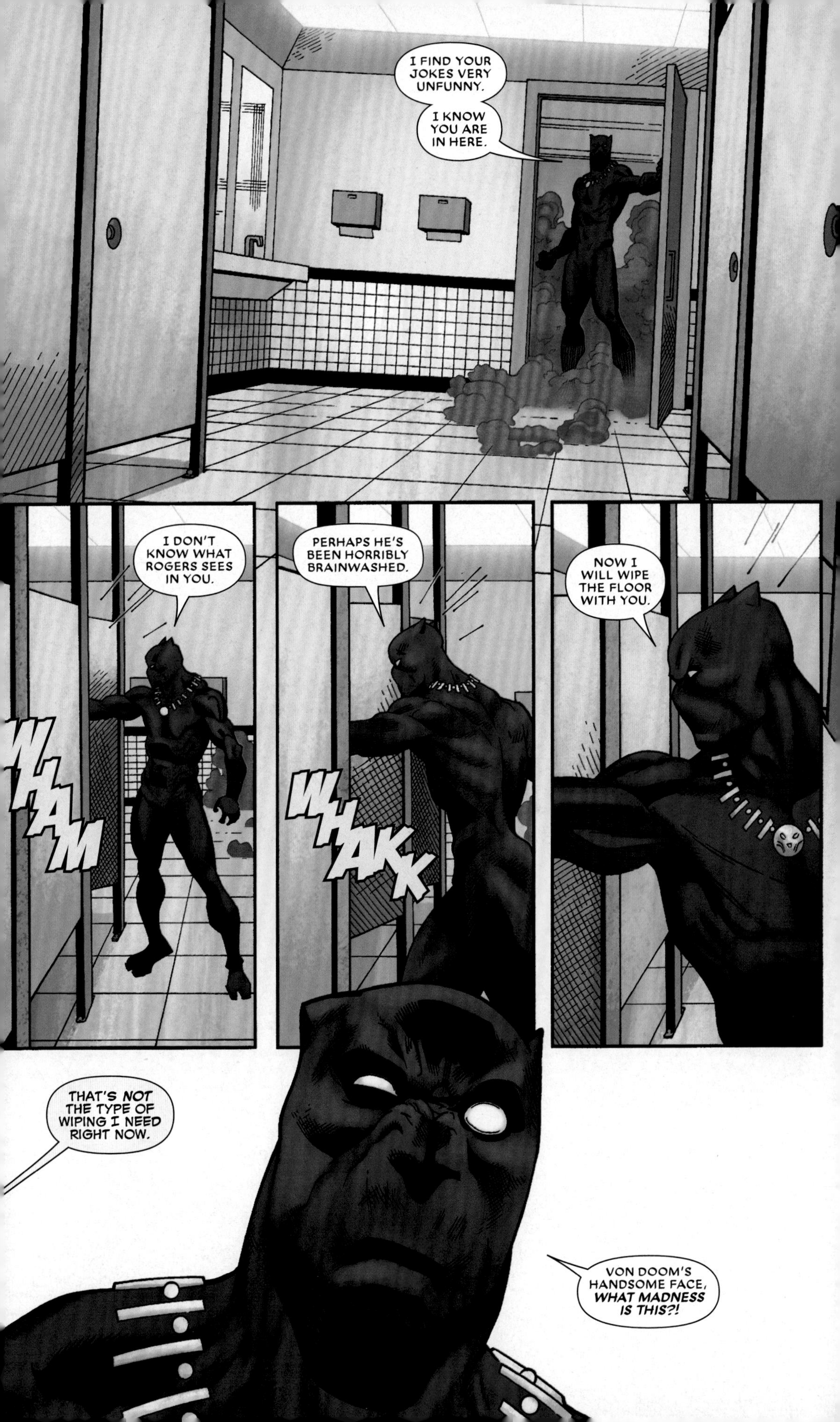
I FIND YOUR JOKES VERY UNFUNNY.
I KNOW YOU ARE IN HERE.
I DON'T KNOW WHAT ROGERS SEES IN YOU.
WHAM
PERHAPS HE'S BEEN HORRIBLY BRAINWASHED.
WHAKK
NOW I WILL WIPE THE FLOOR WITH YOU.
THAT'S *NOT* THE TYPE OF WIPING I NEED RIGHT NOW.
VON DOOM'S HANDSOME FACE, ***WHAT MADNESS IS THIS?!***

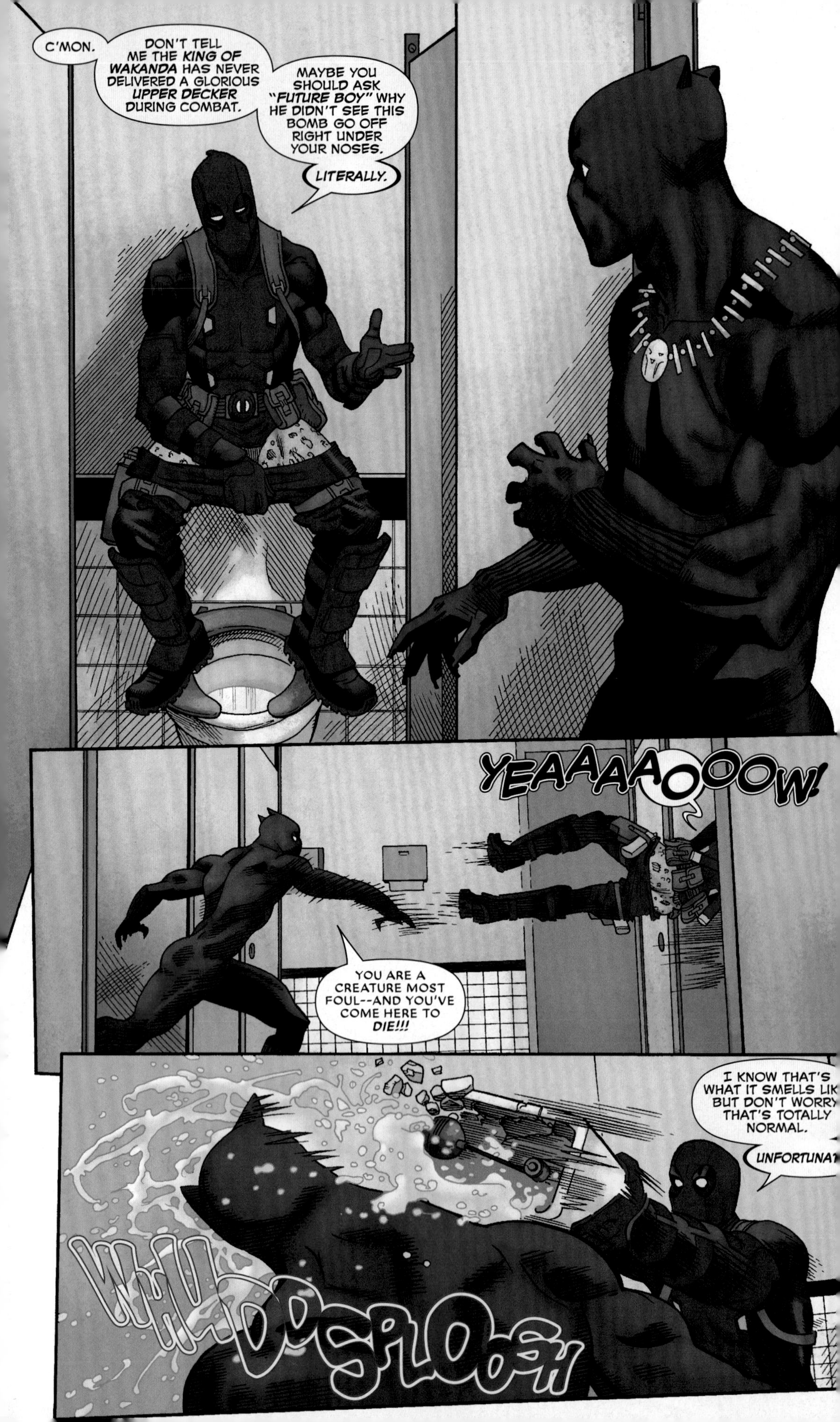
C'MON.
DON'T TELL ME THE KING OF WAKANDA HAS NEVER DELIVERED A GLORIOUS UPPER DECKER DURING COMBAT.
MAYBE YOU SHOULD ASK "FUTURE BOY" WHY HE DIDN'T SEE THIS BOMB GO OFF RIGHT UNDER YOUR NOSES.
LITERALLY.
YEAAAAOOOOW!
YOU ARE A CREATURE MOST FOUL--AND YOU'VE COME HERE TO DIE!!!
I KNOW THAT'S WHAT IT SMELLS LIK BUT DON'T WORRY THAT'S TOTALLY NORMAL.
UNFORTUNA
WHADOOSPLOOSH

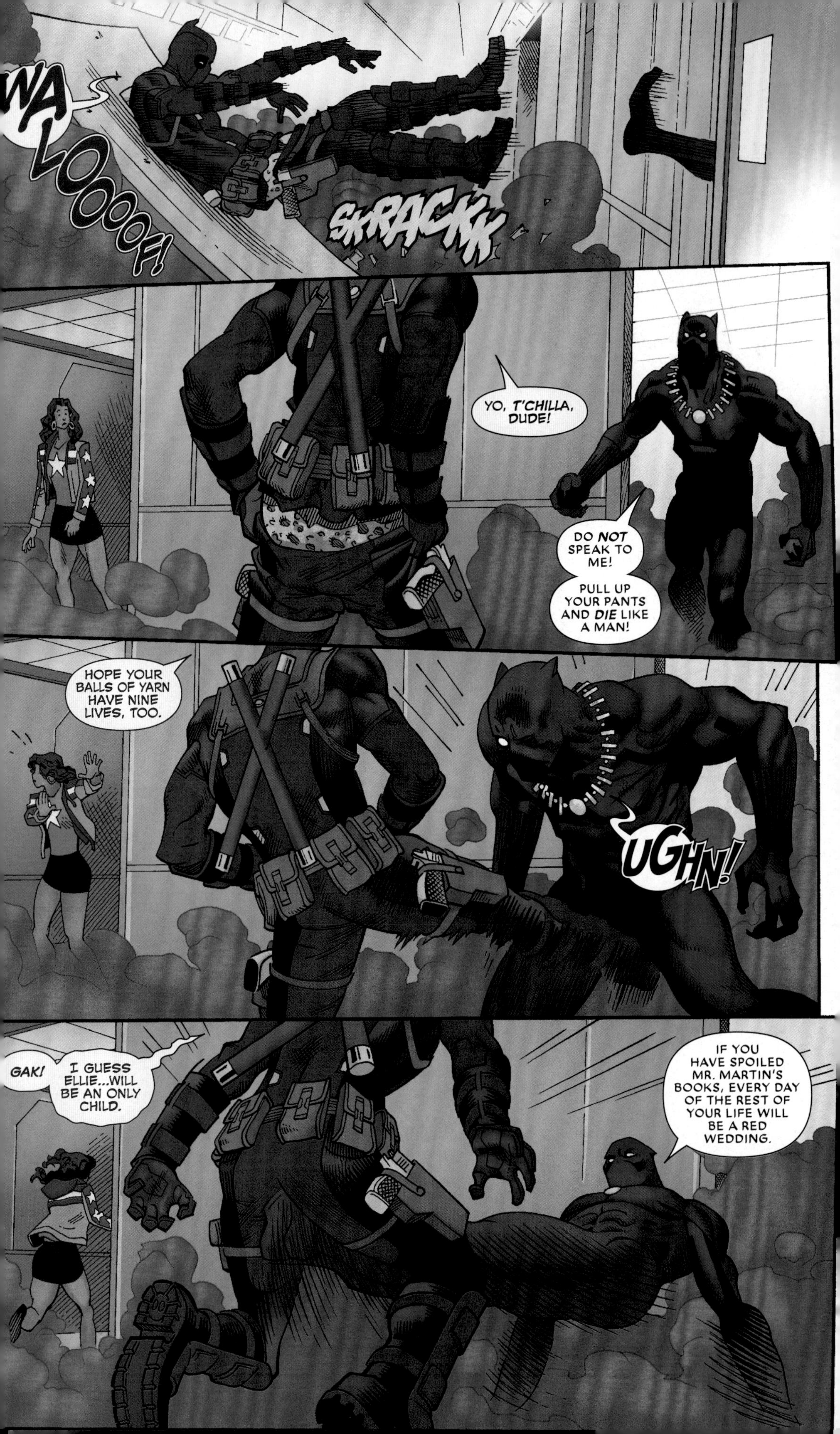
WALOOOOF!
SKRACKK
YO, T'CHILLA, DUDE!
DO NOT SPEAK TO ME!
PULL UP YOUR PANTS AND DIE LIKE A MAN!
HOPE YOUR BALLS OF YARN HAVE NINE LIVES, TOO.
UGHN!
GAK!
I GUESS ELLIE...WILL BE AN ONLY CHILD.
IF YOU HAVE SPOILED MR. MARTIN'S BOOKS, EVERY DAY OF THE REST OF YOUR LIFE WILL BE A RED WEDDING.

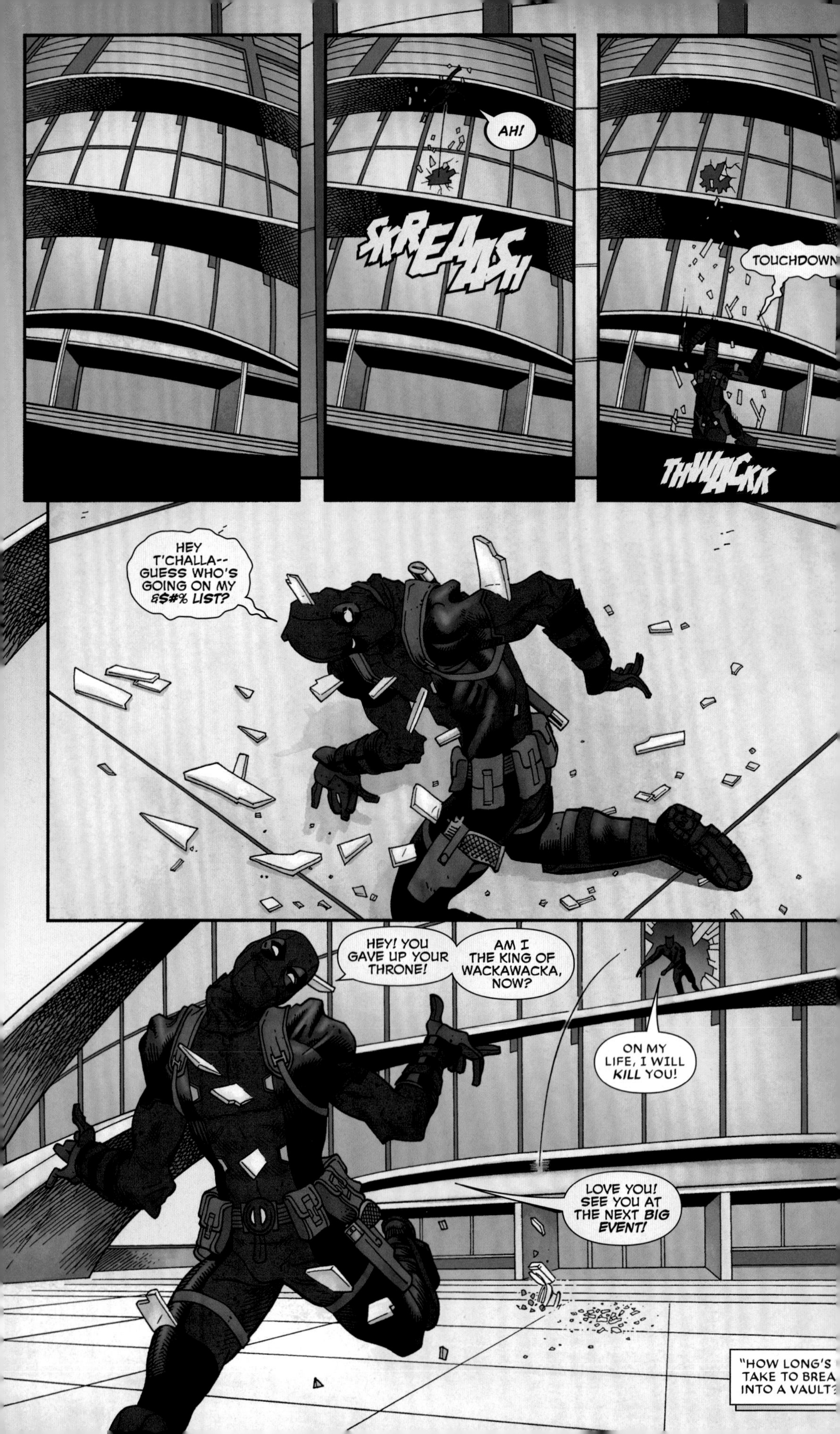
AH!
SKREAASH
TOUCHDOWN
THWACKK
HEY T'CHALLA-- GUESS WHO'S GOING ON MY &$#% LIST?
HEY! YOU GAVE UP YOUR THRONE!
AM I THE KING OF WACKAWACKA, NOW?
ON MY LIFE, I WILL KILL YOU!
LOVE YOU! SEE YOU AT THE NEXT BIG EVENT!
"HOW LONG'S TAKE TO BREA INTO A VAULT?

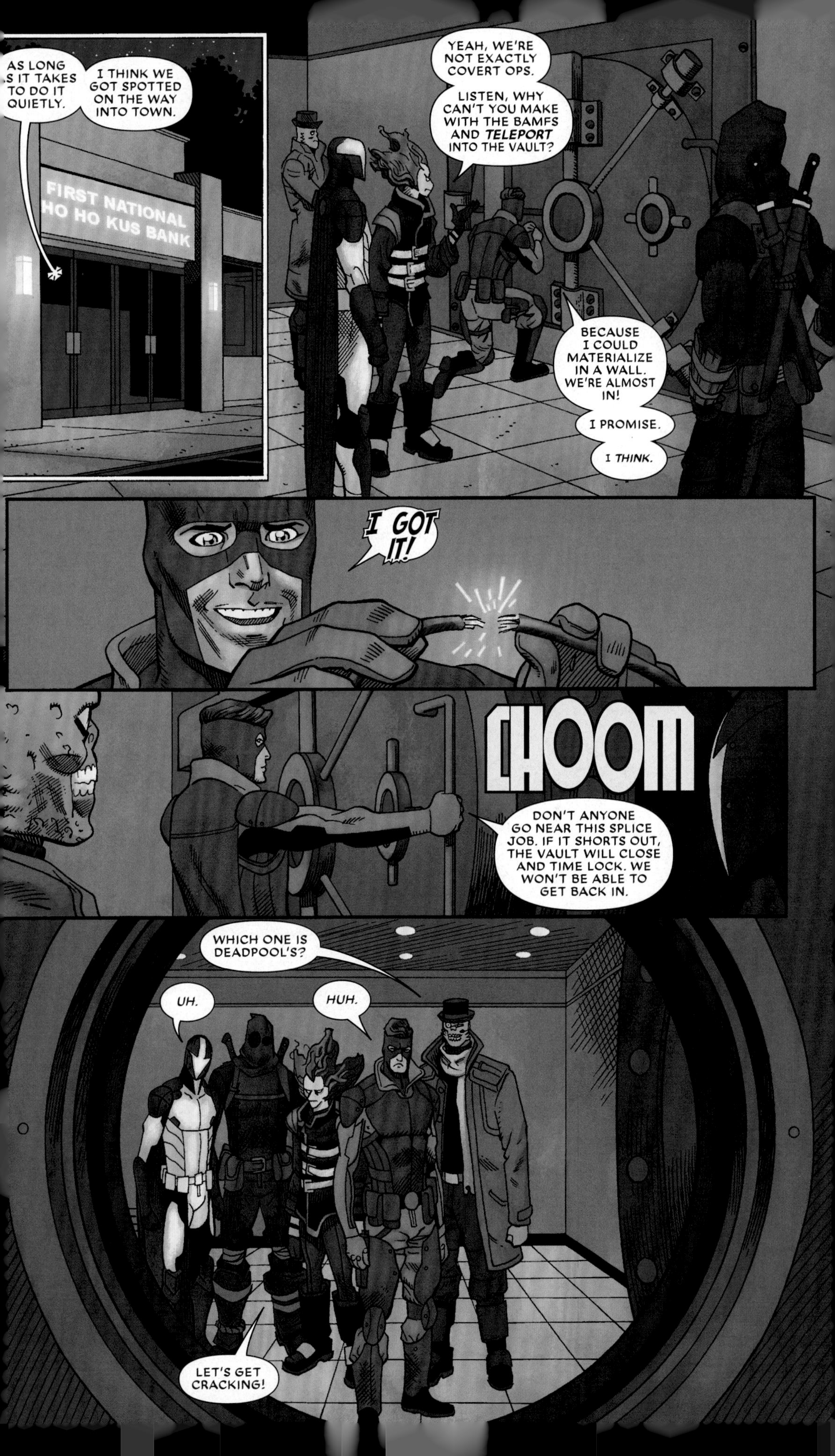

AS LONG S IT TAKES TO DO IT QUIETLY.
I THINK WE GOT SPOTTED ON THE WAY INTO TOWN.
FIRST NATIONAL HO HO KUS BANK
YEAH, WE'RE NOT EXACTLY COVERT OPS.
LISTEN, WHY CAN'T YOU MAKE WITH THE BAMFS AND *TELEPORT* INTO THE VAULT?
BECAUSE I COULD MATERIALIZE IN A WALL. WE'RE ALMOST IN!
I PROMISE.
I *THINK*.
I GOT IT!
CHOOM
DON'T ANYONE GO NEAR THIS SPLICE JOB. IF IT SHORTS OUT, THE VAULT WILL CLOSE AND TIME LOCK. WE WON'T BE ABLE TO GET BACK IN.
WHICH ONE IS DEADPOOL'S?
UH.
HUH.
LET'S GET CRACKING!

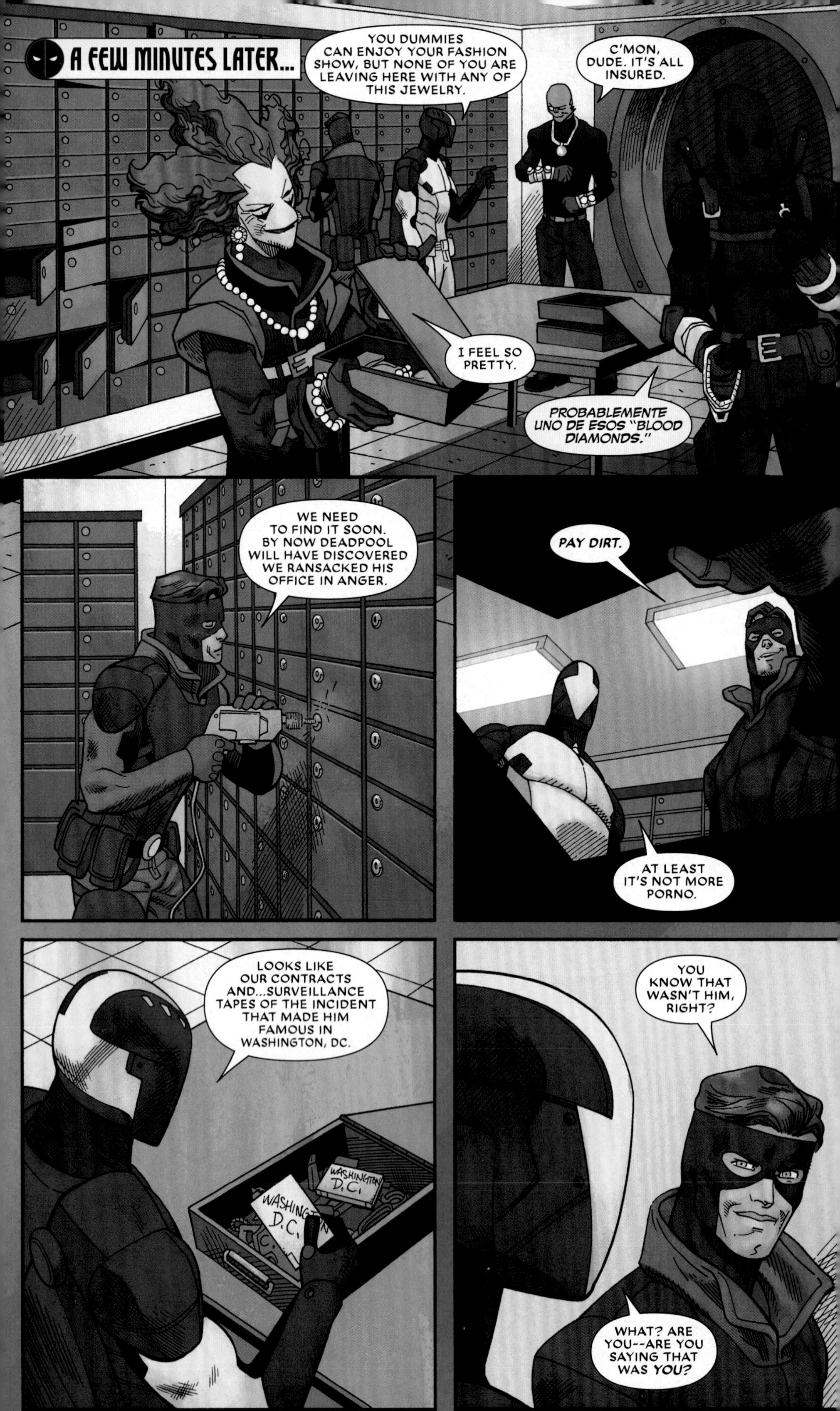

A FEW MINUTES LATER...
YOU DUMMIES CAN ENJOY YOUR FASHION SHOW, BUT NONE OF YOU ARE LEAVING HERE WITH ANY OF THIS JEWELRY.
C'MON, DUDE. IT'S ALL INSURED.
I FEEL SO PRETTY.
PROBABLEMENTE UNO DE ESOS "BLOOD DIAMONDS."
WE NEED TO FIND IT SOON. BY NOW DEADPOOL WILL HAVE DISCOVERED WE RANSACKED HIS OFFICE IN ANGER.
PAY DIRT.
AT LEAST IT'S NOT MORE PORNO.
LOOKS LIKE OUR CONTRACTS AND...SURVEILLANCE TAPES OF THE INCIDENT THAT MADE HIM FAMOUS IN WASHINGTON, DC.
WASHINGTON D.C.
WASHINGTON D.C.
YOU KNOW THAT WASN'T HIM, RIGHT?
WHAT? ARE YOU--ARE YOU SAYING THAT WAS YOU?

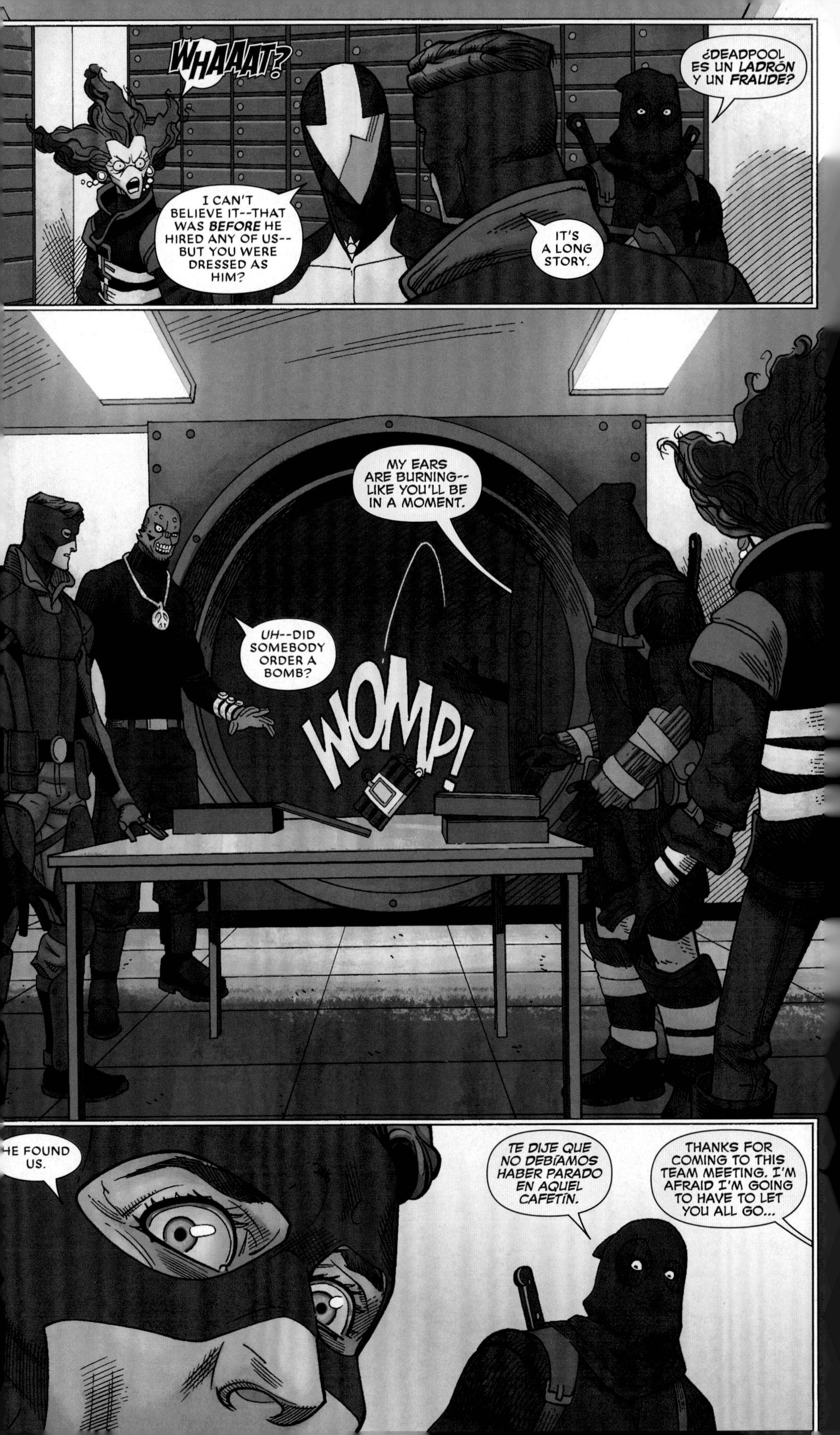
WHAAAT?
I CAN'T BELIEVE IT--THAT WAS *BEFORE* HE HIRED ANY OF US--BUT YOU WERE DRESSED AS HIM?
IT'S A LONG STORY.
¿DEADPOOL ES UN *LADRÓN* Y UN *FRAUDE?*
MY EARS ARE BURNING--LIKE YOU'LL BE IN A MOMENT.
UH--DID SOMEBODY ORDER A BOMB?
WOMP!
HE FOUND US.
TE DIJE QUE NO DEBÍAMOS HABER PARADO EN AQUEL CAFETÍN.
THANKS FOR COMING TO THIS TEAM MEETING. I'M AFRAID I'M GOING TO HAVE TO LET YOU ALL GO...

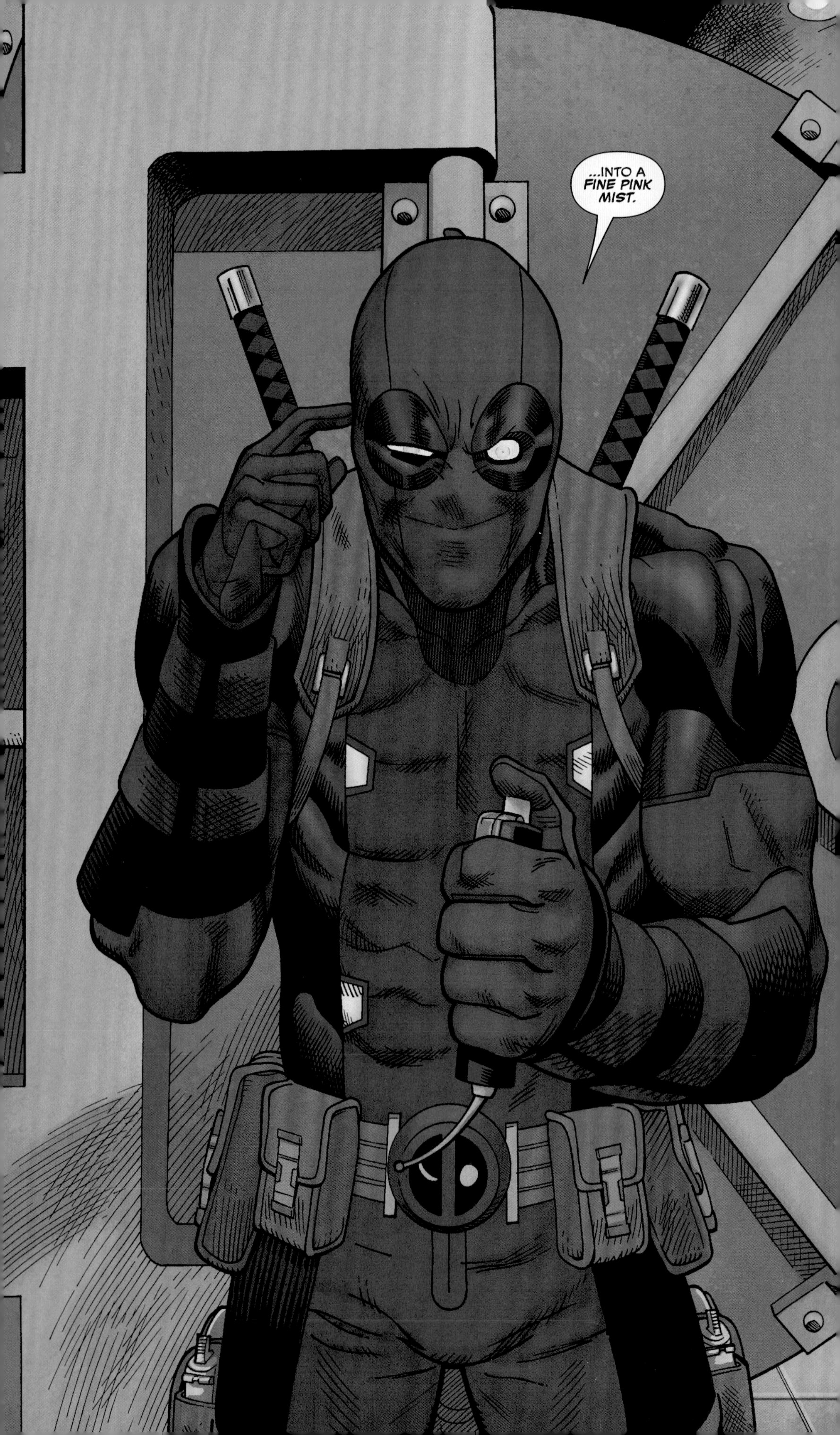
...INTO A FINE PINK MIST.

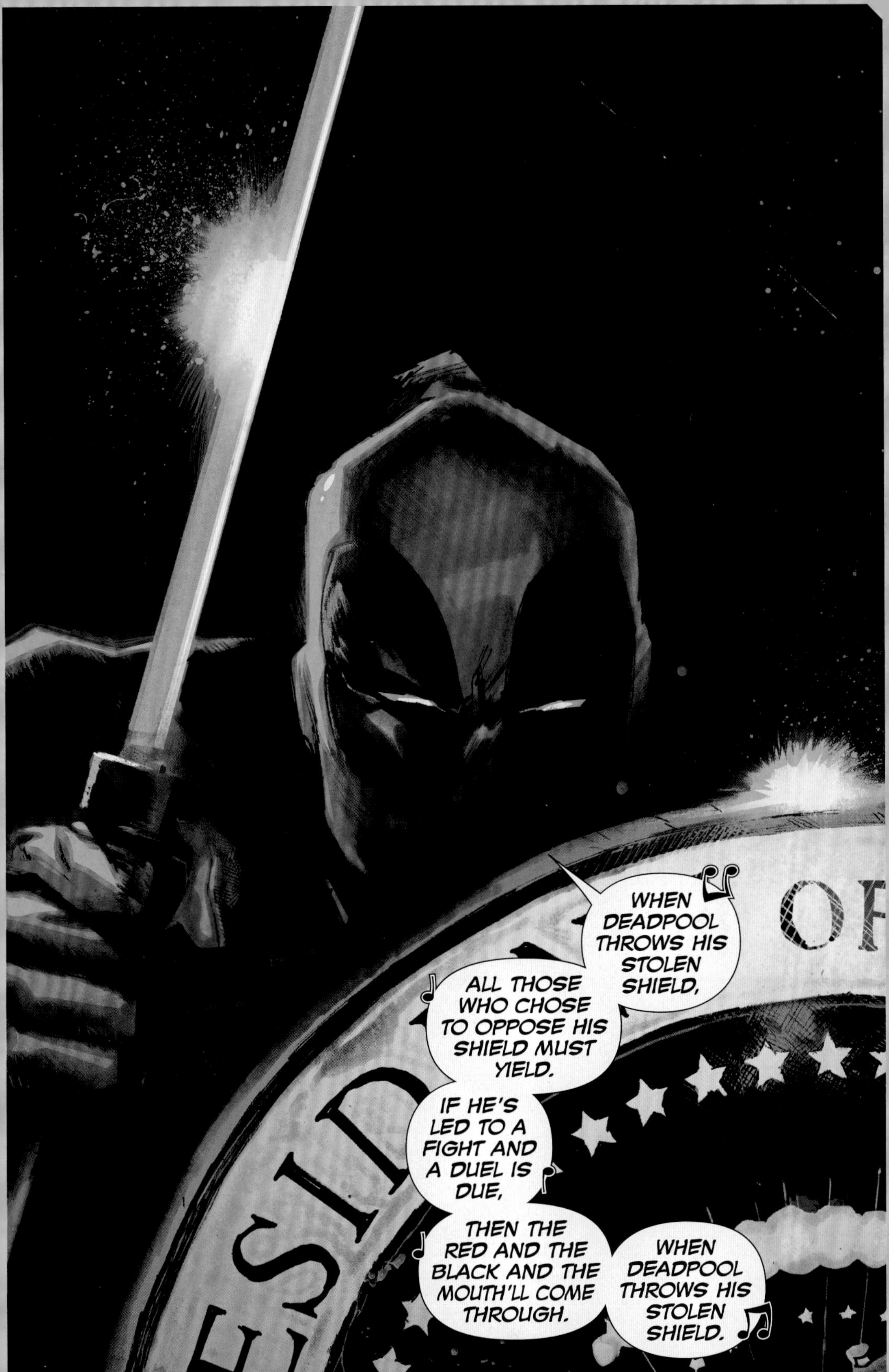
WHEN DEADPOOL THROWS HIS STOLEN SHIELD,
ALL THOSE WHO CHOSE TO OPPOSE HIS SHIELD MUST YIELD.
IF HE'S LED TO A FIGHT AND A DUEL IS DUE,
THEN THE RED AND THE BLACK AND THE MOUTH'LL COME THROUGH.
WHEN DEADPOOL THROWS HIS STOLEN SHIELD.

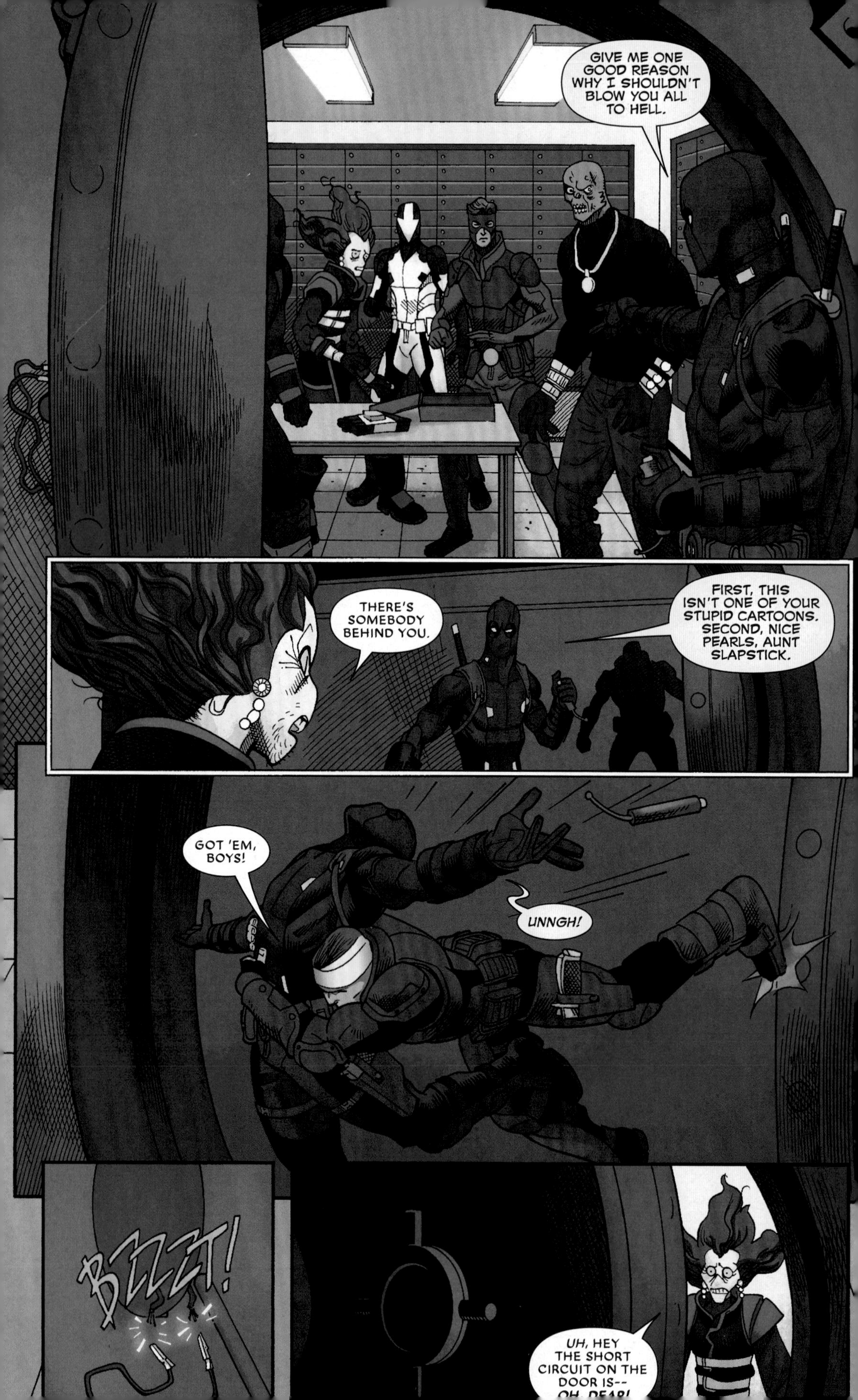
GIVE ME ONE GOOD REASON WHY I SHOULDN'T BLOW YOU ALL TO HELL.
THERE'S SOMEBODY BEHIND YOU.
FIRST, THIS ISN'T ONE OF YOUR STUPID CARTOONS. SECOND, NICE PEARLS, AUNT SLAPSTICK.
GOT 'EM, BOYS!
UNNGH!
BZZZT!
UH, HEY THE SHORT CIRCUIT ON THE DOOR IS--

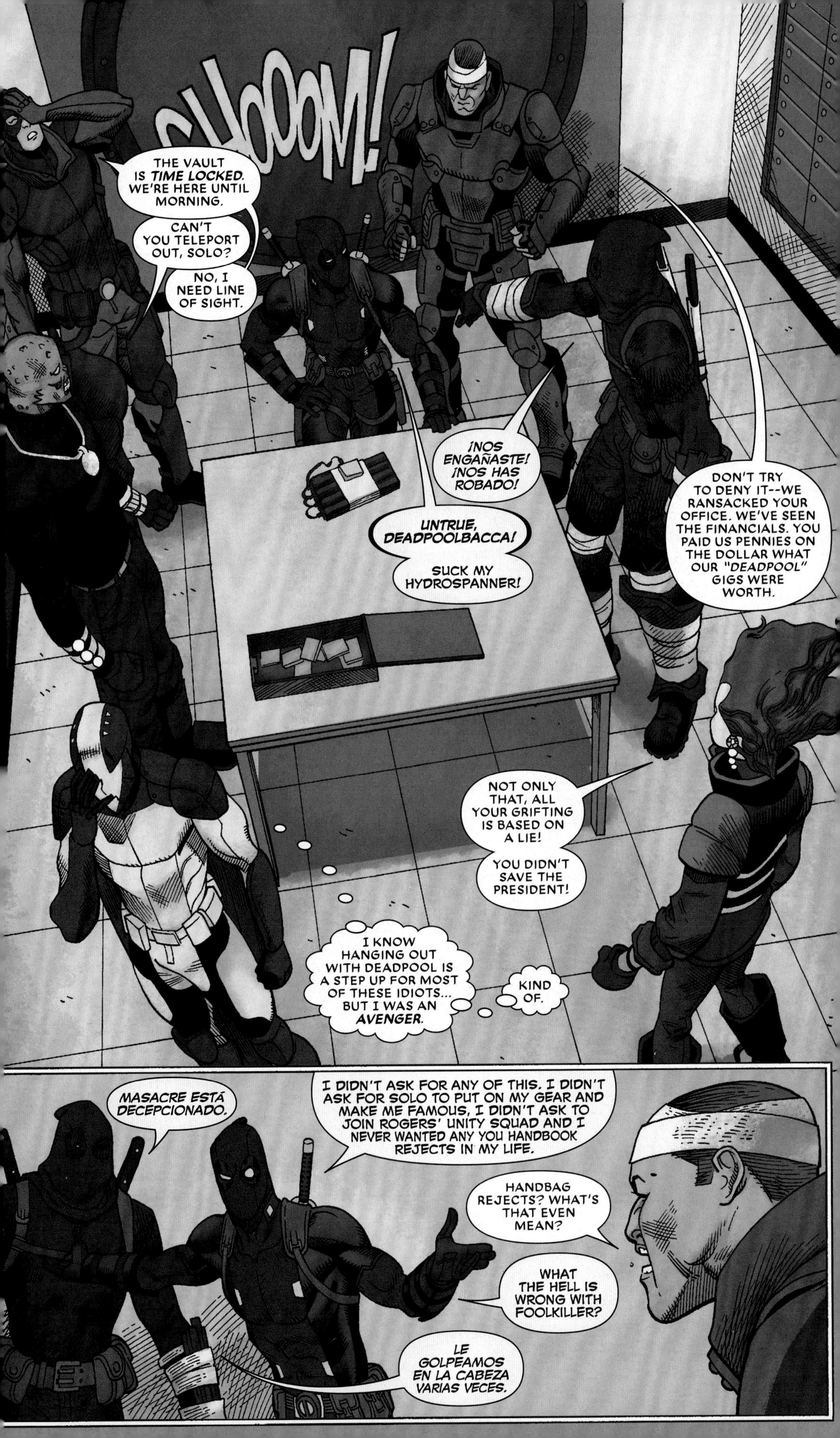
SHOOOM!
THE VAULT IS TIME LOCKED. WE'RE HERE UNTIL MORNING.
CAN'T YOU TELEPORT OUT, SOLO?
NO, I NEED LINE OF SIGHT.
¡NOS ENGAÑASTE! ¡NOS HAS ROBADO!
UNTRUE, DEADPOOLBACCA!
SUCK MY HYDROSPANNER!
DON'T TRY TO DENY IT--WE RANSACKED YOUR OFFICE. WE'VE SEEN THE FINANCIALS. YOU PAID US PENNIES ON THE DOLLAR WHAT OUR "DEADPOOL" GIGS WERE WORTH.
NOT ONLY THAT, ALL YOUR GRIFTING IS BASED ON A LIE!
YOU DIDN'T SAVE THE PRESIDENT!
I KNOW HANGING OUT WITH DEADPOOL IS A STEP UP FOR MOST OF THESE IDIOTS... BUT I WAS AN AVENGER.
KIND OF.
MASACRE ESTÁ DECEPCIONADO.
I DIDN'T ASK FOR ANY OF THIS. I DIDN'T ASK FOR SOLO TO PUT ON MY GEAR AND MAKE ME FAMOUS, I DIDN'T ASK TO JOIN ROGERS' UNITY SQUAD AND I NEVER WANTED ANY YOU HANDBOOK REJECTS IN MY LIFE.
HANDBAG REJECTS? WHAT'S THAT EVEN MEAN?
WHAT THE HELL IS WRONG WITH FOOLKILLER?
LE GOLPEAMOS EN LA CABEZA VARIAS VECES.

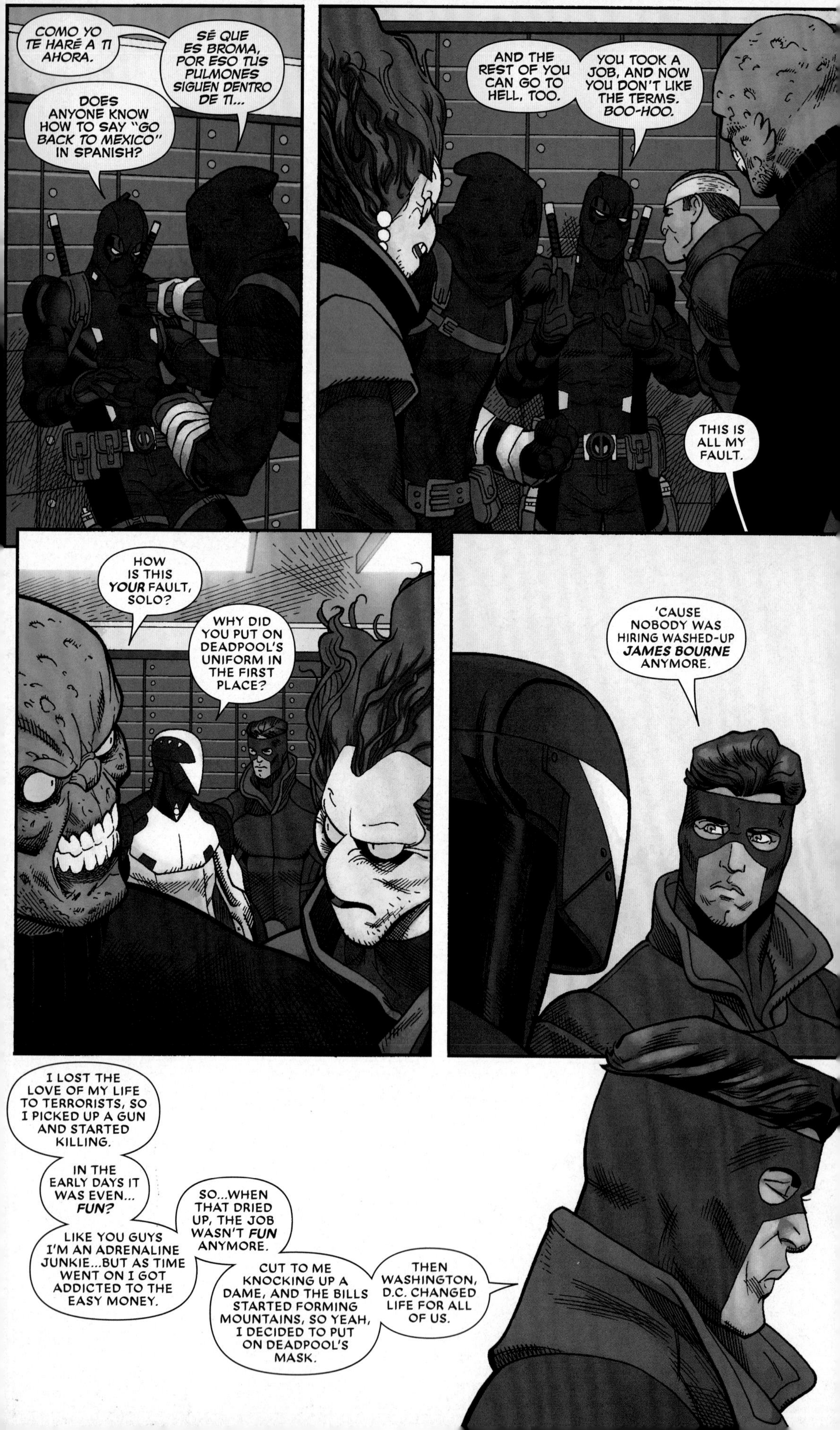
COMO YO TE HARÉ A TI AHORA.
SÉ QUE ES BROMA, POR ESO TUS PULMONES SIGUEN DENTRO DE TI...
DOES ANYONE KNOW HOW TO SAY "GO BACK TO MEXICO" IN SPANISH?
AND THE REST OF YOU CAN GO TO HELL, TOO.
YOU TOOK A JOB, AND NOW YOU DON'T LIKE THE TERMS. BOO-HOO.
THIS IS ALL MY FAULT.
HOW IS THIS YOUR FAULT, SOLO?
WHY DID YOU PUT ON DEADPOOL'S UNIFORM IN THE FIRST PLACE?
'CAUSE NOBODY WAS HIRING WASHED-UP JAMES BOURNE ANYMORE.
I LOST THE LOVE OF MY LIFE TO TERRORISTS, SO I PICKED UP A GUN AND STARTED KILLING.
IN THE EARLY DAYS IT WAS EVEN... FUN?
LIKE YOU GUYS I'M AN ADRENALINE JUNKIE...BUT AS TIME WENT ON I GOT ADDICTED TO THE EASY MONEY.
SO...WHEN THAT DRIED UP, THE JOB WASN'T FUN ANYMORE.
CUT TO ME KNOCKING UP A DAME, AND THE BILLS STARTED FORMING MOUNTAINS, SO YEAH, I DECIDED TO PUT ON DEADPOOL'S MASK.
THEN WASHINGTON, D.C. CHANGED LIFE FOR ALL OF US.

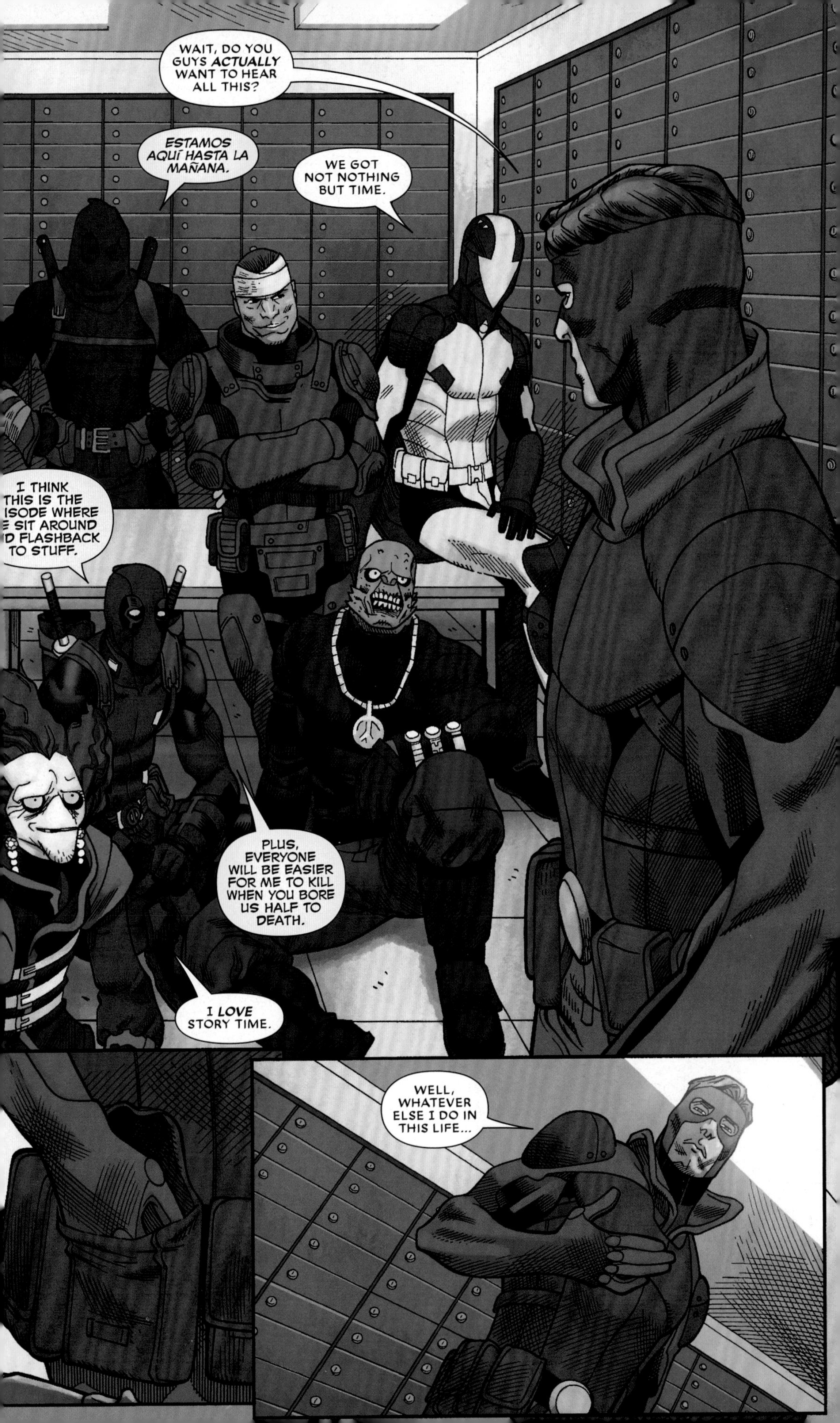

WAIT, DO YOU GUYS *ACTUALLY* WANT TO HEAR ALL THIS?
ESTAMOS AQUÍ HASTA LA MAÑANA.
WE GOT NOT NOTHING BUT TIME.
I THINK THIS IS THE ISODE WHERE E SIT AROUND D FLASHBACK TO STUFF.
PLUS, EVERYONE WILL BE EASIER FOR ME TO KILL WHEN YOU BORE US HALF TO DEATH.
I *LOVE* STORY TIME.
WELL, WHATEVER ELSE I DO IN THIS LIFE...

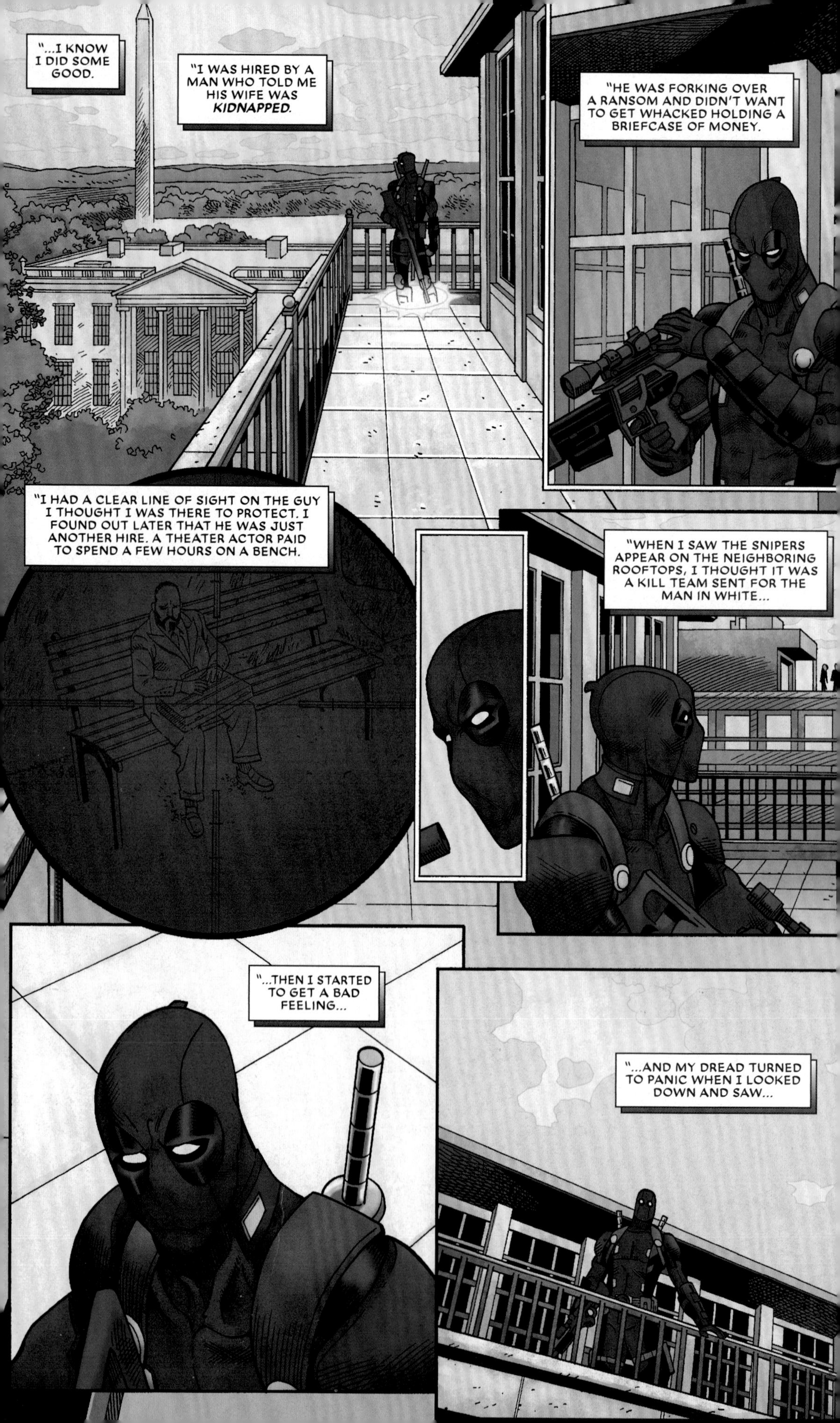
"...I KNOW I DID SOME GOOD.
"I WAS HIRED BY A MAN WHO TOLD ME HIS WIFE WAS *KIDNAPPED.*
"HE WAS FORKING OVER A RANSOM AND DIDN'T WANT TO GET WHACKED HOLDING A BRIEFCASE OF MONEY.
"I HAD A CLEAR LINE OF SIGHT ON THE GUY I THOUGHT I WAS THERE TO PROTECT. I FOUND OUT LATER THAT HE WAS JUST ANOTHER HIRE. A THEATER ACTOR PAID TO SPEND A FEW HOURS ON A BENCH.
"WHEN I SAW THE SNIPERS APPEAR ON THE NEIGHBORING ROOFTOPS, I THOUGHT IT WAS A KILL TEAM SENT FOR THE MAN IN WHITE...
"...THEN I STARTED TO GET A BAD FEELING...
"...AND MY DREAD TURNED TO PANIC WHEN I LOOKED DOWN AND SAW...

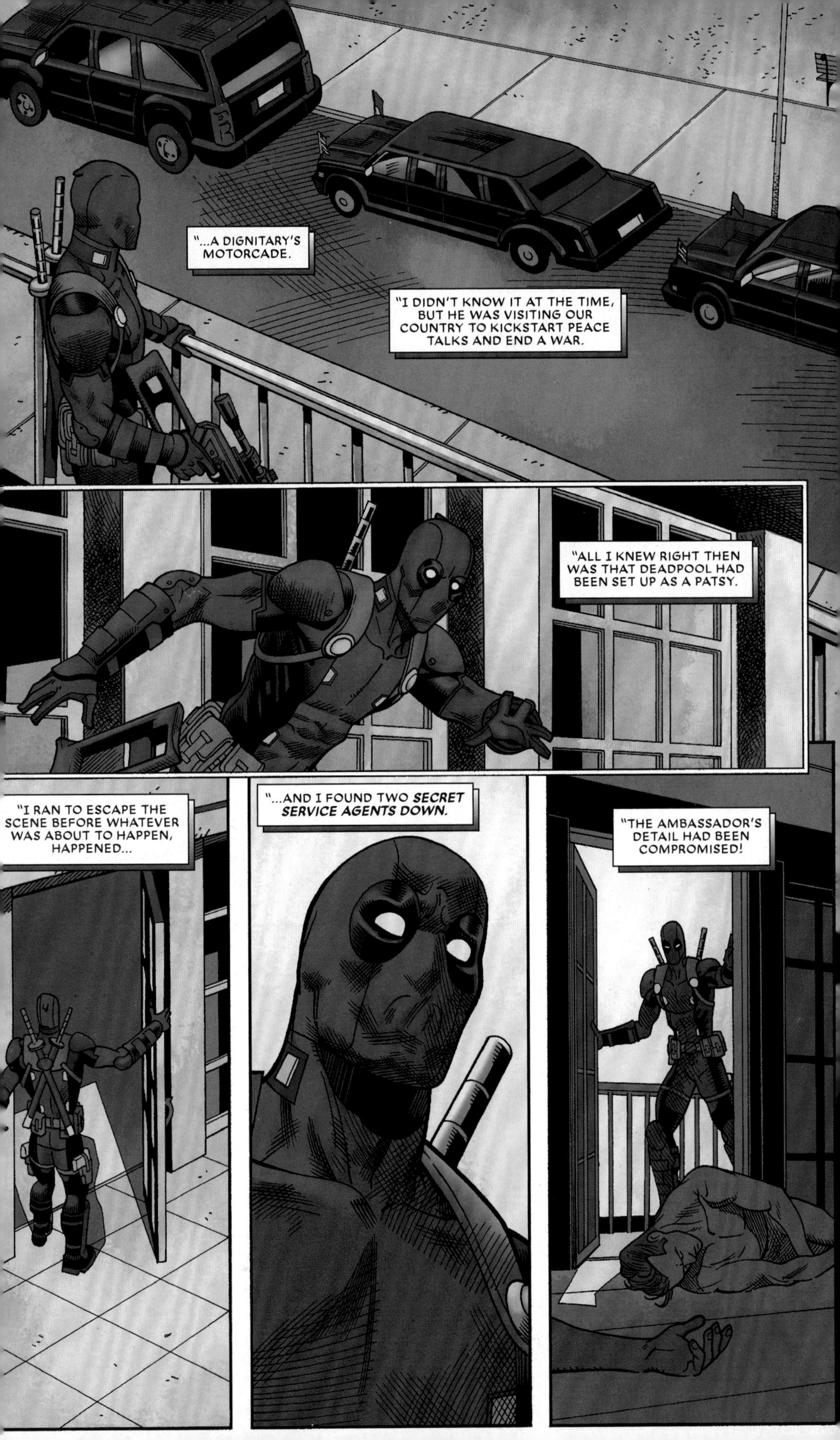
"...A DIGNITARY'S MOTORCADE.
"I DIDN'T KNOW IT AT THE TIME, BUT HE WAS VISITING OUR COUNTRY TO KICKSTART PEACE TALKS AND END A WAR.
"ALL I KNEW RIGHT THEN WAS THAT DEADPOOL HAD BEEN SET UP AS A PATSY.
"I RAN TO ESCAPE THE SCENE BEFORE WHATEVER WAS ABOUT TO HAPPEN, HAPPENED...
"...AND I FOUND TWO SECRET SERVICE AGENTS DOWN.
"THE AMBASSADOR'S DETAIL HAD BEEN COMPROMISED!

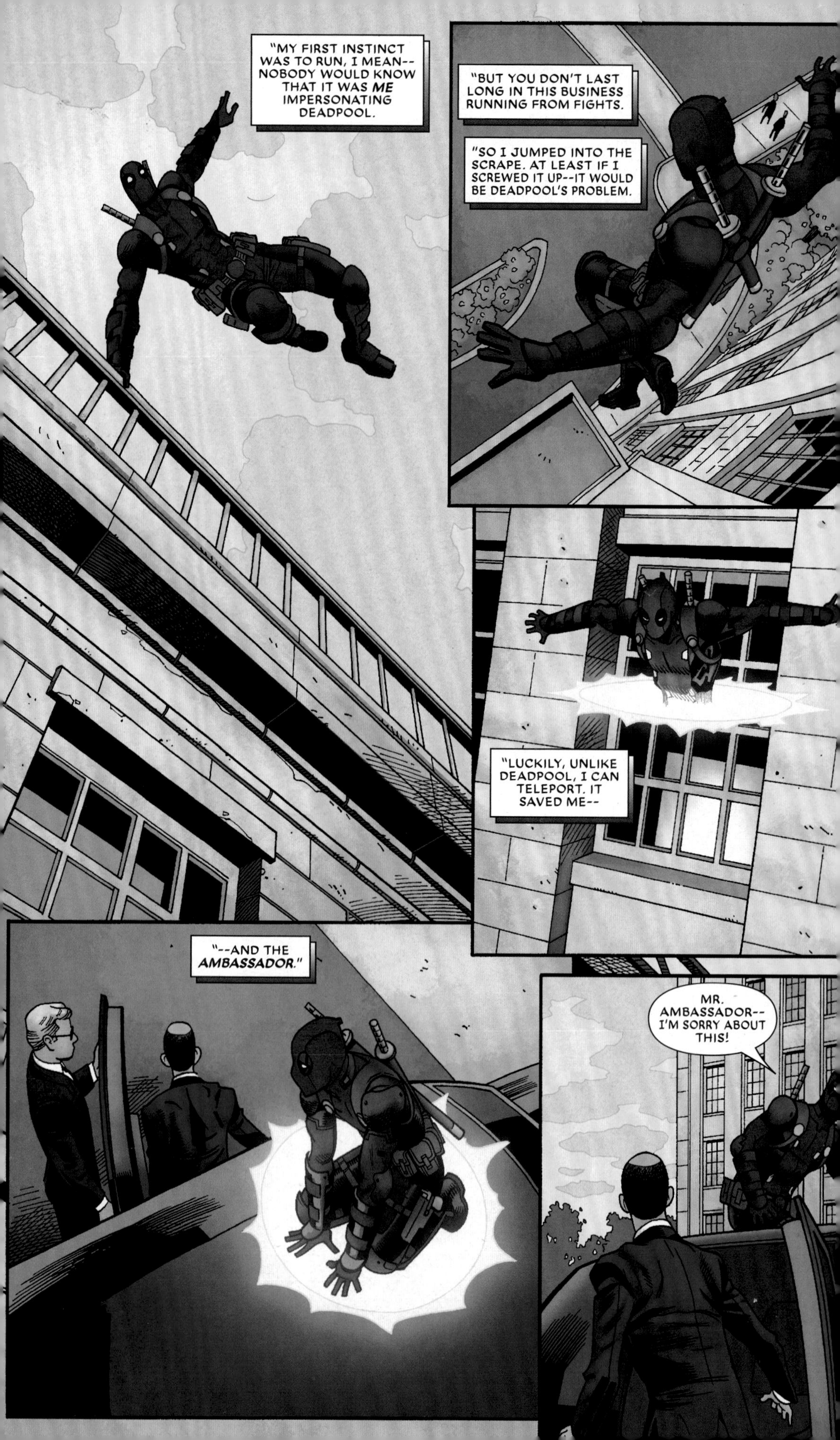
"MY FIRST INSTINCT WAS TO RUN, I MEAN-- NOBODY WOULD KNOW THAT IT WAS ME IMPERSONATING DEADPOOL.
"BUT YOU DON'T LAST LONG IN THIS BUSINESS RUNNING FROM FIGHTS.
"SO I JUMPED INTO THE SCRAPE. AT LEAST IF I SCREWED IT UP--IT WOULD BE DEADPOOL'S PROBLEM.
"LUCKILY, UNLIKE DEADPOOL, I CAN TELEPORT. IT SAVED ME--
"--AND THE AMBASSADOR."
MR. AMBASSADOR-- I'M SORRY ABOUT THIS!

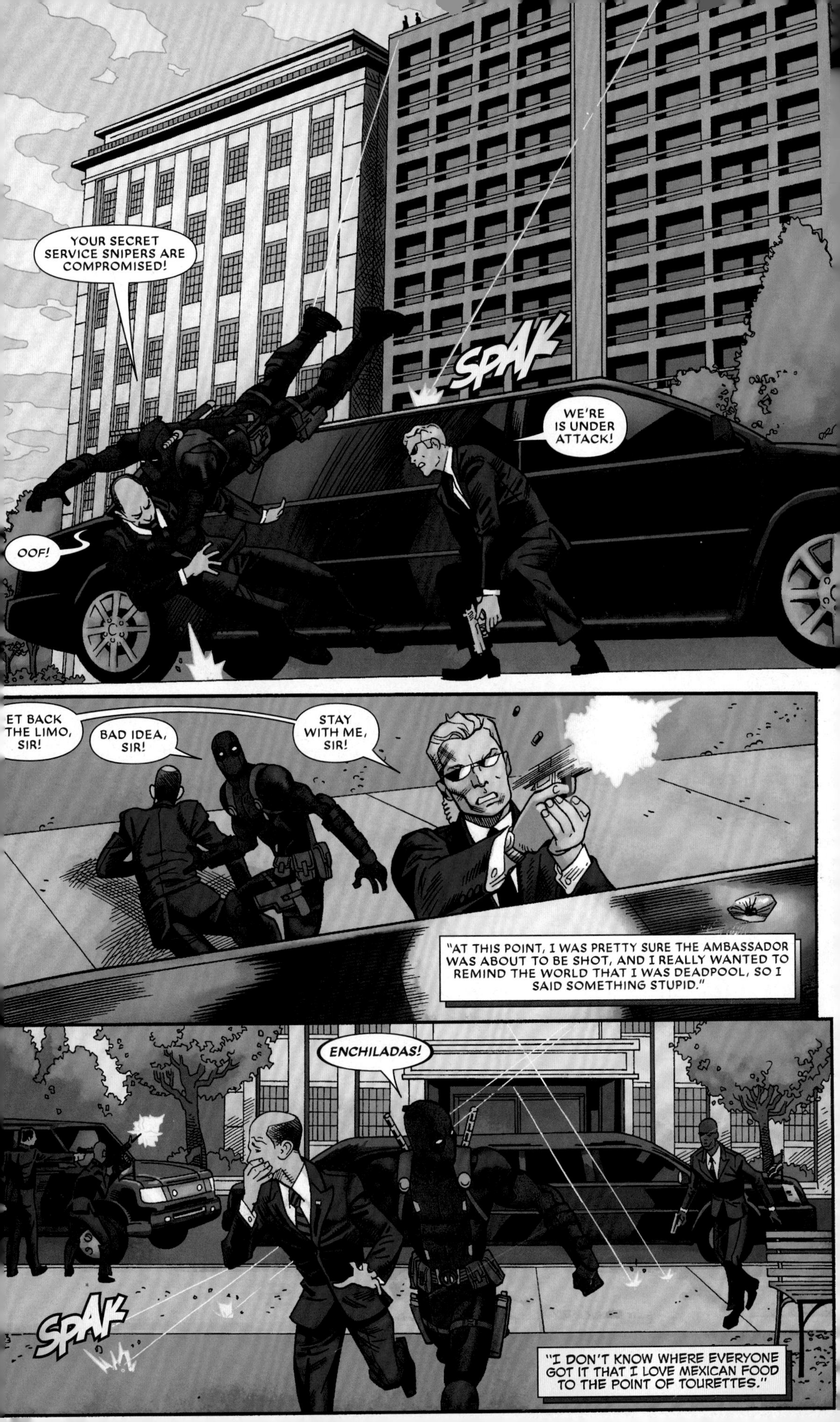
YOUR SECRET SERVICE SNIPERS ARE COMPROMISED!
SPAK
OOF!
WE'RE IS UNDER ATTACK!
ET BACK THE LIMO, SIR!
BAD IDEA, SIR!
STAY WITH ME, SIR!
"AT THIS POINT, I WAS PRETTY SURE THE AMBASSADOR WAS ABOUT TO BE SHOT, AND I REALLY WANTED TO REMIND THE WORLD THAT I WAS DEADPOOL, SO I SAID SOMETHING STUPID."
ENCHILADAS!
SPAK
"I DON'T KNOW WHERE EVERYONE GOT IT THAT I LOVE MEXICAN FOOD TO THE POINT OF TOURETTES."

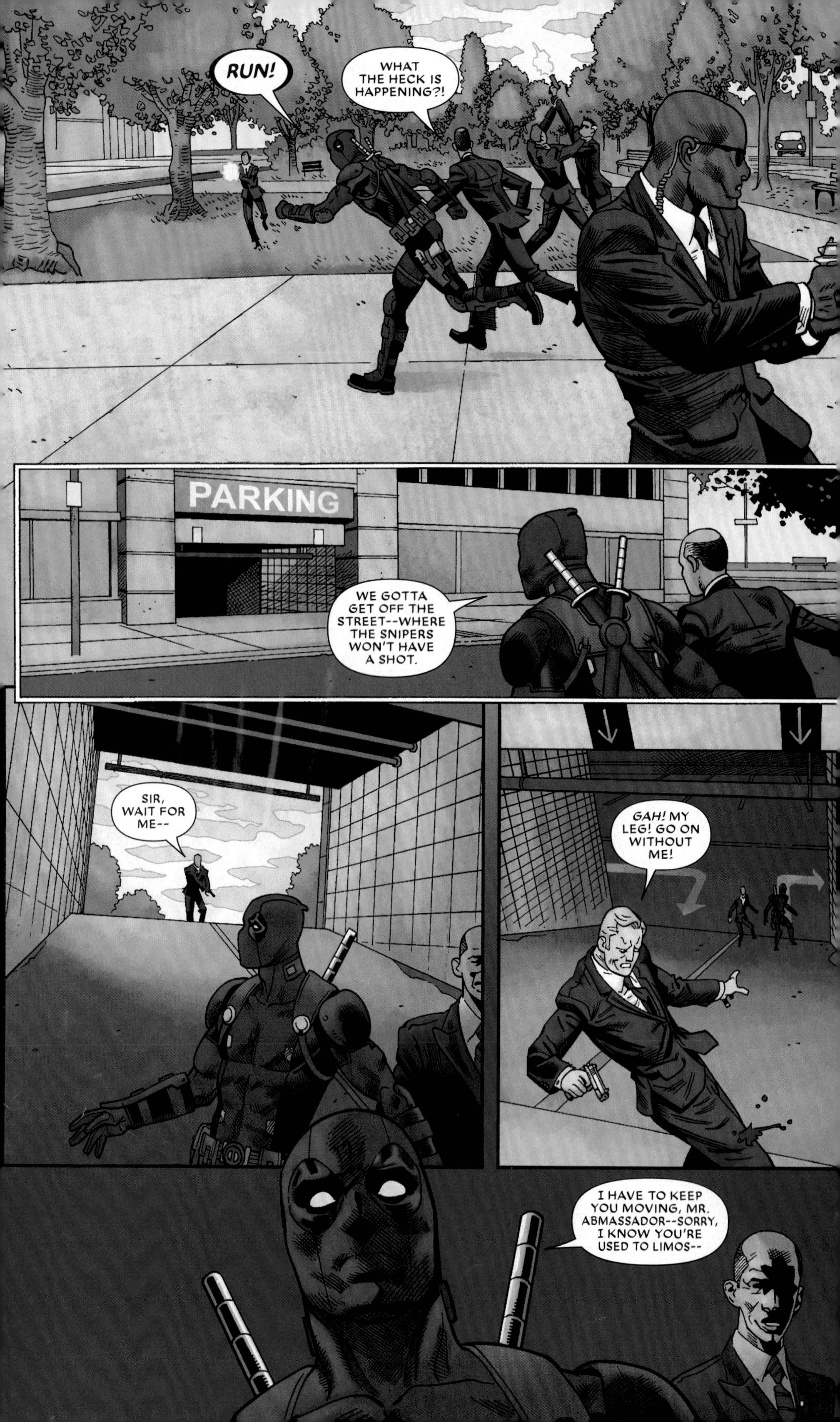
RUN!
WHAT THE HECK IS HAPPENING?!
PARKING
WE GOTTA GET OFF THE STREET--WHERE THE SNIPERS WON'T HAVE A SHOT.
SIR, WAIT FOR ME--
GAH! MY LEG! GO ON WITHOUT ME!
I HAVE TO KEEP YOU MOVING, MR. ABMASSADOR--SORRY, I KNOW YOU'RE USED TO LIMOS--

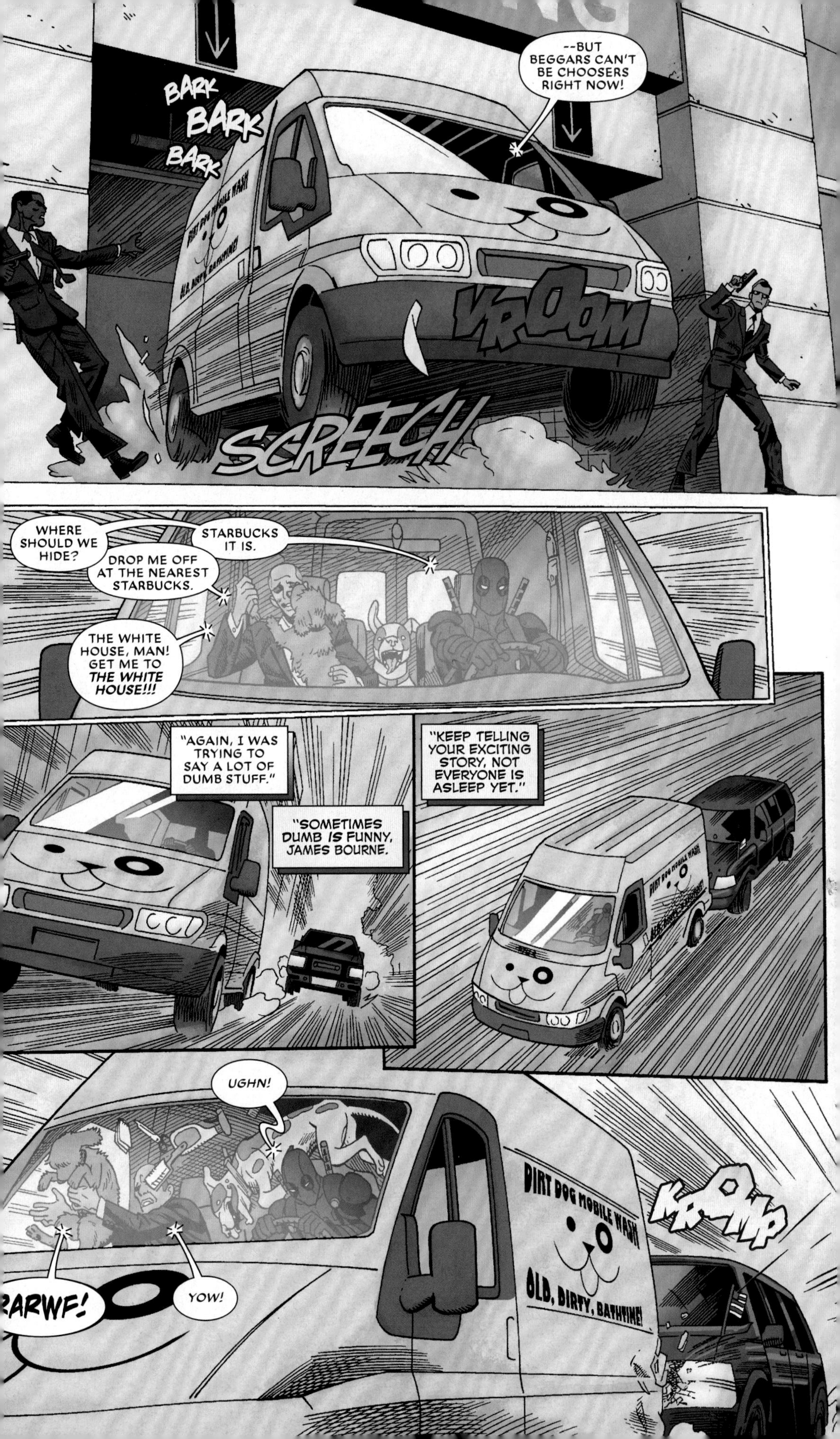

BARK
BARK
BARK
--BUT BEGGARS CAN'T BE CHOOSERS RIGHT NOW!
DIRT DOG MOBILE WASH
OLD, DIRTY, BATHTIME!
VROOM
SCREECH
WHERE SHOULD WE HIDE?
DROP ME OFF AT THE NEAREST STARBUCKS.
STARBUCKS IT IS.
THE WHITE HOUSE, MAN! GET ME TO *THE WHITE HOUSE!!!*
"AGAIN, I WAS TRYING TO SAY A LOT OF DUMB STUFF."
"SOMETIMES DUMB *IS* FUNNY, JAMES BOURNE.
"KEEP TELLING YOUR EXCITING STORY, NOT EVERYONE IS ASLEEP YET."
DIRT DOG MOBILE WASH
UGHN!
RARWF!
YOW!
DIRT DOG MOBILE WASH
OLD, DIRTY, BATHTIME!
KA-OMP

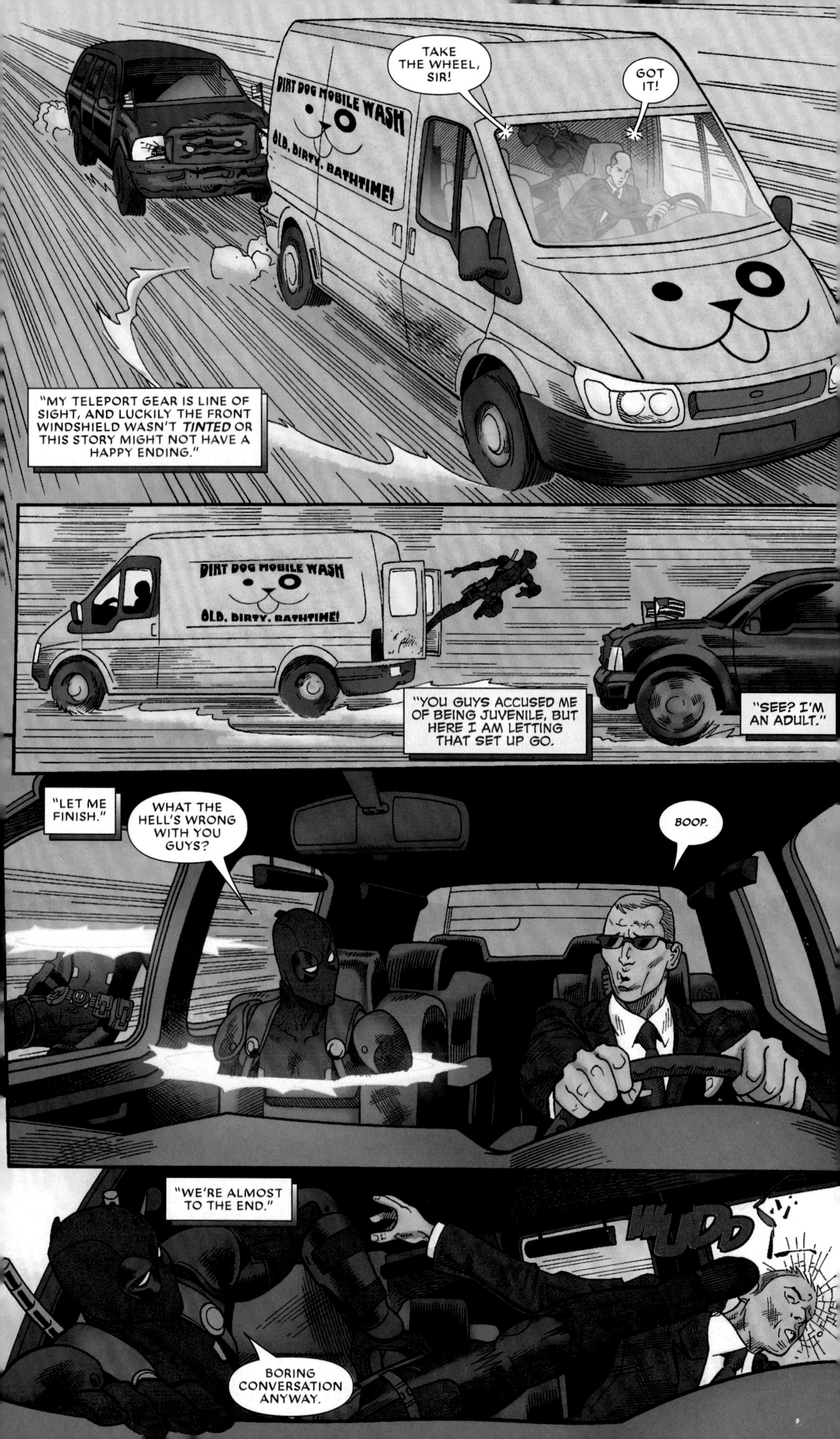
TAKE THE WHEEL, SIR!
GOT IT!
DIRT DOG MOBILE WASH
OLD, DIRTY, BATHTIME!
"MY TELEPORT GEAR IS LINE OF SIGHT, AND LUCKILY THE FRONT WINDSHIELD WASN'T *TINTED* OR THIS STORY MIGHT NOT HAVE A HAPPY ENDING."
DIRT DOG MOBILE WASH
OLD, DIRTY, BATHTIME!
"YOU GUYS ACCUSED ME OF BEING JUVENILE, BUT HERE I AM LETTING THAT SET UP GO.
"SEE? I'M AN ADULT."
"LET ME FINISH."
WHAT THE HELL'S WRONG WITH YOU GUYS?
BOOP.
"WE'RE ALMOST TO THE END."
WUDD
BORING CONVERSATION ANYWAY.

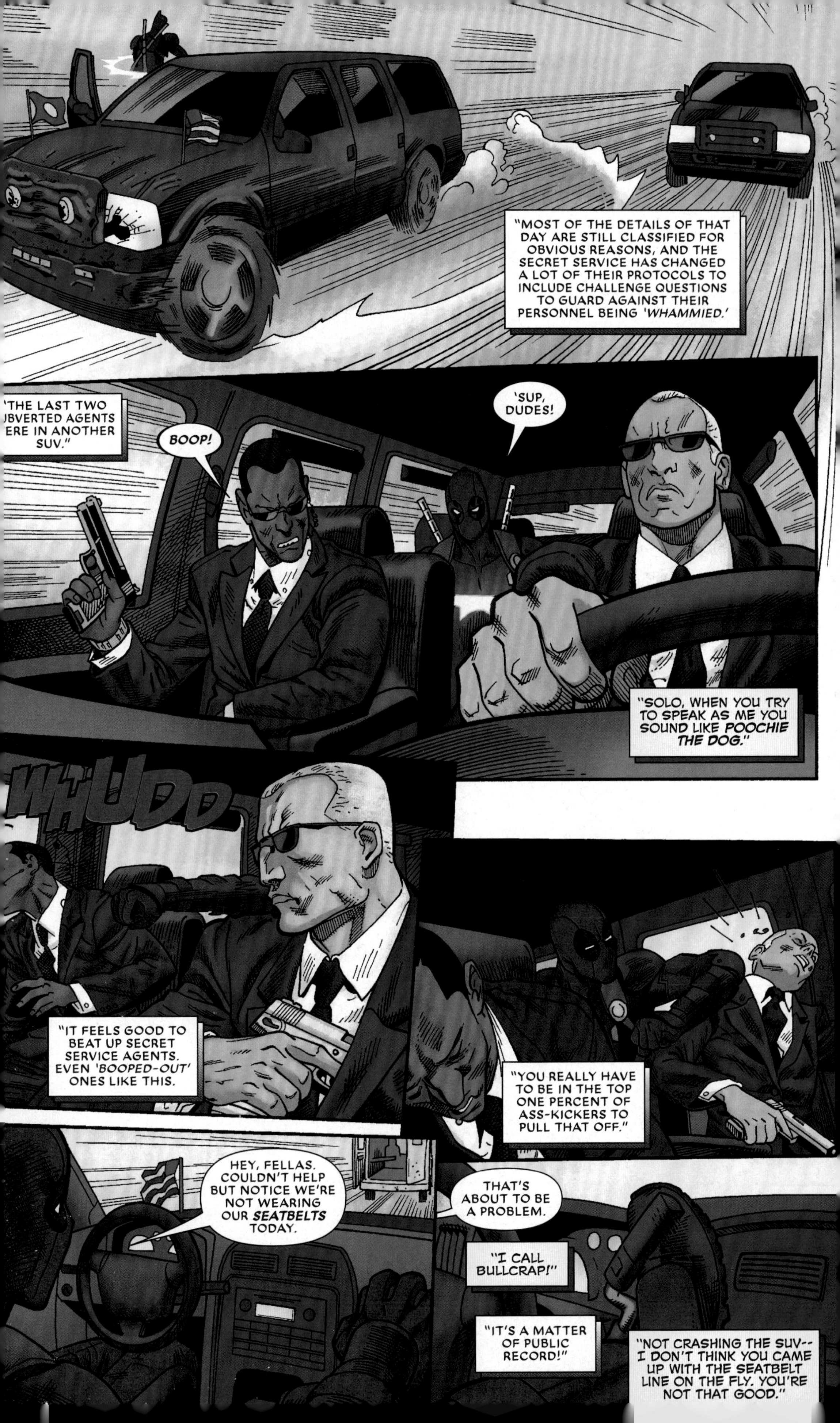
"MOST OF THE DETAILS OF THAT DAY ARE STILL CLASSIFIED FOR OBVIOUS REASONS, AND THE SECRET SERVICE HAS CHANGED A LOT OF THEIR PROTOCOLS TO INCLUDE CHALLENGE QUESTIONS TO GUARD AGAINST THEIR PERSONNEL BEING 'WHAMMIED.'
"THE LAST TWO UBVERTED AGENTS ERE IN ANOTHER SUV."
BOOP!
'SUP, DUDES!
"SOLO, WHEN YOU TRY TO SPEAK AS ME YOU SOUND LIKE POOCHIE THE DOG."
WHUDD
"IT FEELS GOOD TO BEAT UP SECRET SERVICE AGENTS. EVEN 'BOOPED-OUT' ONES LIKE THIS.
"YOU REALLY HAVE TO BE IN THE TOP ONE PERCENT OF ASS-KICKERS TO PULL THAT OFF."
HEY, FELLAS. COULDN'T HELP BUT NOTICE WE'RE NOT WEARING OUR SEATBELTS TODAY.
THAT'S ABOUT TO BE A PROBLEM.
"I CALL BULLCRAP!"
"IT'S A MATTER OF PUBLIC RECORD!"
"NOT CRASHING THE SUV--I DON'T THINK YOU CAME UP WITH THE SEATBELT LINE ON THE FLY. YOU'RE NOT THAT GOOD."

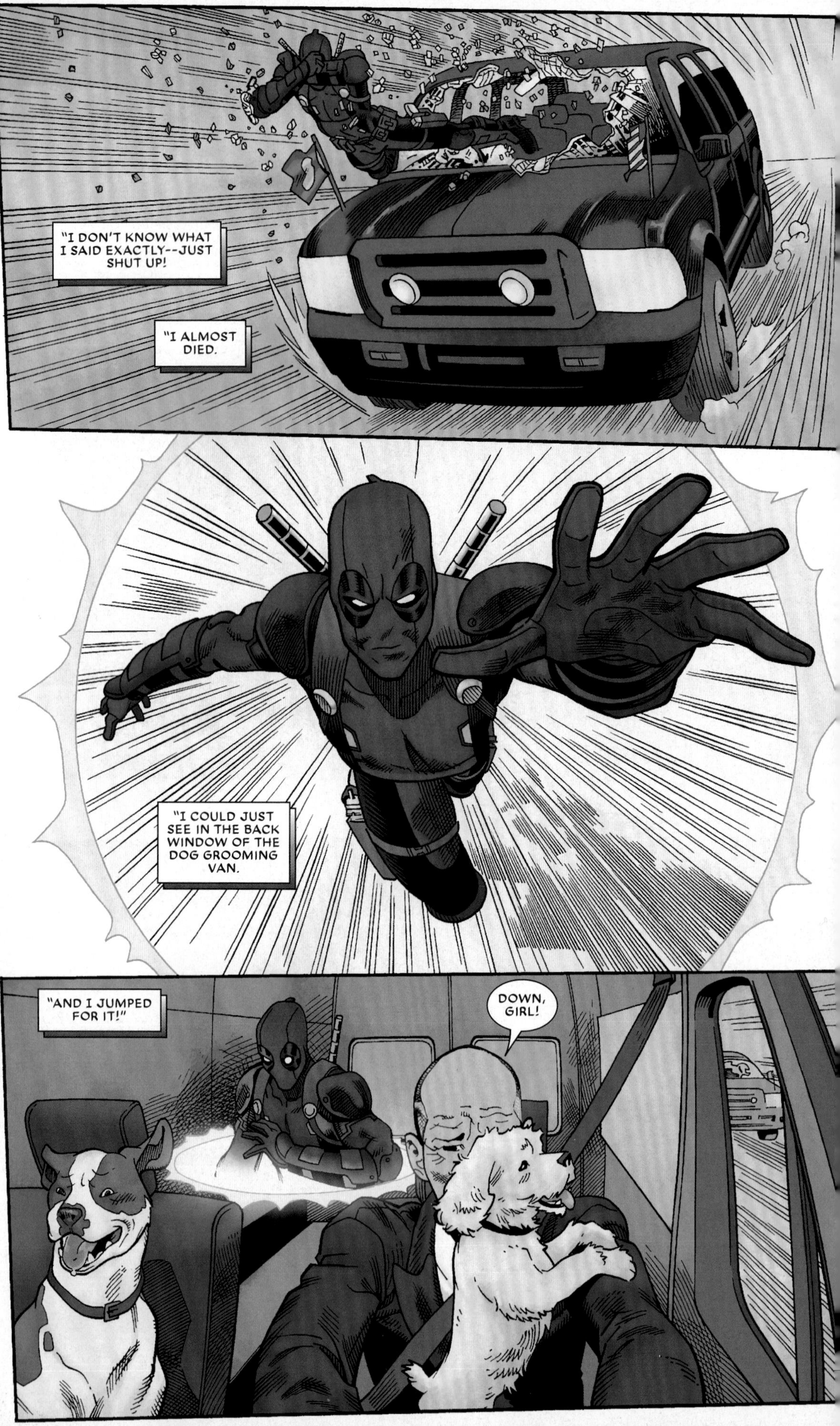
"I DON'T KNOW WHAT I SAID EXACTLY--JUST SHUT UP!
"I ALMOST DIED.
"I COULD JUST SEE IN THE BACK WINDOW OF THE DOG GROOMING VAN.
"AND I JUMPED FOR IT!"
DOWN, GIRL!

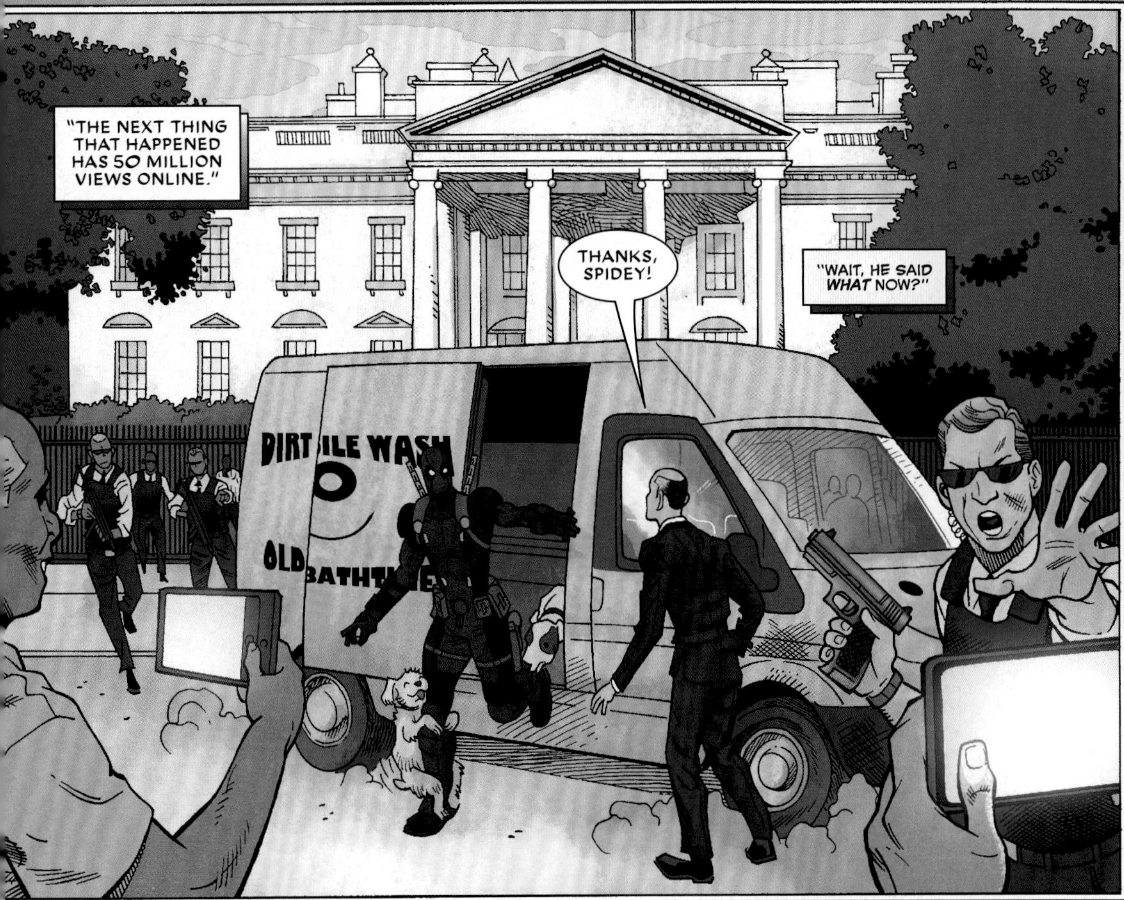
"THE NEXT THING THAT HAPPENED HAS 50 MILLION VIEWS ONLINE."
THANKS, SPIDEY!
"WAIT, HE SAID WHAT NOW?"
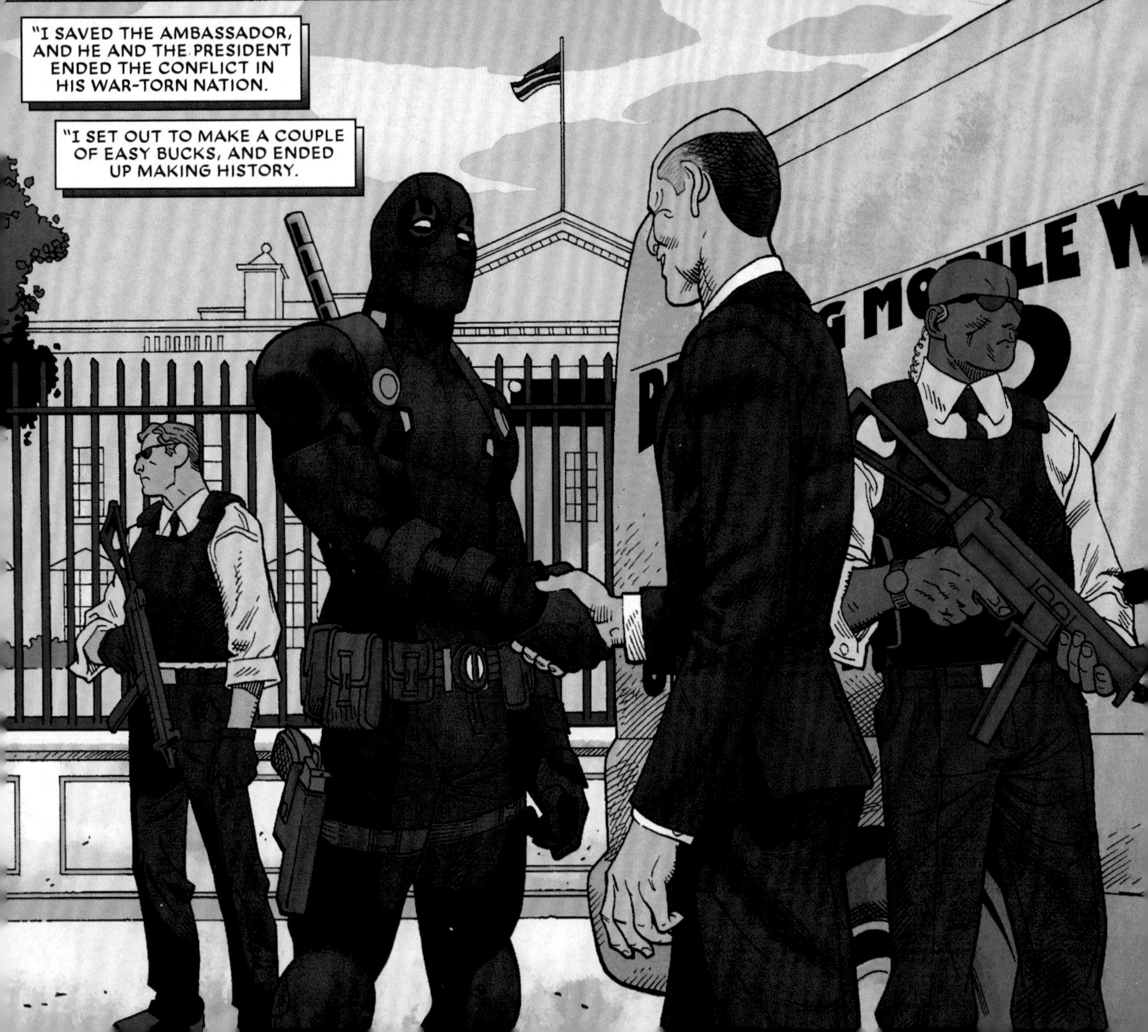
"I SAVED THE AMBASSADOR, AND HE AND THE PRESIDENT ENDED THE CONFLICT IN HIS WAR-TORN NATION.
"I SET OUT TO MAKE A COUPLE OF EASY BUCKS, AND ENDED UP MAKING HISTORY.

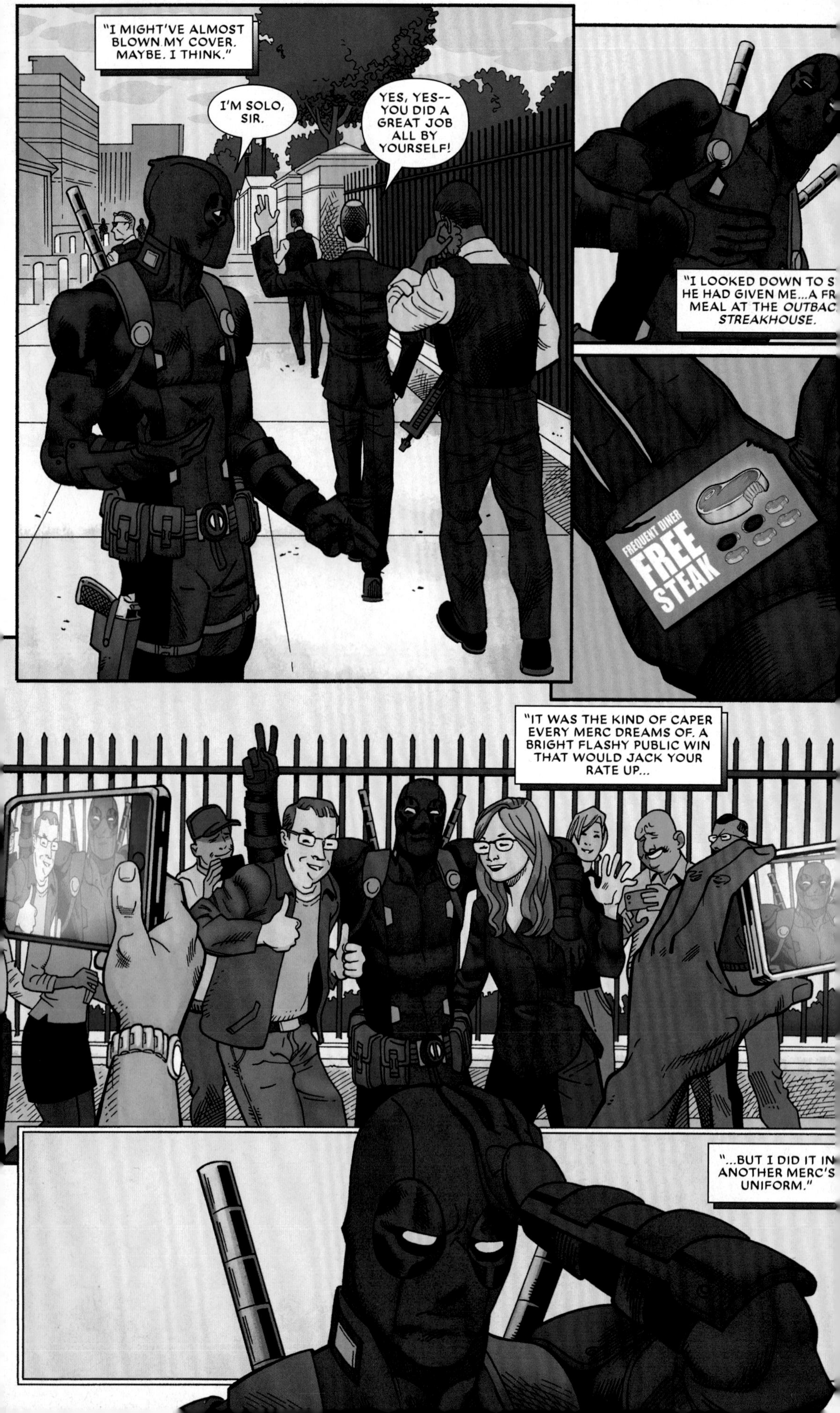
"I MIGHT'VE ALMOST BLOWN MY COVER. MAYBE. I THINK."
I'M SOLO, SIR.
YES, YES-- YOU DID A GREAT JOB ALL BY YOURSELF!
"I LOOKED DOWN TO S
HE HAD GIVEN ME...A FR
MEAL AT THE OUTBAC
STREAKHOUSE.
FREQUENT DINER
FREE STEAK
"IT WAS THE KIND OF CAPER EVERY MERC DREAMS OF. A BRIGHT FLASHY PUBLIC WIN THAT WOULD JACK YOUR RATE UP...
"...BUT I DID IT IN ANOTHER MERC'S UNIFORM."

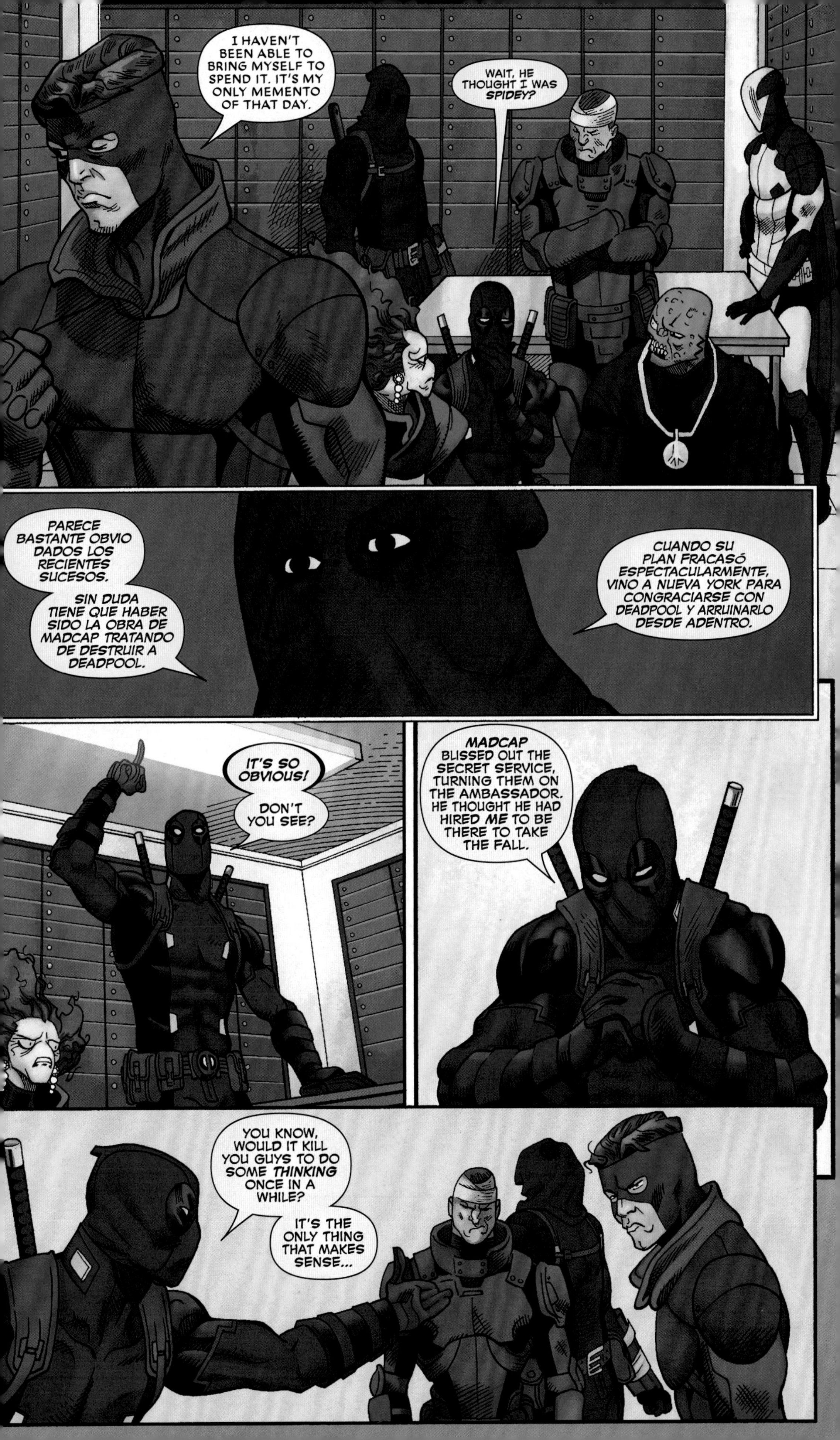

I HAVEN'T BEEN ABLE TO BRING MYSELF TO SPEND IT. IT'S MY ONLY MEMENTO OF THAT DAY.
WAIT, HE THOUGHT I WAS *SPIDEY?*
PARECE BASTANTE OBVIO DADOS LOS RECIENTES SUCESOS.
SIN DUDA TIENE QUE HABER SIDO LA OBRA DE MADCAP TRATANDO DE DESTRUIR A DEADPOOL.
CUANDO SU PLAN FRACASÓ ESPECTACULARMENTE, VINO A NUEVA YORK PARA CONGRACIARSE CON DEADPOOL Y ARRUINARLO DESDE ADENTRO.
IT'S SO OBVIOUS!
DON'T YOU SEE?
MADCAP BLISSED OUT THE SECRET SERVICE, TURNING THEM ON THE AMBASSADOR. HE THOUGHT HE HAD HIRED *ME* TO BE THERE TO TAKE THE FALL.
YOU KNOW, WOULD IT KILL YOU GUYS TO DO SOME *THINKING* ONCE IN A WHILE?
IT'S THE ONLY THING THAT MAKES SENSE...

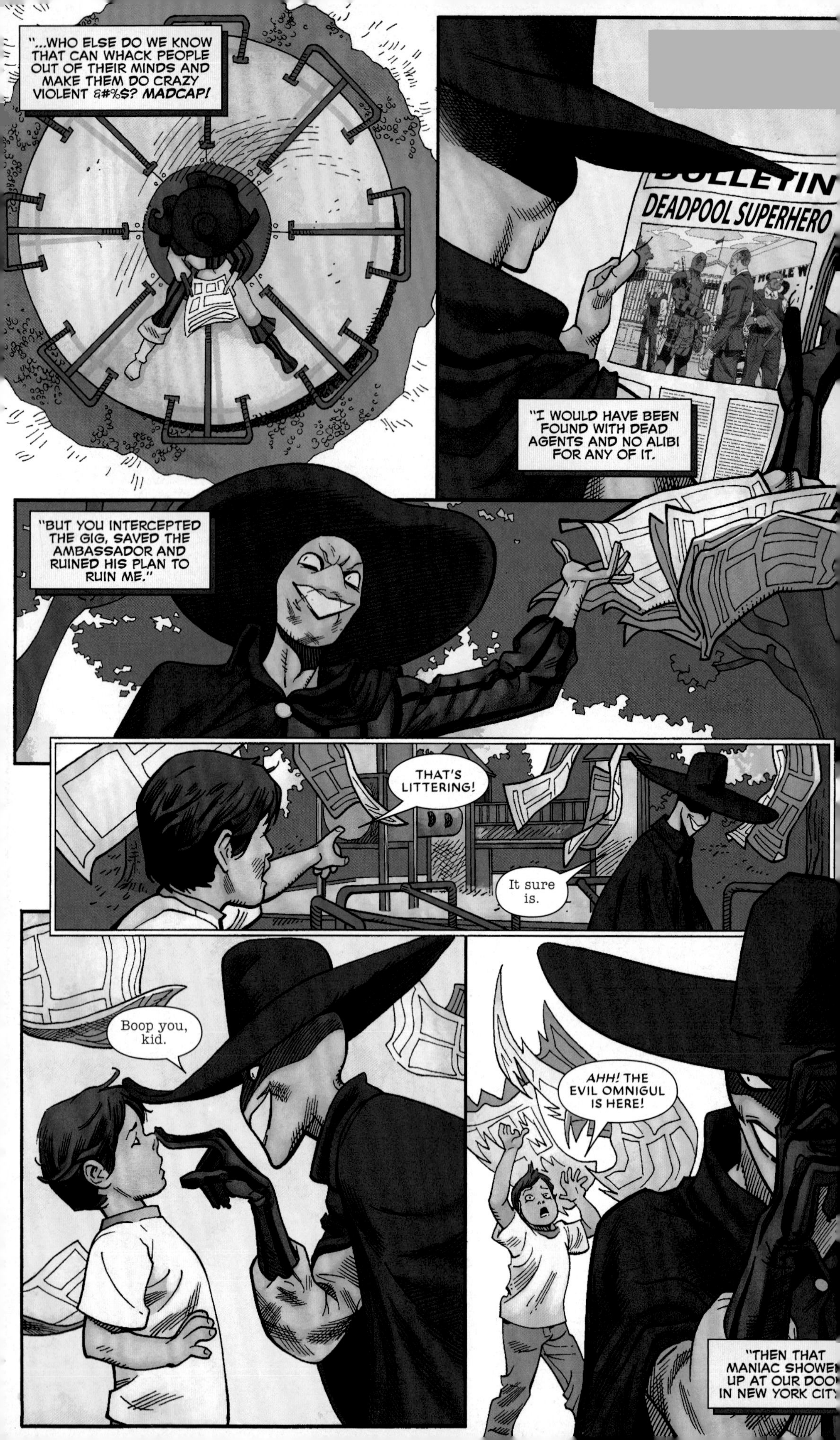

"...WHO ELSE DO WE KNOW THAT CAN WHACK PEOPLE OUT OF THEIR MINDS AND MAKE THEM DO CRAZY VIOLENT &#%$? *MADCAP!*
BULLETIN
DEADPOOL SUPERHERO
"I WOULD HAVE BEEN FOUND WITH DEAD AGENTS AND NO ALIBI FOR ANY OF IT.
"BUT YOU INTERCEPTED THE GIG, SAVED THE AMBASSADOR AND RUINED HIS PLAN TO RUIN ME."
THAT'S LITTERING!
It sure is.
Boop you, kid.
AHH! THE EVIL OMNIGUL IS HERE!
"THEN THAT MANIAC SHOWE UP AT OUR DOO IN NEW YORK CIT

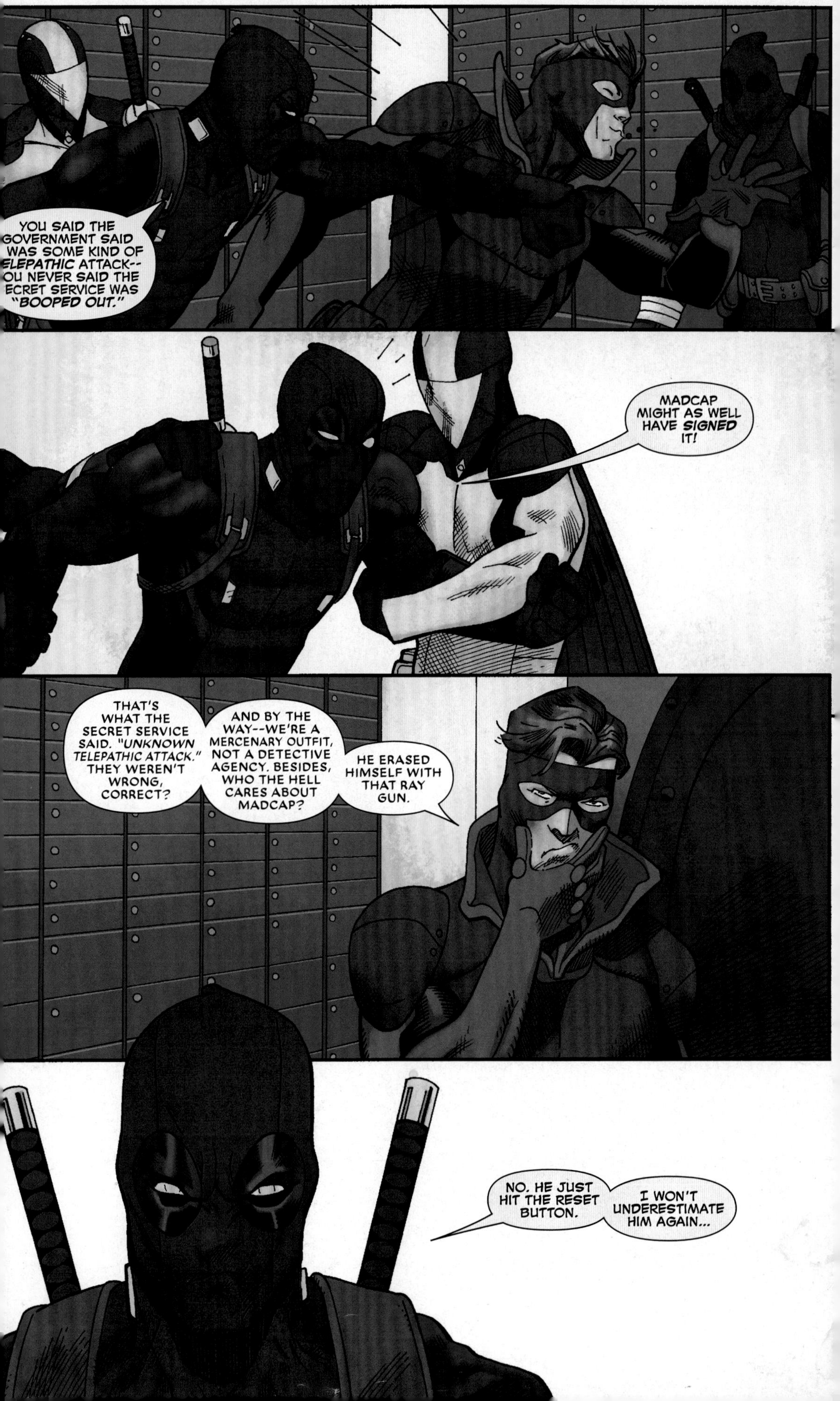
YOU SAID THE GOVERNMENT SAID WAS SOME KIND OF ELEPATHIC ATTACK-- OU NEVER SAID THE ECRET SERVICE WAS "BOOPED OUT."
MADCAP MIGHT AS WELL HAVE SIGNED IT!
THAT'S WHAT THE SECRET SERVICE SAID. "UNKNOWN TELEPATHIC ATTACK." THEY WEREN'T WRONG, CORRECT?
AND BY THE WAY--WE'RE A MERCENARY OUTFIT, NOT A DETECTIVE AGENCY. BESIDES, WHO THE HELL CARES ABOUT MADCAP?
HE ERASED HIMSELF WITH THAT RAY GUN.
NO. HE JUST HIT THE RESET BUTTON.
I WON'T UNDERESTIMATE HIM AGAIN...

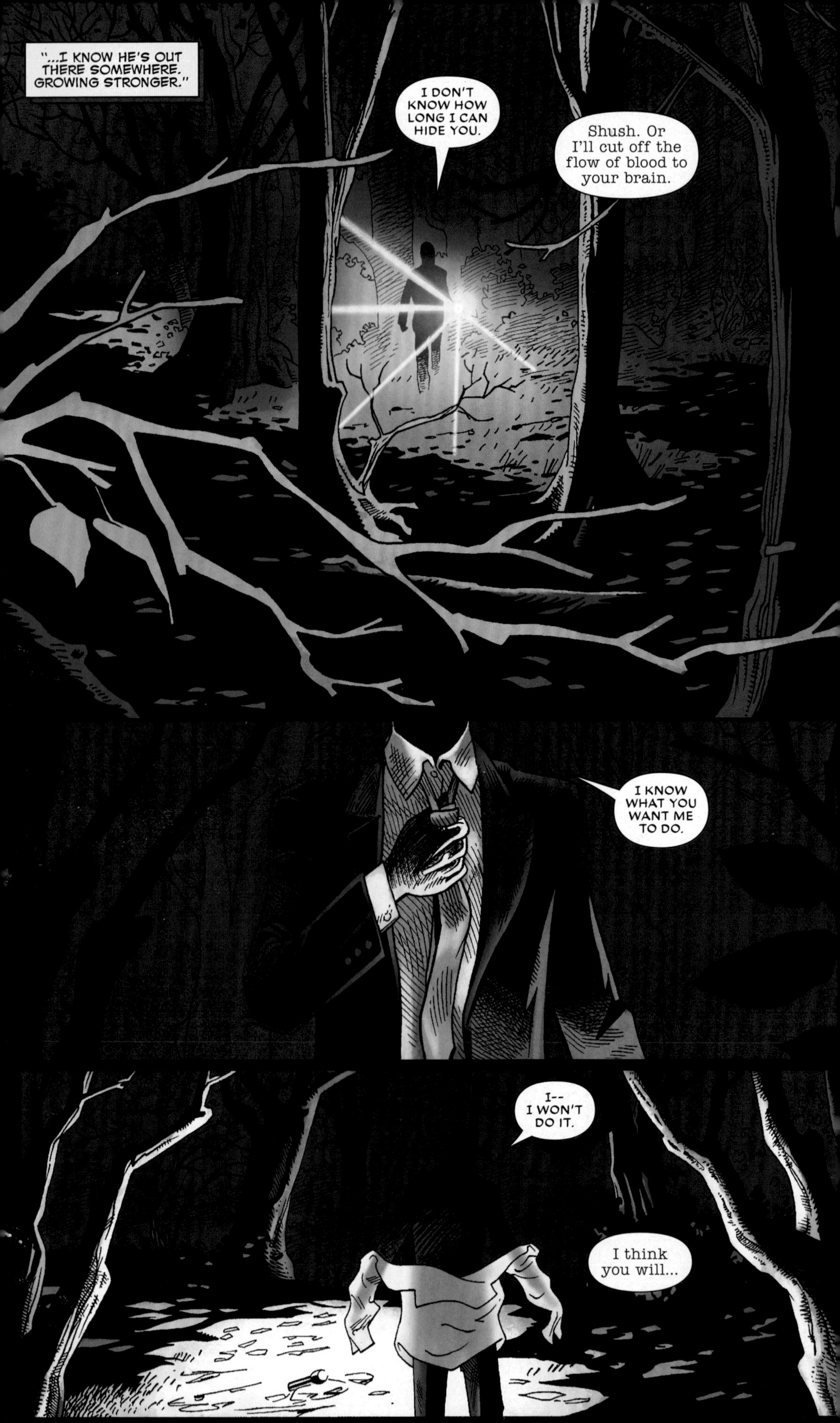
"...I KNOW HE'S OUT THERE SOMEWHERE. GROWING STRONGER."
I DON'T KNOW HOW LONG I CAN HIDE YOU.
Shush. Or I'll cut off the flow of blood to your brain.
I KNOW WHAT YOU WANT ME TO DO.
I-- I WON'T DO IT.
I think you will...

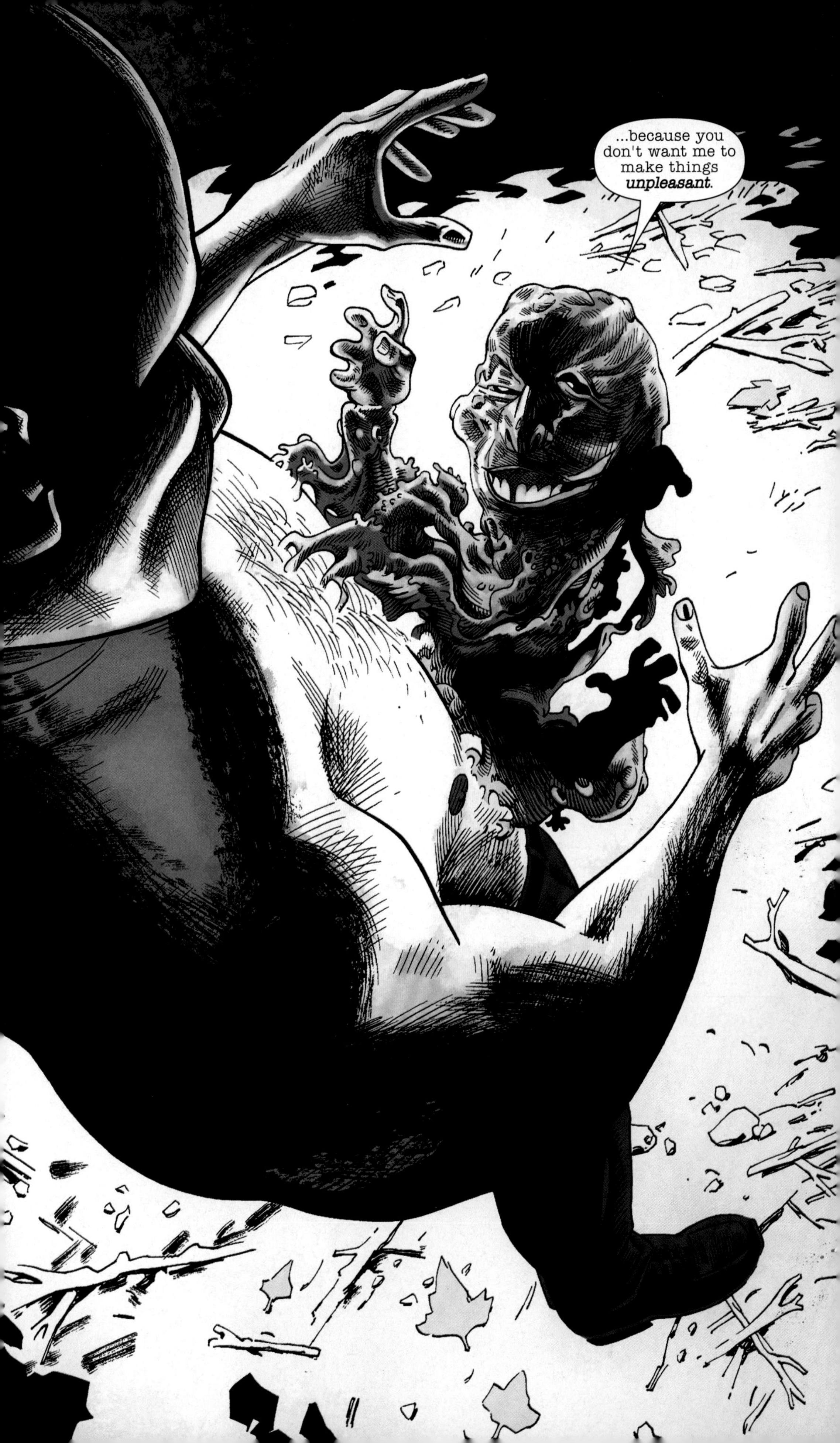
...because you don't want me to make things unpleasant.

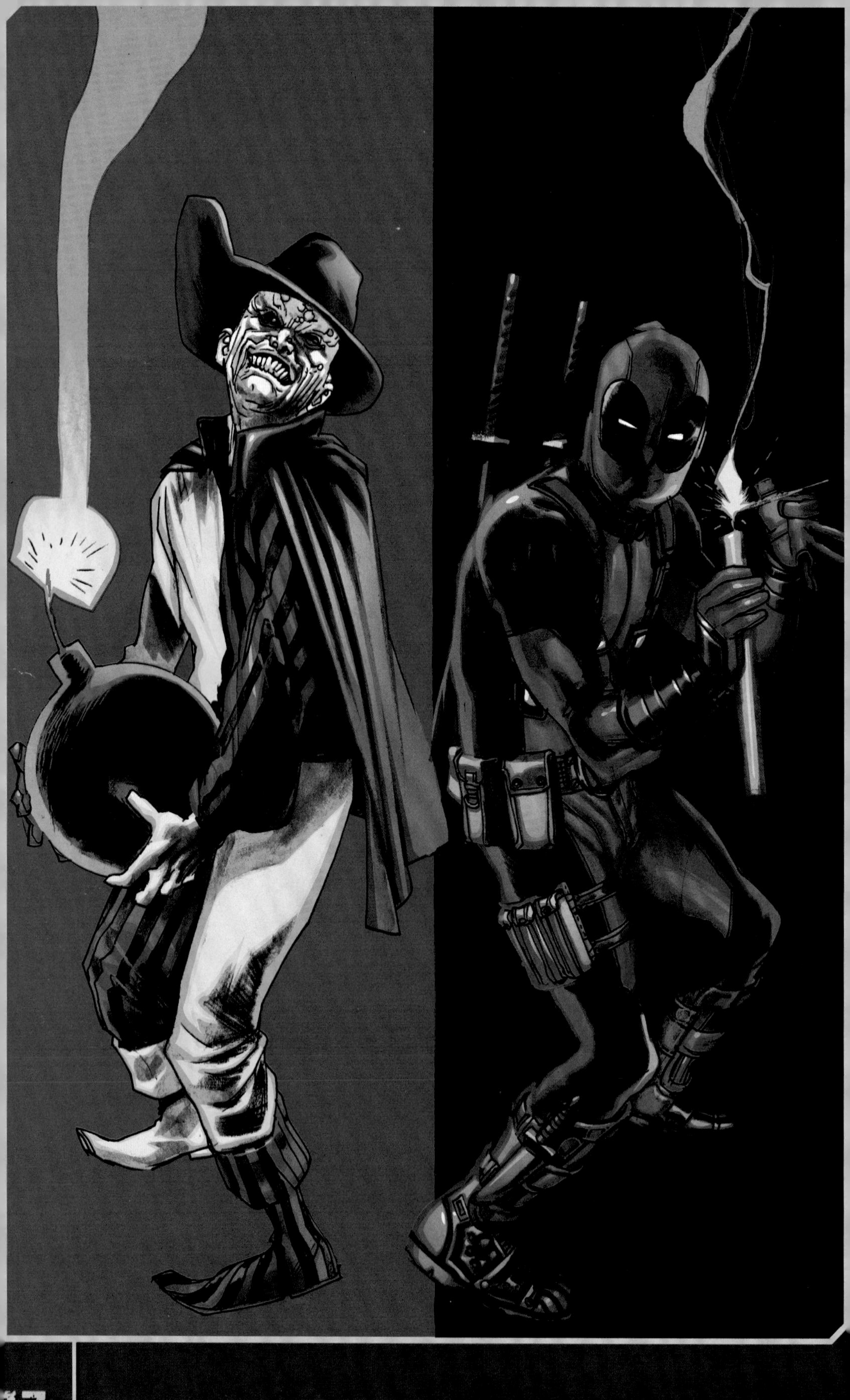

17 DEADPOOL'S UNCIVIL WAR - PART FOUR

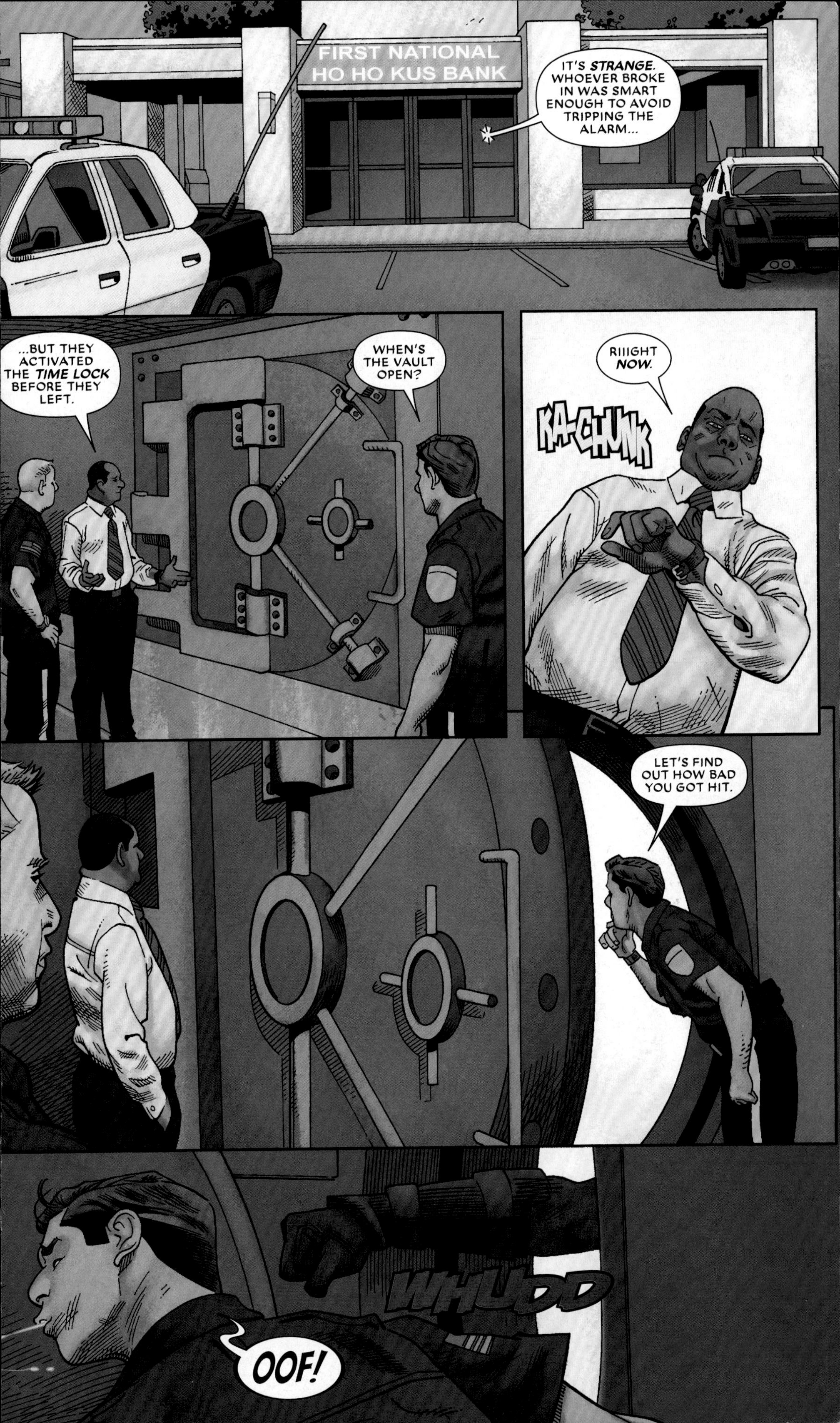
FIRST NATIONAL
HO HO KUS BANK
IT'S STRANGE. WHOEVER BROKE IN WAS SMART ENOUGH TO AVOID TRIPPING THE ALARM...
...BUT THEY ACTIVATED THE TIME LOCK BEFORE THEY LEFT.
WHEN'S THE VAULT OPEN?
RIIIGHT NOW.
KA-CHUNK
LET'S FIND OUT HOW BAD YOU GOT HIT.
WHUDD
OOF!

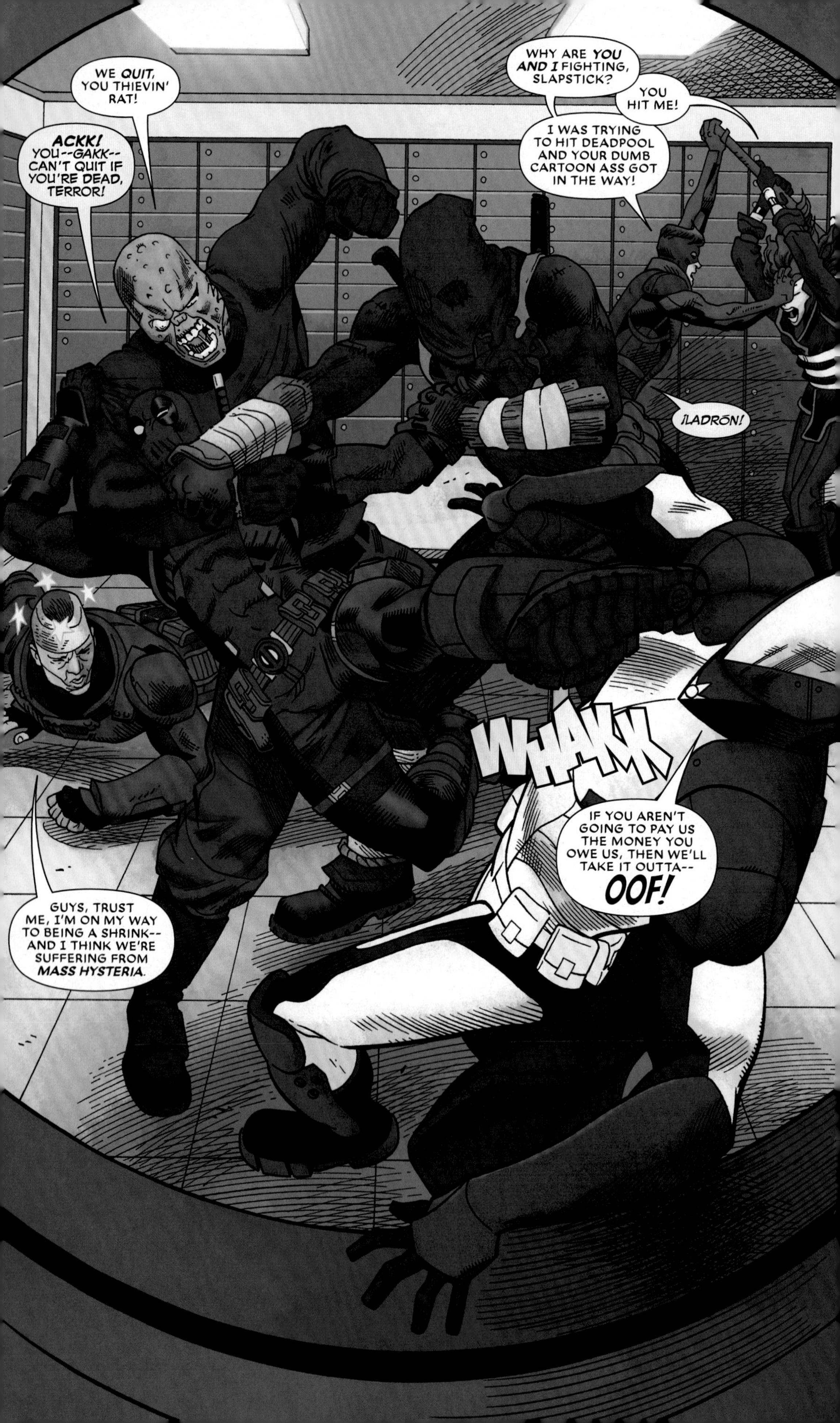
WE QUIT, YOU THIEVIN' RAT!
ACKK! YOU--GAKK--CAN'T QUIT IF YOU'RE DEAD, TERROR!
WHY ARE YOU AND I FIGHTING, SLAPSTICK?
YOU HIT ME!
I WAS TRYING TO HIT DEADPOOL AND YOUR DUMB CARTOON ASS GOT IN THE WAY!
¡LADRÓN!
WHAKK
IF YOU AREN'T GOING TO PAY US THE MONEY YOU OWE US, THEN WE'LL TAKE IT OUTTA-- OOF!
GUYS, TRUST ME, I'M ON MY WAY TO BEING A SHRINK--AND I THINK WE'RE SUFFERING FROM MASS HYSTERIA.

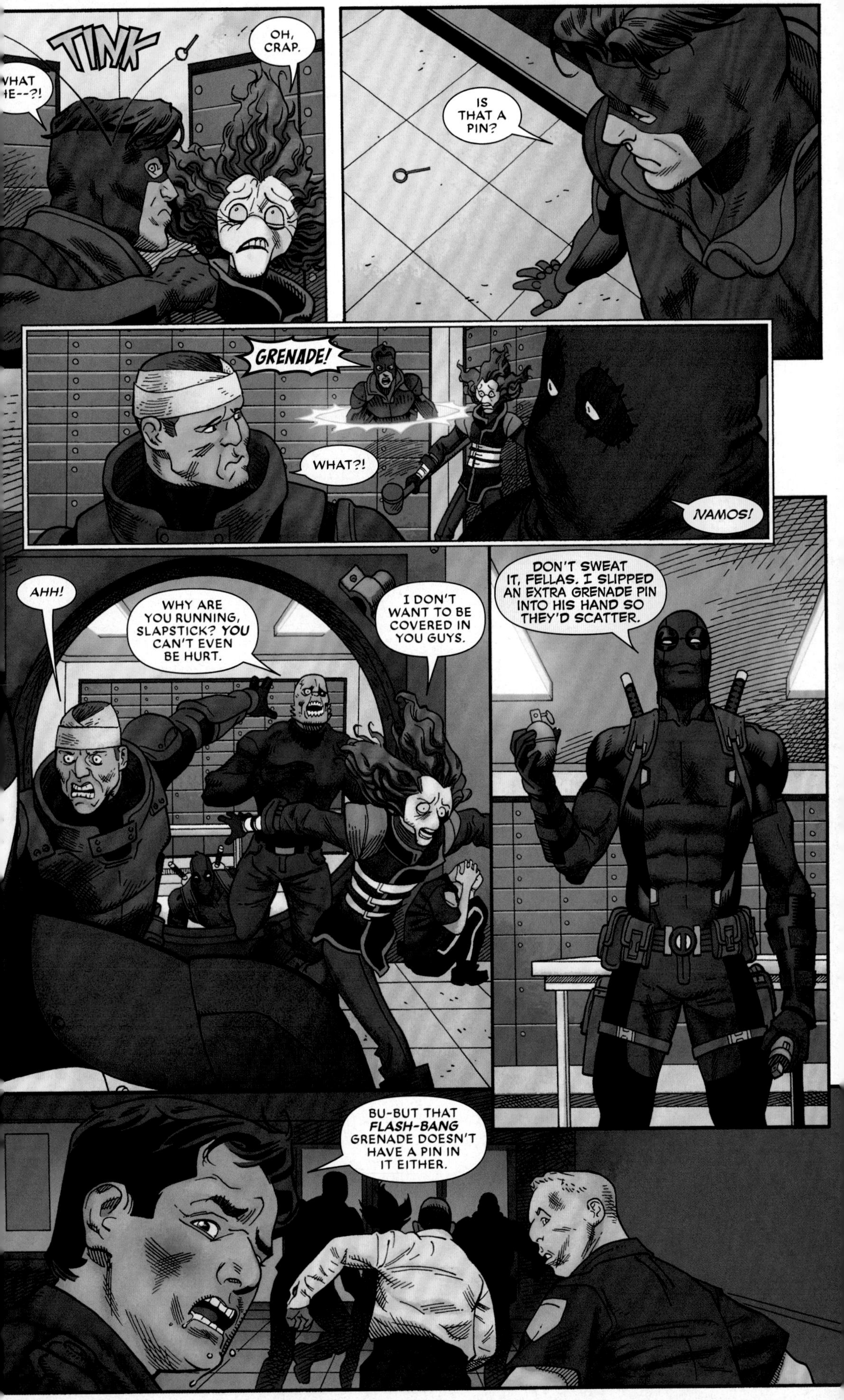
TINK
WHAT HE--?!
OH, CRAP.
IS THAT A PIN?
GRENADE!
WHAT?!
¡VAMOS!
AHH!
WHY ARE YOU RUNNING, SLAPSTICK? YOU CAN'T EVEN BE HURT.
I DON'T WANT TO BE COVERED IN YOU GUYS.
DON'T SWEAT IT, FELLAS. I SLIPPED AN EXTRA GRENADE PIN INTO HIS HAND SO THEY'D SCATTER.
BU-BUT THAT FLASH-BANG GRENADE DOESN'T HAVE A PIN IN IT EITHER.

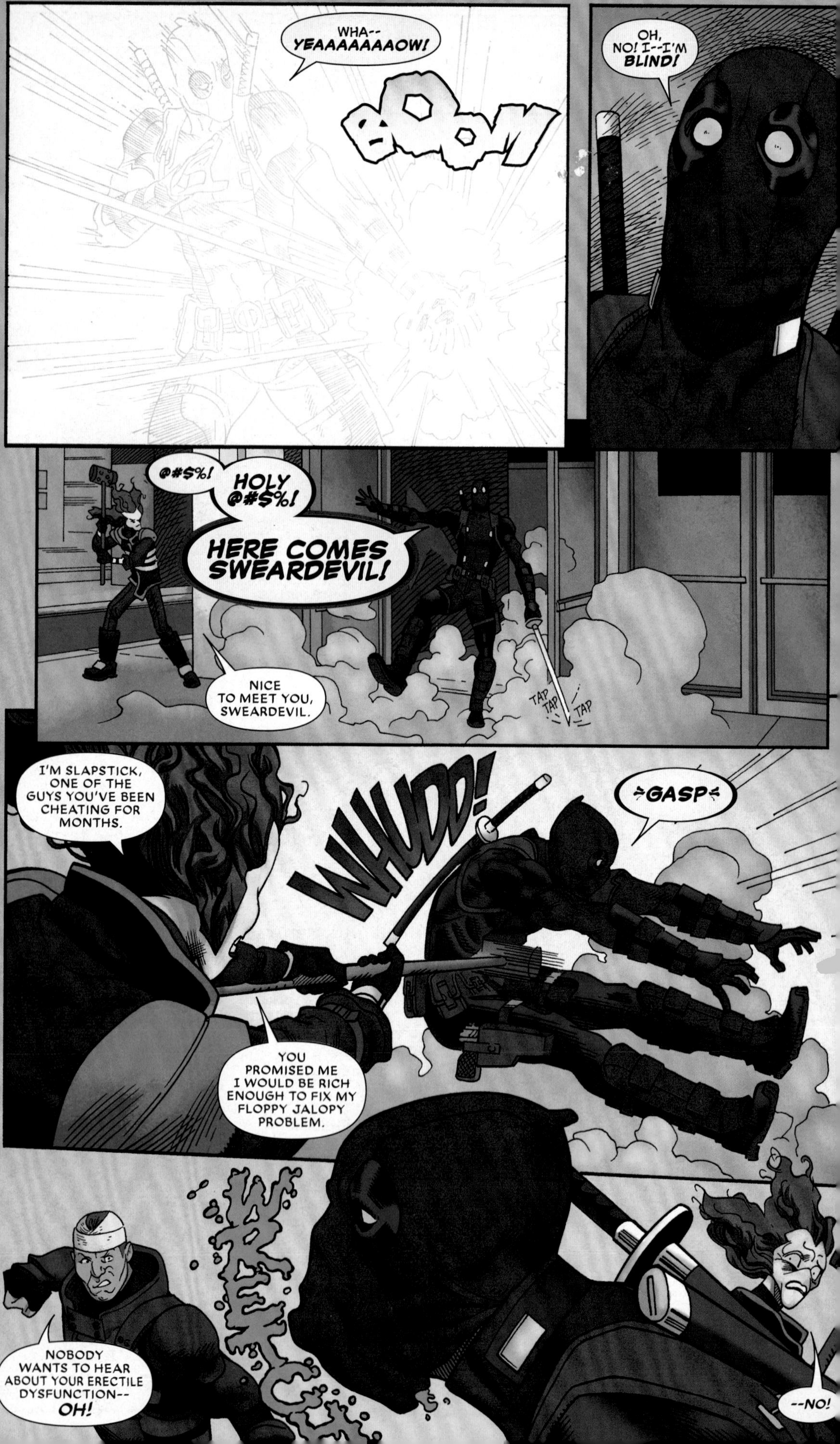
WHA-- YEAAAAAAAOW!
BOOM
OH, NO! I--I'M BLIND!
@#$%!
HOLY @#$%!
HERE COMES SWEARDEVIL!
NICE TO MEET YOU, SWEARDEVIL.
TAP TAP TAP
I'M SLAPSTICK, ONE OF THE GUYS YOU'VE BEEN CHEATING FOR MONTHS.
WHUDD!
GASP
YOU PROMISED ME I WOULD BE RICH ENOUGH TO FIX MY FLOPPY JALOPY PROBLEM.
NOBODY WANTS TO HEAR ABOUT YOUR ERECTILE DYSFUNCTION-- OH!
--NO!

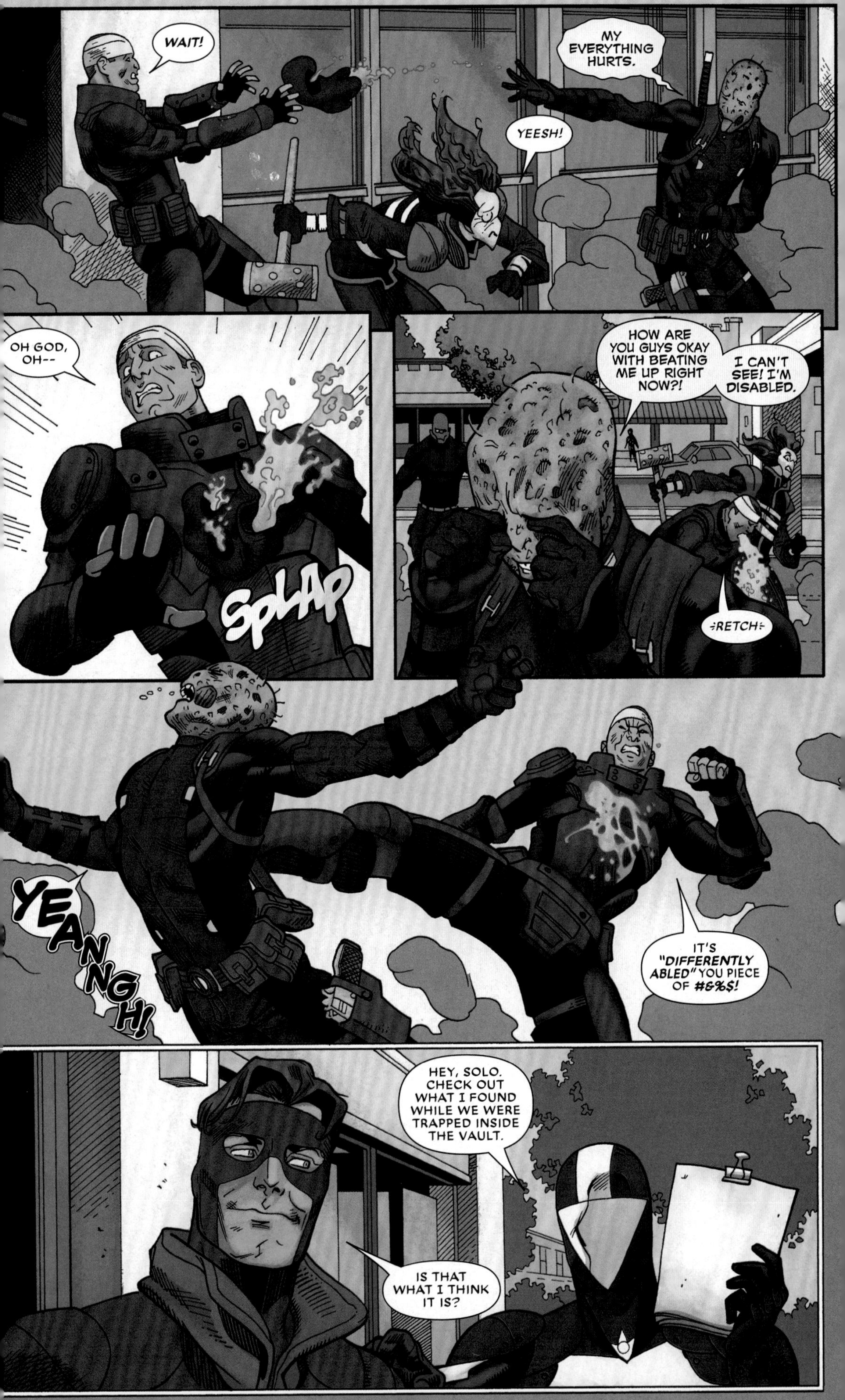
WAIT!
MY EVERYTHING HURTS.
YEESH!
OH GOD, OH--
SpLAP
HOW ARE YOU GUYS OKAY WITH BEATING ME UP RIGHT NOW?!
I CAN'T SEE! I'M DISABLED.
RETCH
YEANNGH!
IT'S "DIFFERENTLY ABLED" YOU PIECE OF #&%$!
HEY, SOLO. CHECK OUT WHAT I FOUND WHILE WE WERE TRAPPED INSIDE THE VAULT.
IS THAT WHAT I THINK IT IS?

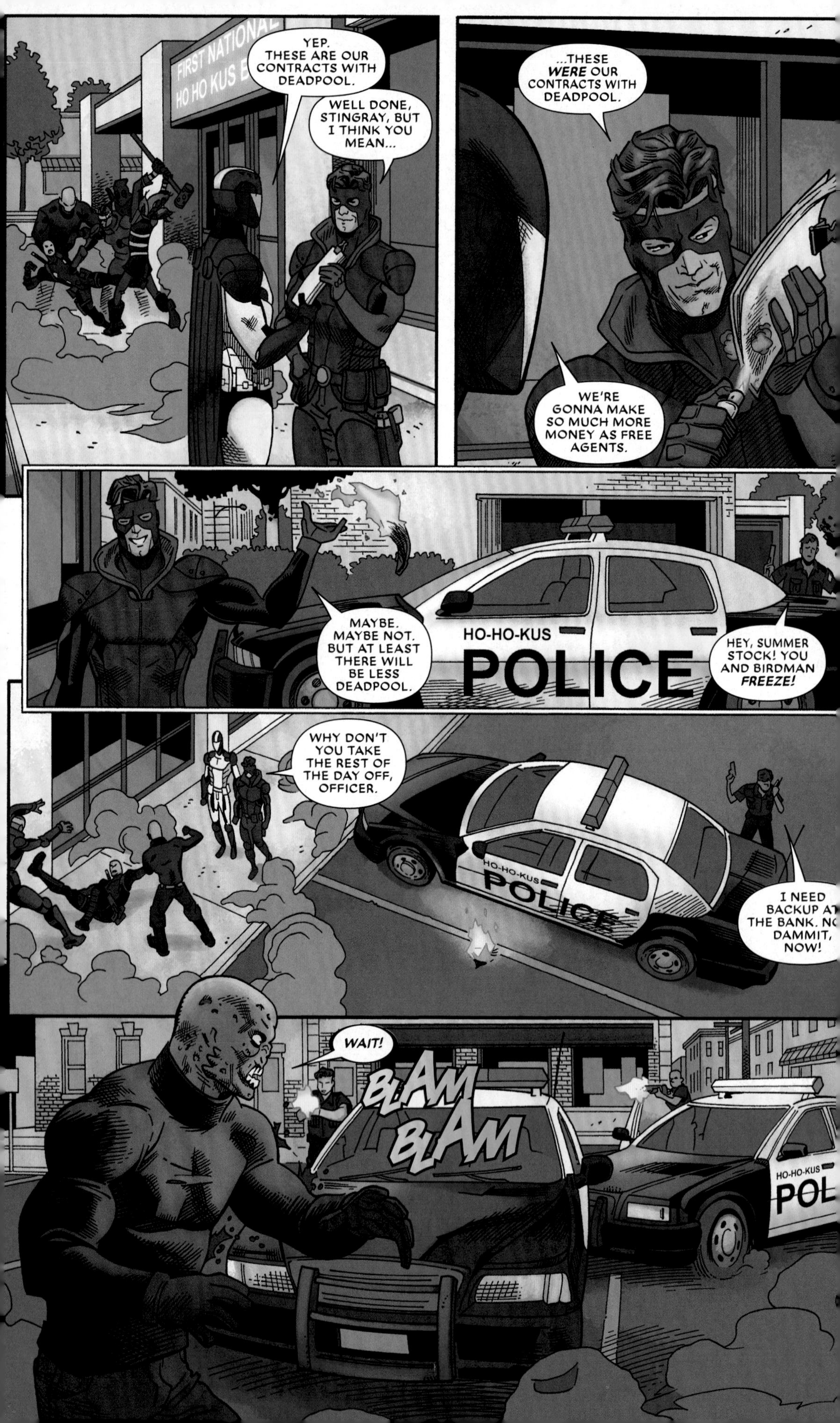
FIRST NATIONAL
HO HO KUS B
YEP. THESE ARE OUR CONTRACTS WITH DEADPOOL.
WELL DONE, STINGRAY, BUT I THINK YOU MEAN...
...THESE *WERE* OUR CONTRACTS WITH DEADPOOL.
WE'RE GONNA MAKE SO MUCH MORE MONEY AS FREE AGENTS.
MAYBE. MAYBE NOT. BUT AT LEAST THERE WILL BE LESS DEADPOOL.
HO-HO-KUS
POLICE
HEY, SUMMER STOCK! YOU AND BIRDMAN *FREEZE!*
WHY DON'T YOU TAKE THE REST OF THE DAY OFF, OFFICER.
HO-HO-KUS
POLICE
I NEED BACKUP AT THE BANK. NO DAMMIT, NOW!
WAIT!
BLAM
BLAM
HO-HO-KUS
POL

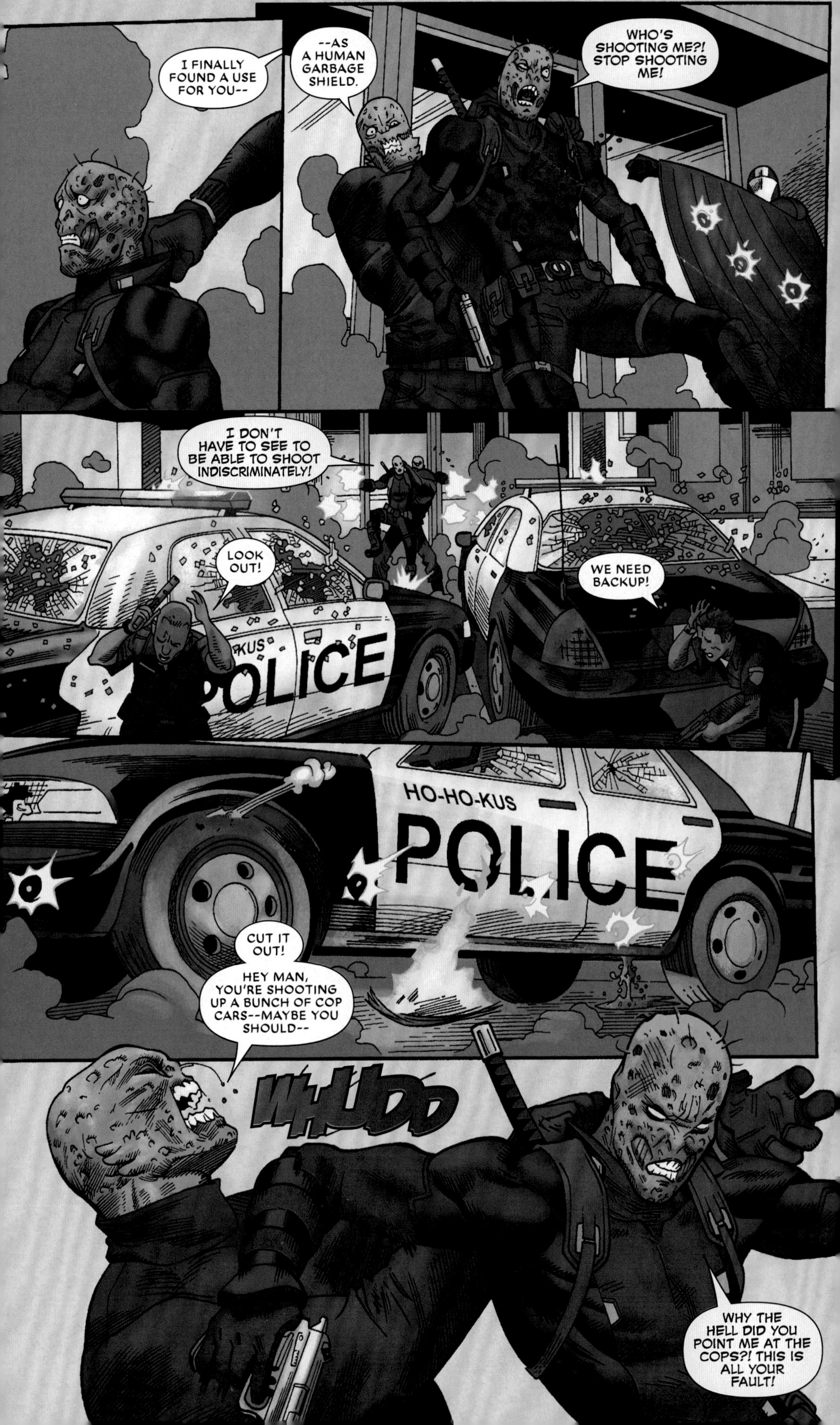
I FINALLY FOUND A USE FOR YOU--
--AS A HUMAN GARBAGE SHIELD.
WHO'S SHOOTING ME?! STOP SHOOTING ME!
I DON'T HAVE TO SEE TO BE ABLE TO SHOOT INDISCRIMINATELY!
LOOK OUT!
KUS
POLICE
WE NEED BACKUP!
HO-HO-KUS
POLICE
CUT IT OUT!
HEY MAN, YOU'RE SHOOTING UP A BUNCH OF COP CARS--MAYBE YOU SHOULD--
WHUDD
WHY THE HELL DID YOU POINT ME AT THE COPS?! THIS IS ALL YOUR FAULT!

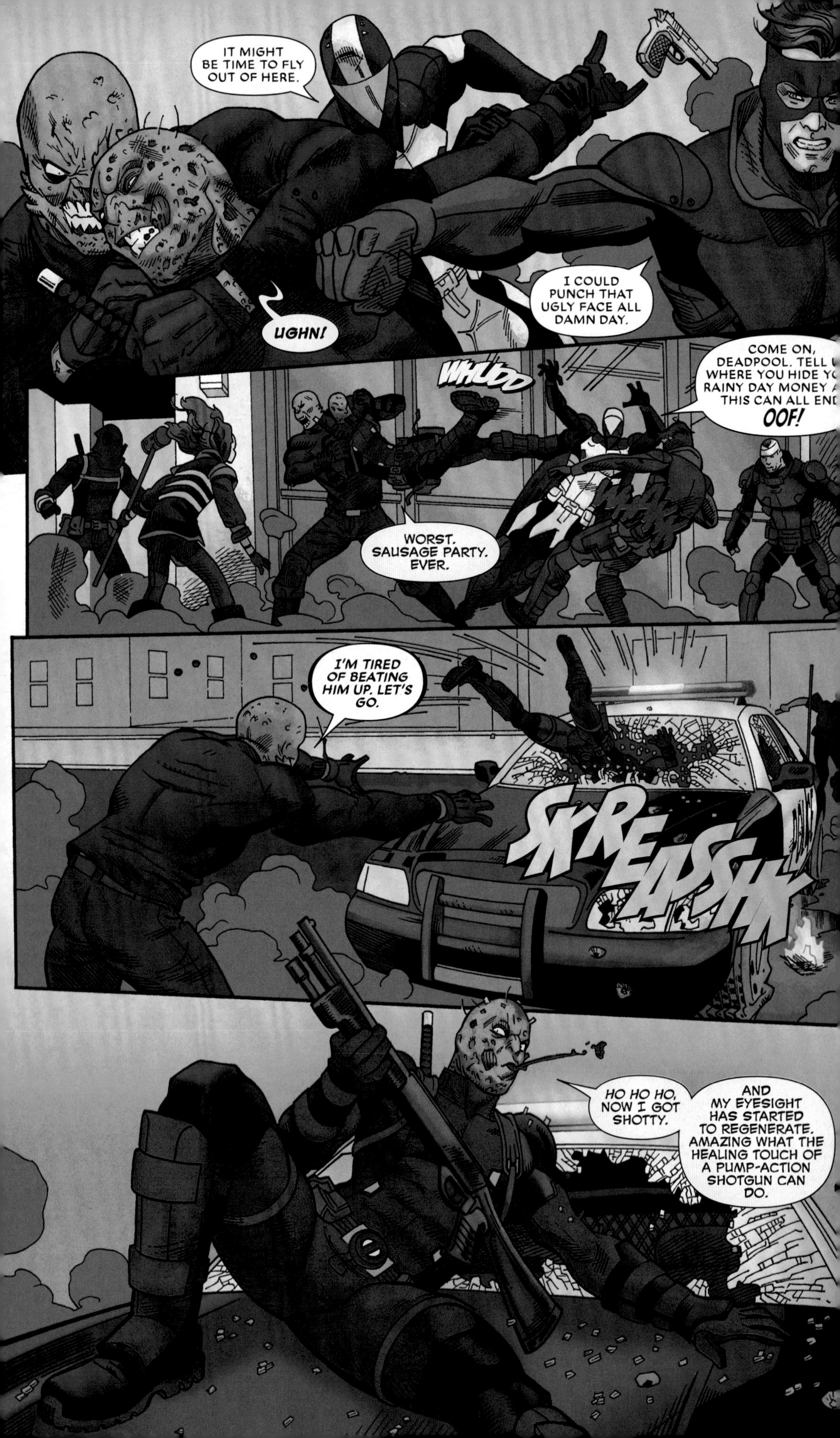
IT MIGHT BE TIME TO FLY OUT OF HERE.
UGHN!
I COULD PUNCH THAT UGLY FACE ALL DAMN DAY.
WHUDD
COME ON, DEADPOOL. TELL U WHERE YOU HIDE YO RAINY DAY MONEY A THIS CAN ALL END
OOF!
WORST. SAUSAGE PARTY. EVER.
I'M TIRED OF BEATING HIM UP. LET'S GO.
SKREASH
HO HO HO, NOW I GOT SHOTTY.
AND MY EYESIGHT HAS STARTED TO REGENERATE. AMAZING WHAT THE HEALING TOUCH OF A PUMP-ACTION SHOTGUN CAN DO.

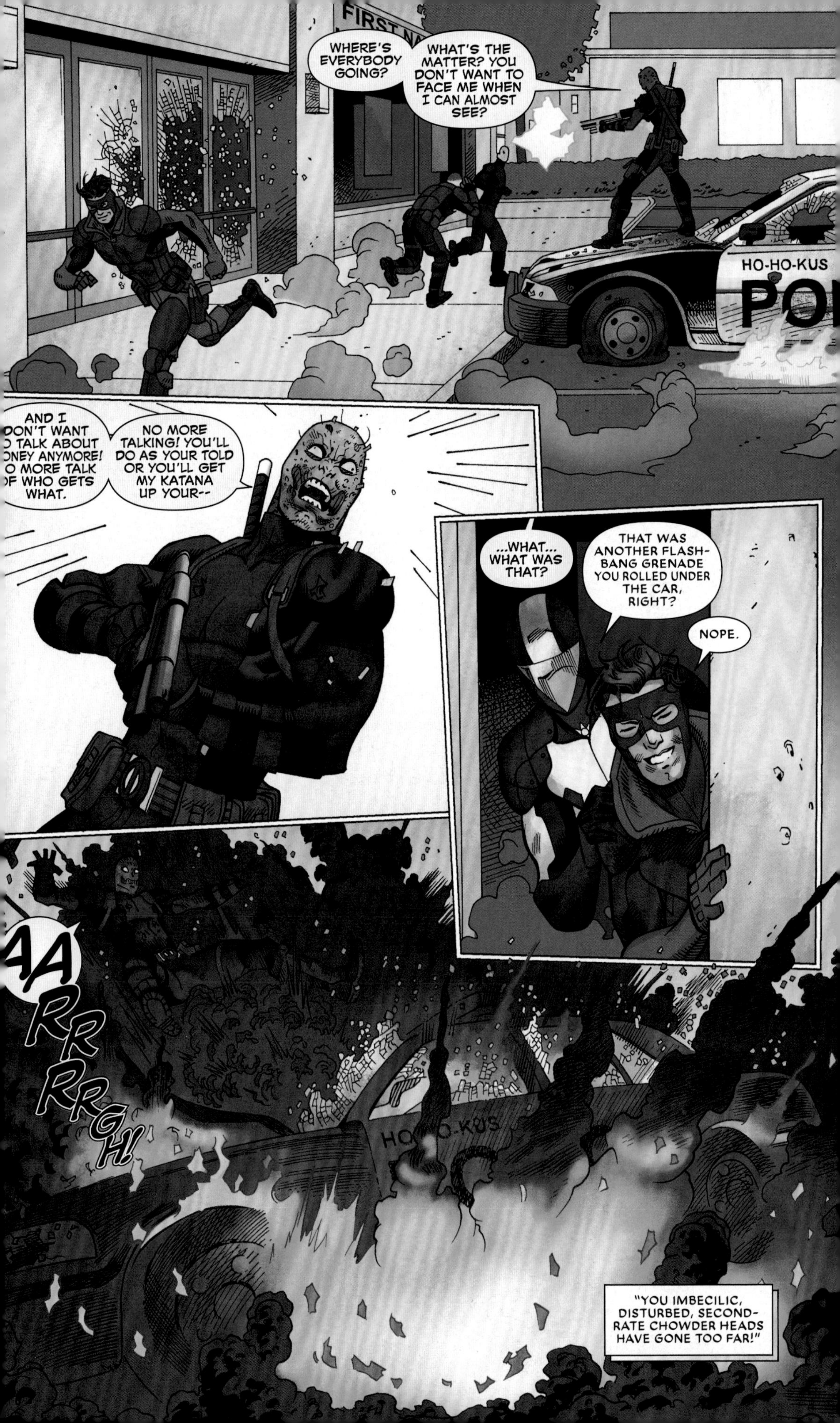
FIRST NA
WHERE'S EVERYBODY GOING?
WHAT'S THE MATTER? YOU DON'T WANT TO FACE ME WHEN I CAN ALMOST SEE?
HO-HO-KUS
PO
AND I DON'T WANT TO TALK ABOUT MONEY ANYMORE! NO MORE TALK OF WHO GETS WHAT.
NO MORE TALKING! YOU'LL DO AS YOUR TOLD OR YOU'LL GET MY KATANA UP YOUR--
...WHAT... WHAT WAS THAT?
THAT WAS ANOTHER FLASH-BANG GRENADE YOU ROLLED UNDER THE CAR, RIGHT?
NOPE.
AARRRRGH!
HO-HO-KUS
"YOU IMBECILIC, DISTURBED, SECOND-RATE CHOWDER HEADS HAVE GONE TOO FAR!"

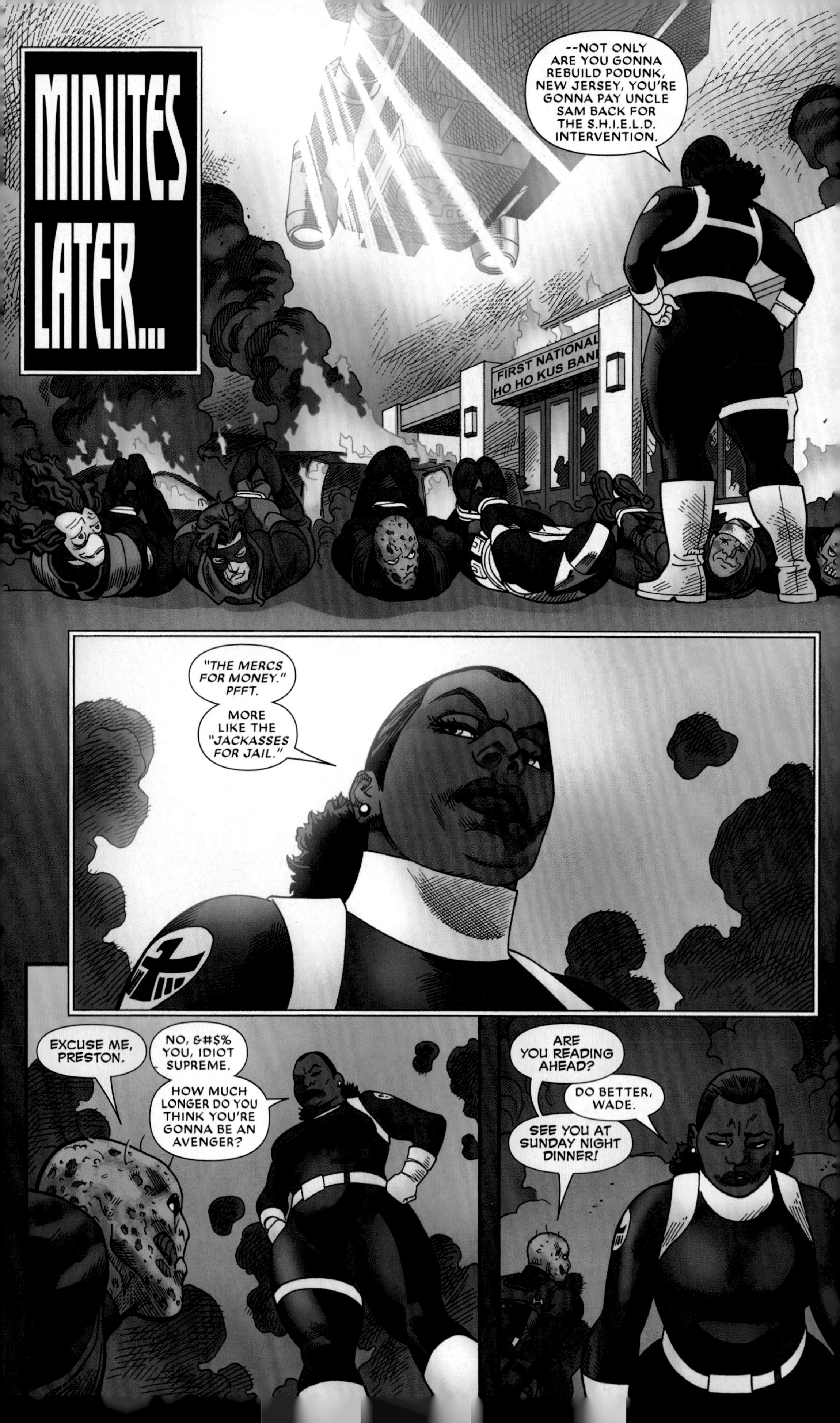
MINUTES LATER...
--NOT ONLY ARE YOU GONNA REBUILD PODUNK, NEW JERSEY, YOU'RE GONNA PAY UNCLE SAM BACK FOR THE S.H.I.E.L.D. INTERVENTION.
FIRST NATIONAL HO HO KUS BANK
"THE MERCS FOR MONEY." PFFT.
MORE LIKE THE "JACKASSES FOR JAIL."
EXCUSE ME, PRESTON.
NO, &#$% YOU, IDIOT SUPREME.
HOW MUCH LONGER DO YOU THINK YOU'RE GONNA BE AN AVENGER?
ARE YOU READING AHEAD?
DO BETTER, WADE.
SEE YOU AT SUNDAY NIGHT DINNER!

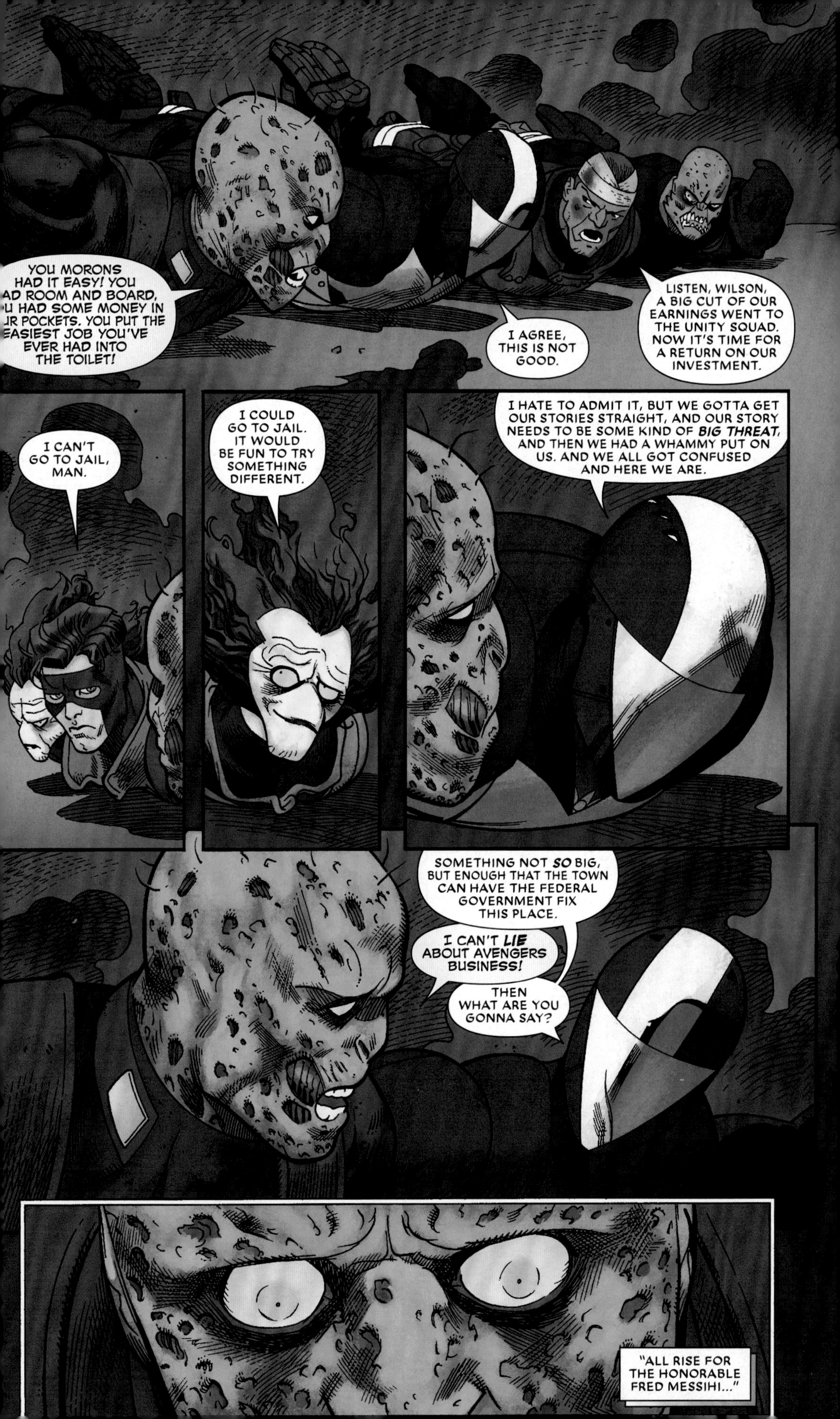
YOU MORONS HAD IT EASY! YOU AD ROOM AND BOARD, U HAD SOME MONEY IN R POCKETS. YOU PUT THE EASIEST JOB YOU'VE EVER HAD INTO THE TOILET!
I AGREE, THIS IS NOT GOOD.
LISTEN, WILSON, A BIG CUT OF OUR EARNINGS WENT TO THE UNITY SQUAD. NOW IT'S TIME FOR A RETURN ON OUR INVESTMENT.
I CAN'T GO TO JAIL, MAN.
I COULD GO TO JAIL. IT WOULD BE FUN TO TRY SOMETHING DIFFERENT.
I HATE TO ADMIT IT, BUT WE GOTTA GET OUR STORIES STRAIGHT, AND OUR STORY NEEDS TO BE SOME KIND OF *BIG THREAT*, AND THEN WE HAD A WHAMMY PUT ON US. AND WE ALL GOT CONFUSED AND HERE WE ARE.
SOMETHING NOT *SO* BIG, BUT ENOUGH THAT THE TOWN CAN HAVE THE FEDERAL GOVERNMENT FIX THIS PLACE.
I CAN'T *LIE* ABOUT AVENGERS BUSINESS!
THEN WHAT ARE YOU GONNA SAY?
"ALL RISE FOR THE HONORABLE FRED MESSIHI..."

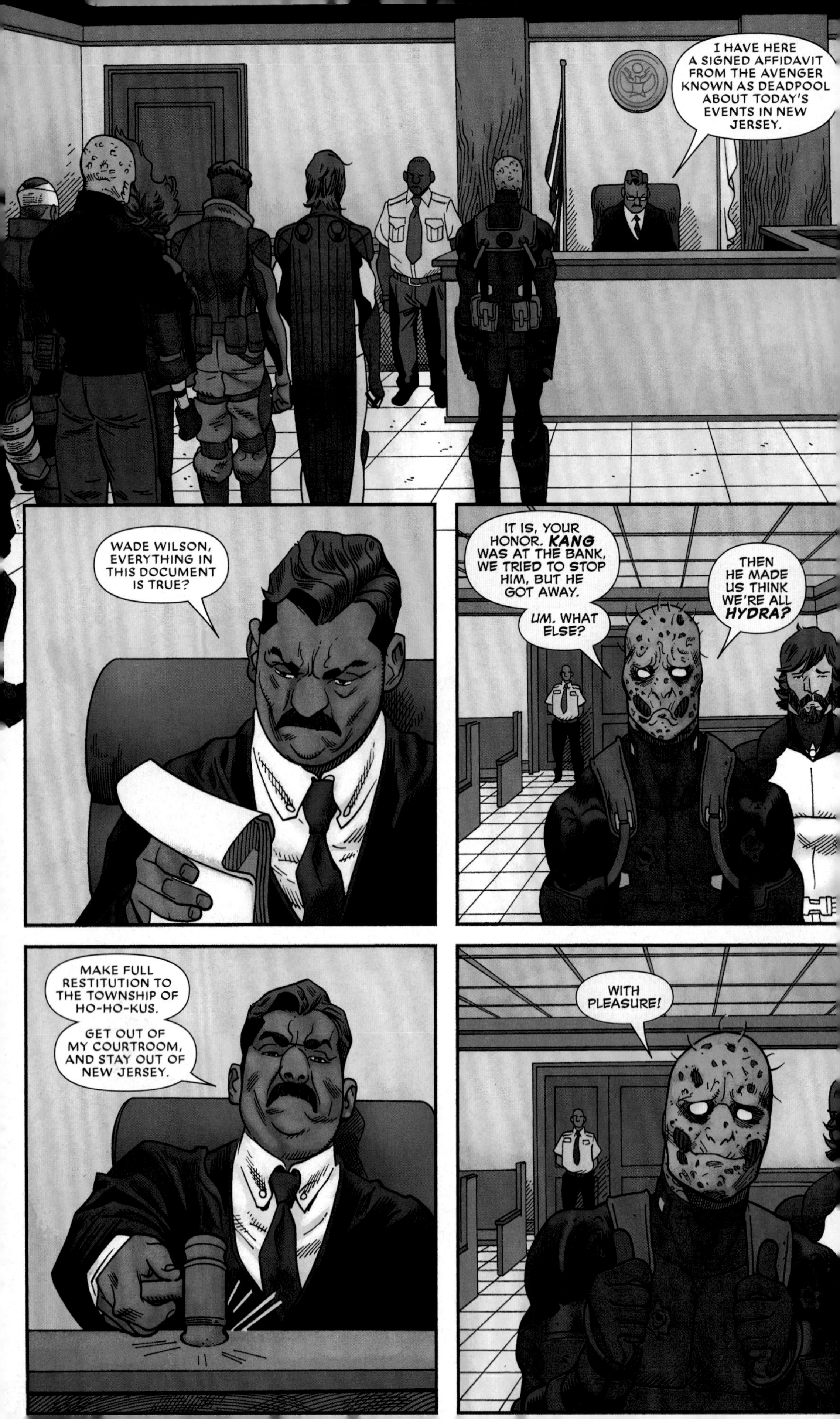
I HAVE HERE A SIGNED AFFIDAVIT FROM THE AVENGER KNOWN AS DEADPOOL ABOUT TODAY'S EVENTS IN NEW JERSEY.
WADE WILSON, EVERYTHING IN THIS DOCUMENT IS TRUE?
IT IS, YOUR HONOR. KANG WAS AT THE BANK, WE TRIED TO STOP HIM, BUT HE GOT AWAY.
UM. WHAT ELSE?
THEN HE MADE US THINK WE'RE ALL HYDRA?
MAKE FULL RESTITUTION TO THE TOWNSHIP OF HO-HO-KUS.
GET OUT OF MY COURTROOM, AND STAY OUT OF NEW JERSEY.
WITH PLEASURE!

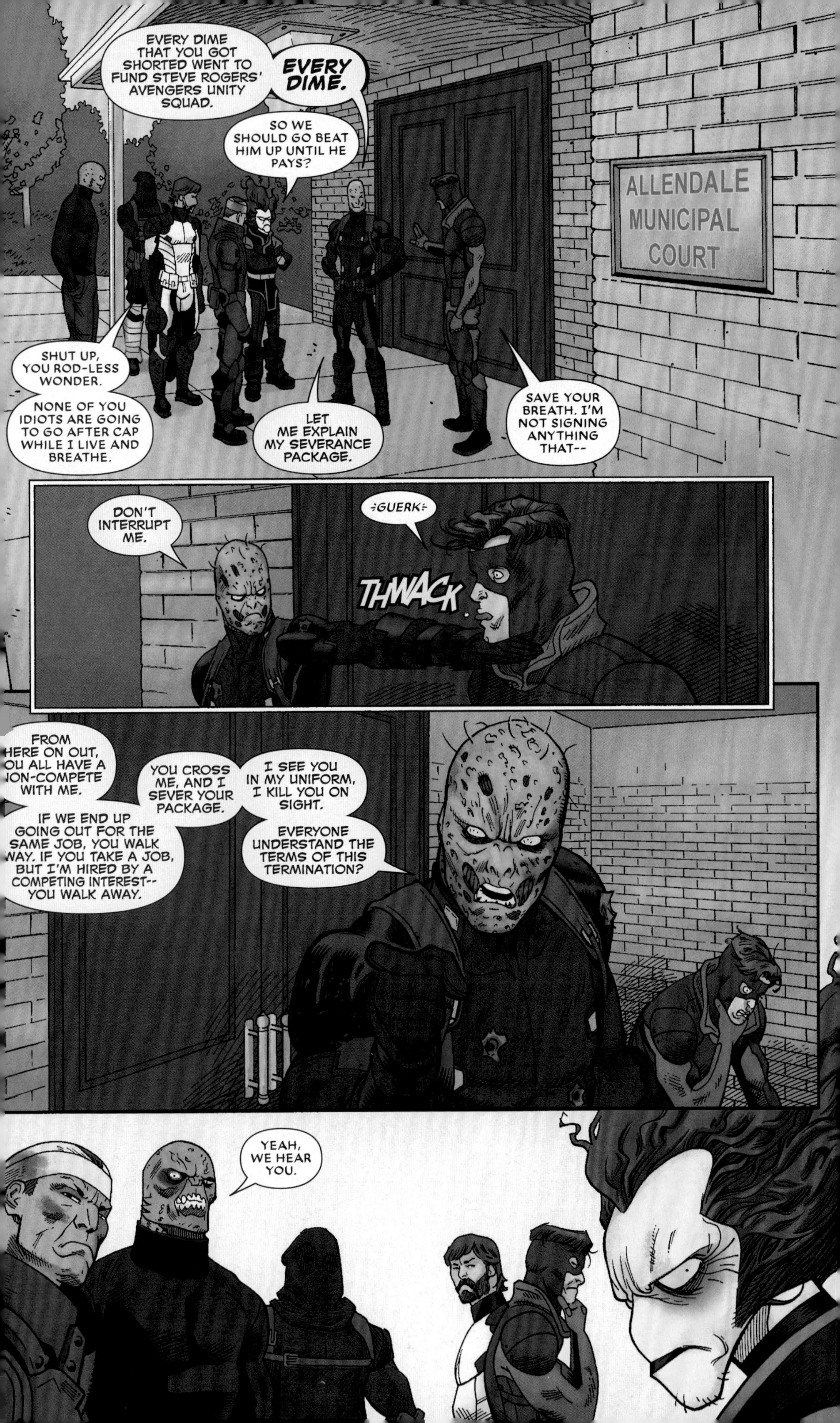
EVERY DIME THAT YOU GOT SHORTED WENT TO FUND STEVE ROGERS' AVENGERS UNITY SQUAD.
EVERY DIME.
SO WE SHOULD GO BEAT HIM UP UNTIL HE PAYS?
ALLENDALE MUNICIPAL COURT
SHUT UP, YOU ROD-LESS WONDER.
NONE OF YOU IDIOTS ARE GOING TO GO AFTER CAP WHILE I LIVE AND BREATHE.
LET ME EXPLAIN MY SEVERANCE PACKAGE.
SAVE YOUR BREATH. I'M NOT SIGNING ANYTHING THAT--
DON'T INTERRUPT ME.
GUERK
THWACK
FROM HERE ON OUT, YOU ALL HAVE A NON-COMPETE WITH ME.
IF WE END UP GOING OUT FOR THE SAME JOB, YOU WALK AWAY. IF YOU TAKE A JOB, BUT I'M HIRED BY A COMPETING INTEREST-- YOU WALK AWAY.
YOU CROSS ME, AND I SEVER YOUR PACKAGE.
I SEE YOU IN MY UNIFORM, I KILL YOU ON SIGHT.
EVERYONE UNDERSTAND THE TERMS OF THIS TERMINATION?
YEAH, WE HEAR YOU.

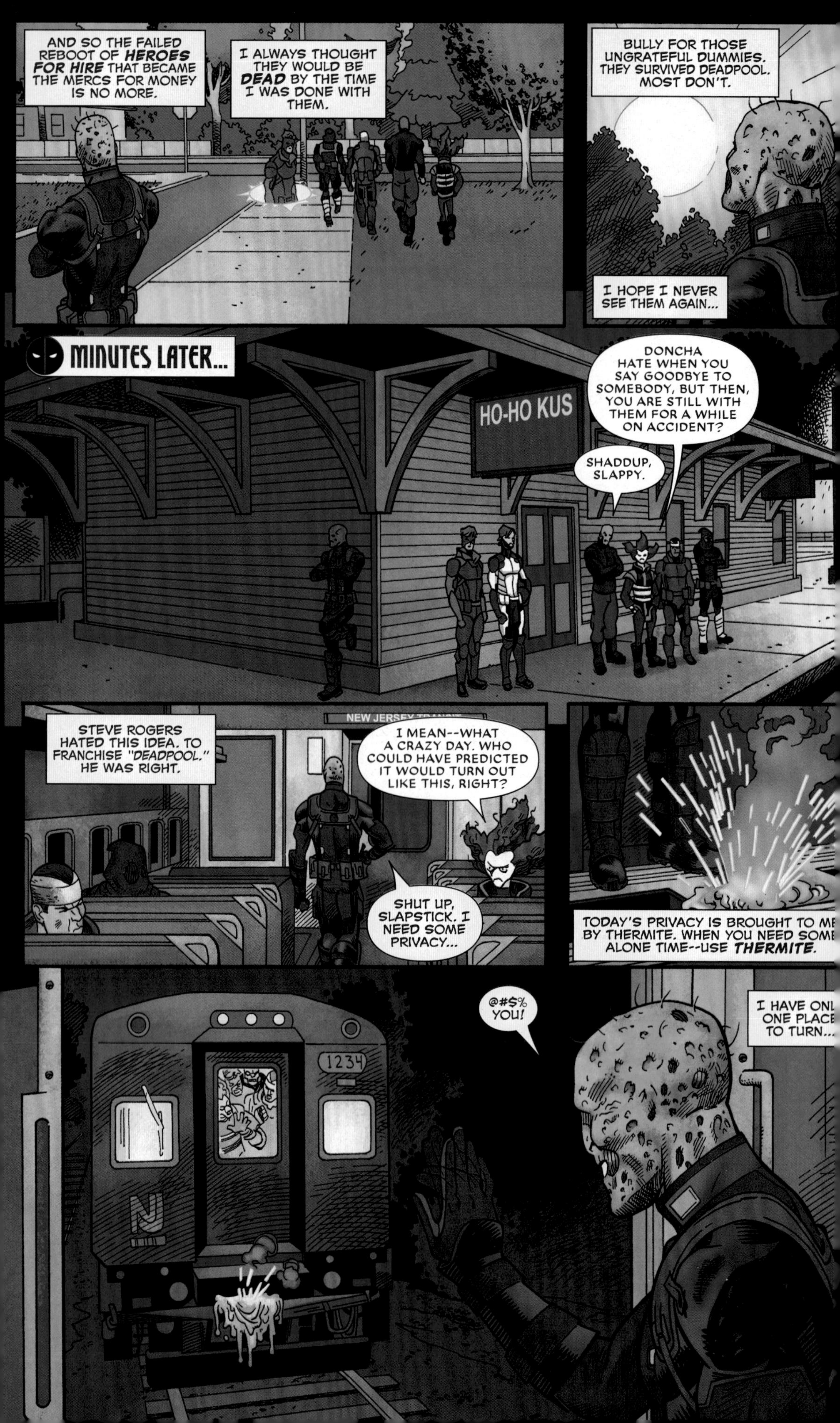

AND SO THE FAILED REBOOT OF **HEROES FOR HIRE** THAT BECAME THE MERCS FOR MONEY IS NO MORE.
I ALWAYS THOUGHT THEY WOULD BE **DEAD** BY THE TIME I WAS DONE WITH THEM.
BULLY FOR THOSE UNGRATEFUL DUMMIES. THEY SURVIVED DEADPOOL. MOST DON'T.
I HOPE I NEVER SEE THEM AGAIN...
MINUTES LATER...
HO-HO KUS
DONCHA HATE WHEN YOU SAY GOODBYE TO SOMEBODY, BUT THEN, YOU ARE STILL WITH THEM FOR A WHILE ON ACCIDENT?
SHADDUP, SLAPPY.
STEVE ROGERS HATED THIS IDEA. TO FRANCHISE "DEADPOOL." HE WAS RIGHT.
I MEAN--WHAT A CRAZY DAY. WHO COULD HAVE PREDICTED IT WOULD TURN OUT LIKE THIS, RIGHT?
SHUT UP, SLAPSTICK. I NEED SOME PRIVACY...
TODAY'S PRIVACY IS BROUGHT TO ME BY THERMITE. WHEN YOU NEED SOME ALONE TIME--USE **THERMITE**.
1234
@#$% YOU!
I HAVE ONLY ONE PLACE TO TURN...

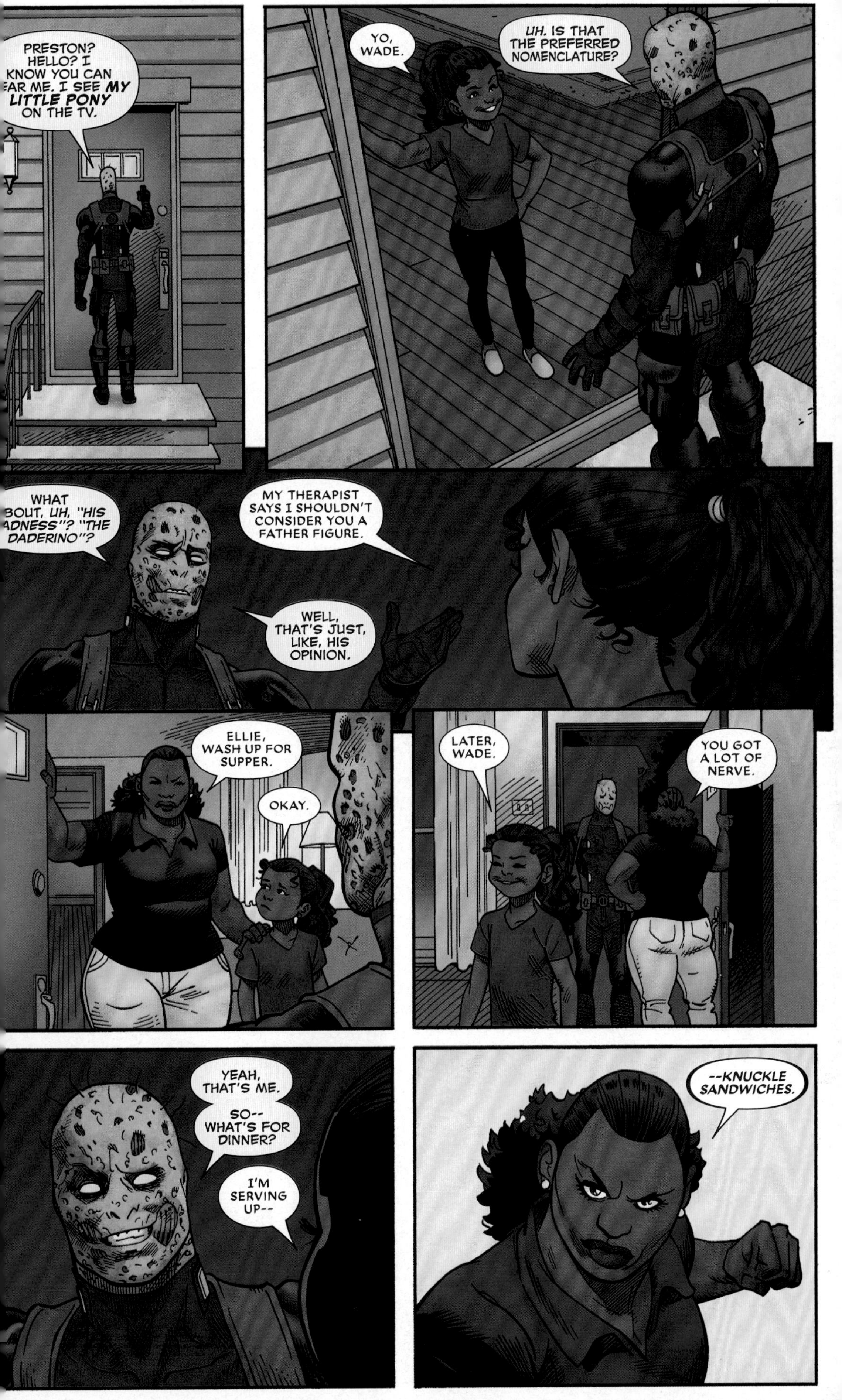
PRESTON? HELLO? I KNOW YOU CAN HEAR ME. I SEE MY LITTLE PONY ON THE TV.
YO, WADE.
UH. IS THAT THE PREFERRED NOMENCLATURE?
WHAT ABOUT, UH, "HIS DADNESS"? "THE DADERINO"?
MY THERAPIST SAYS I SHOULDN'T CONSIDER YOU A FATHER FIGURE.
WELL, THAT'S JUST, LIKE, HIS OPINION.
ELLIE, WASH UP FOR SUPPER.
OKAY.
LATER, WADE.
YOU GOT A LOT OF NERVE.
YEAH, THAT'S ME.
SO-- WHAT'S FOR DINNER?
I'M SERVING UP--
--KNUCKLE SANDWICHES.

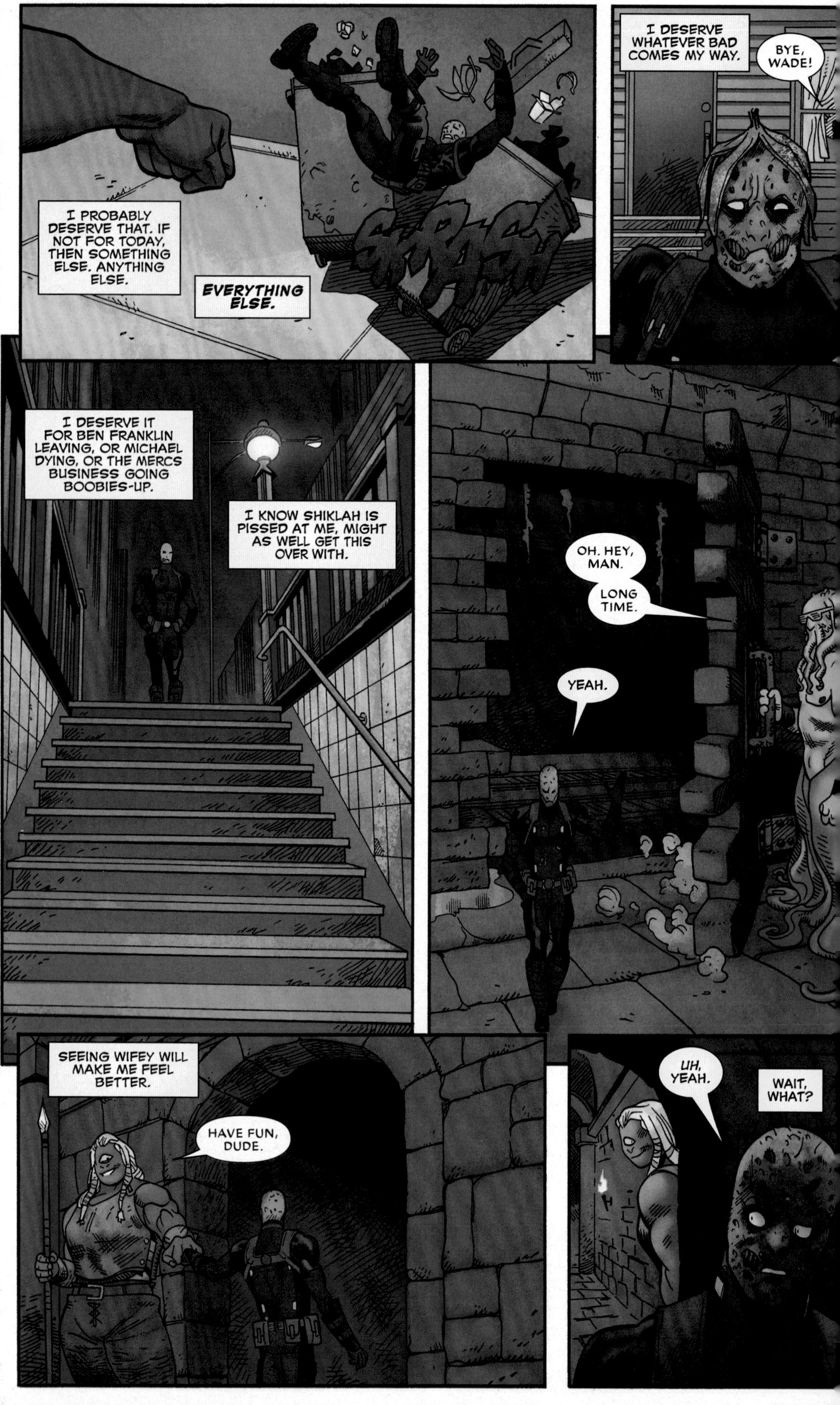
I PROBABLY DESERVE THAT. IF NOT FOR TODAY, THEN SOMETHING ELSE. ANYTHING ELSE.
EVERYTHING ELSE.
SPLASH
I DESERVE WHATEVER BAD COMES MY WAY.
BYE, WADE!
I DESERVE IT FOR BEN FRANKLIN LEAVING, OR MICHAEL DYING, OR THE MERCS BUSINESS GOING BOOBIES-UP.
I KNOW SHIKLAH IS PISSED AT ME, MIGHT AS WELL GET THIS OVER WITH.
OH. HEY, MAN.
LONG TIME.
YEAH.
SEEING WIFEY WILL MAKE ME FEEL BETTER.
HAVE FUN, DUDE.
UH, YEAH.
WAIT, WHAT?

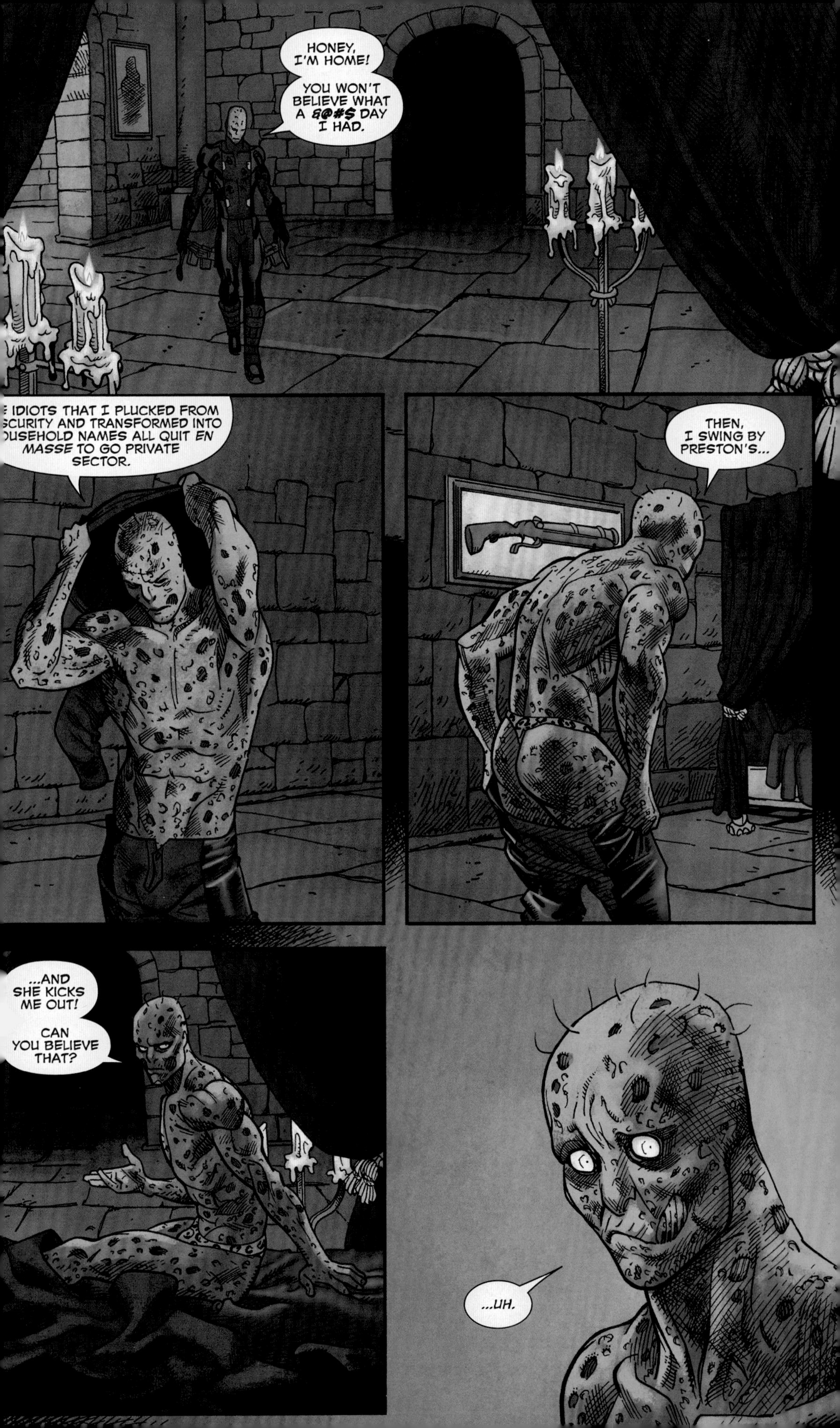
HONEY, I'M HOME!
YOU WON'T BELIEVE WHAT A &@#$ DAY I HAD.
E IDIOTS THAT I PLUCKED FROM SCURITY AND TRANSFORMED INTO OUSEHOLD NAMES ALL QUIT EN MASSE TO GO PRIVATE SECTOR.
THEN, I SWING BY PRESTON'S...
...AND SHE KICKS ME OUT!
CAN YOU BELIEVE THAT?
...UH.

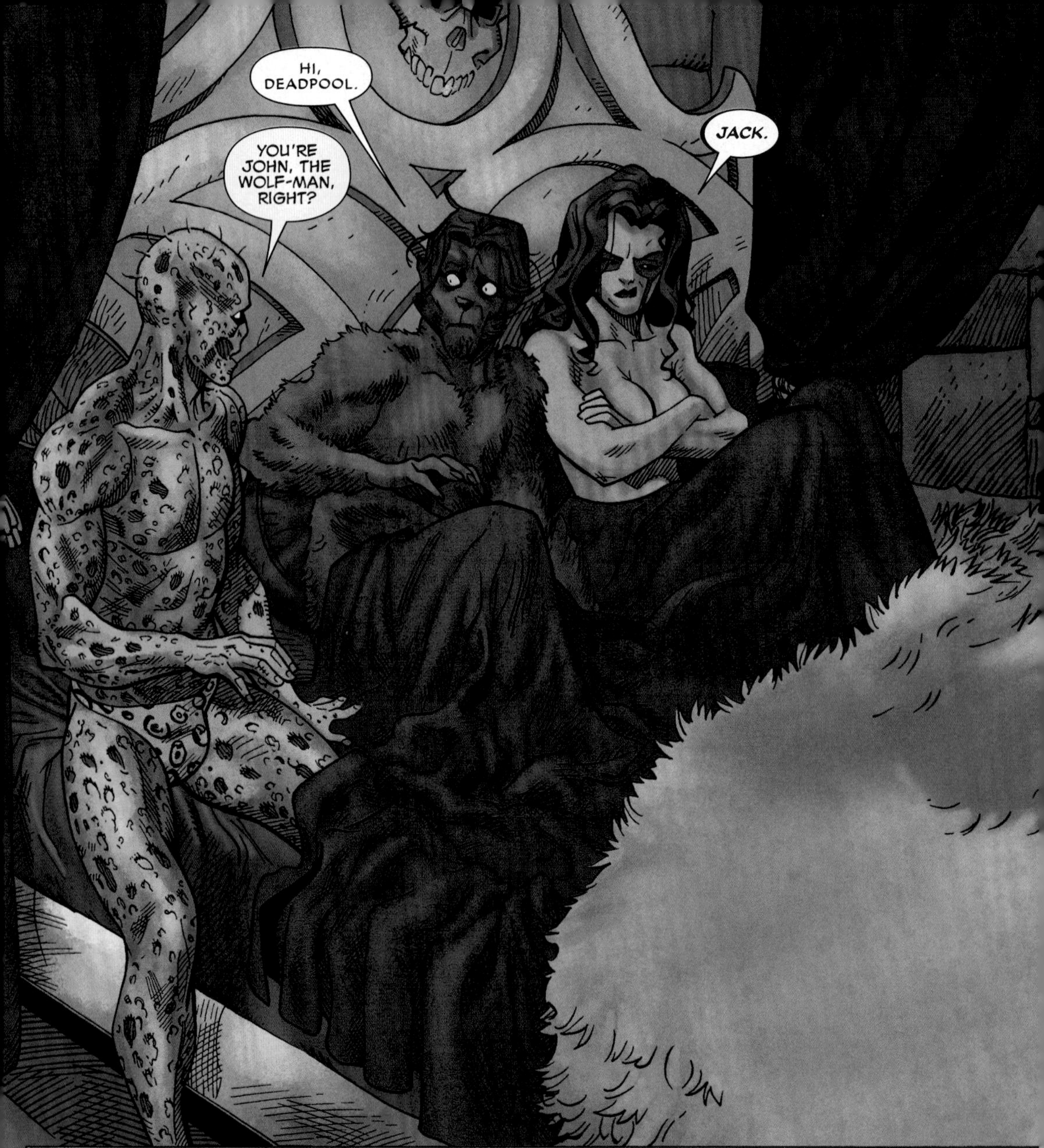
HI, DEADPOOL.
YOU'RE JOHN, THE WOLF-MAN, RIGHT?
JACK.

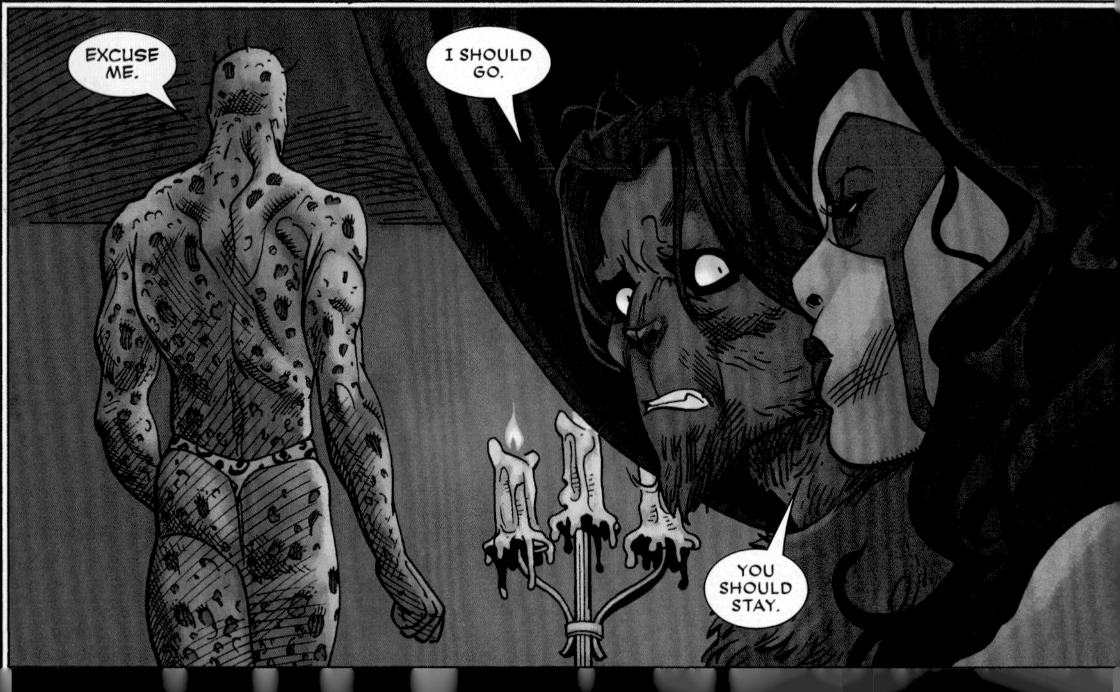
EXCUSE ME.
I SHOULD GO.
YOU SHOULD STAY.

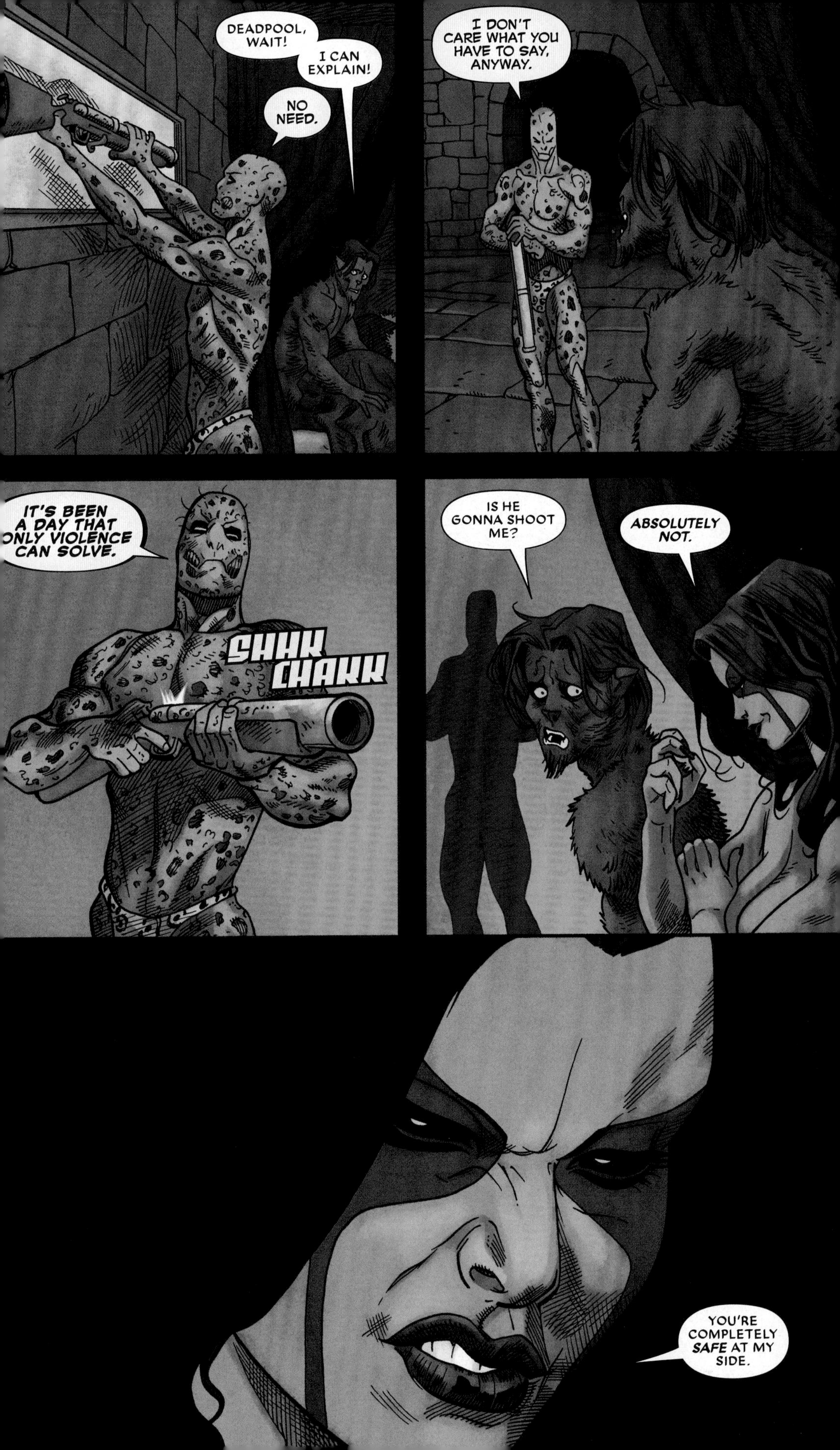
DEADPOOL, WAIT!
I CAN EXPLAIN!
NO NEED.
I DON'T CARE WHAT YOU HAVE TO SAY, ANYWAY.
IT'S BEEN A DAY THAT ONLY VIOLENCE CAN SOLVE.
SHHK CHAKK
IS HE GONNA SHOOT ME?
ABSOLUTELY NOT.
YOU'RE COMPLETELY SAFE AT MY SIDE.

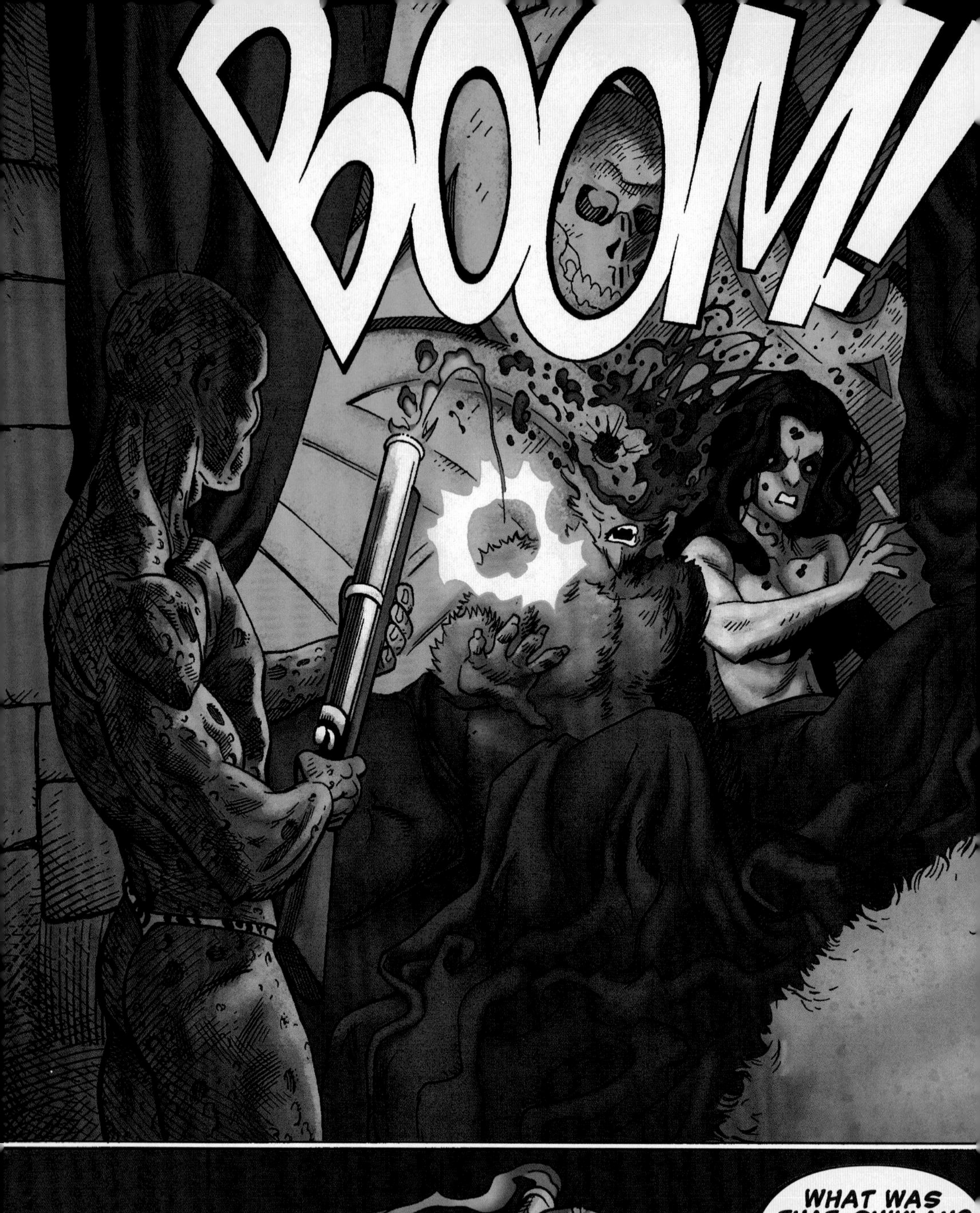
BOOM!

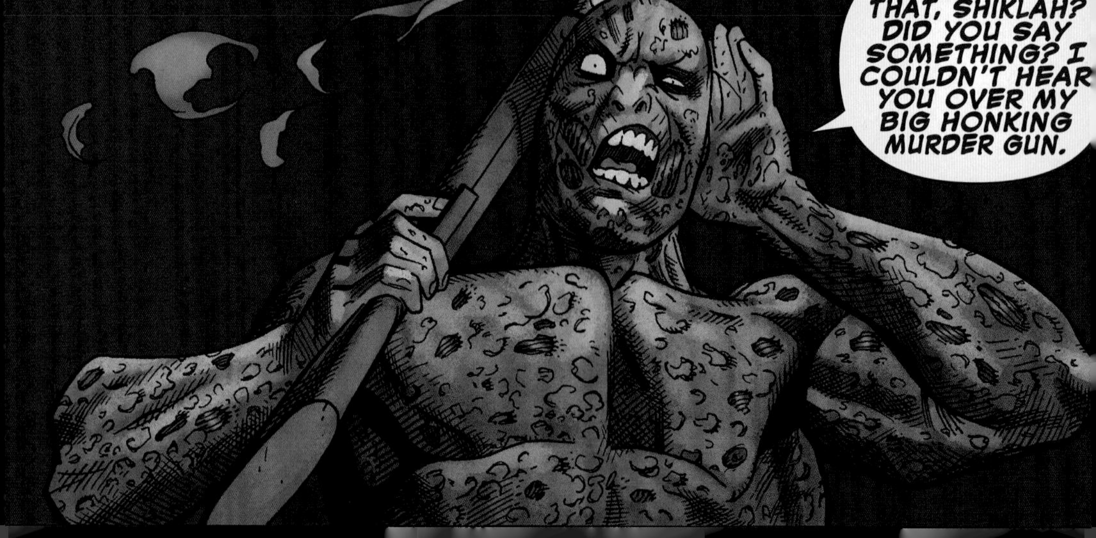
WHAT WAS THAT, SHIKLAH? DID YOU SAY SOMETHING? I COULDN'T HEAR YOU OVER MY BIG HONKING MURDER GUN.

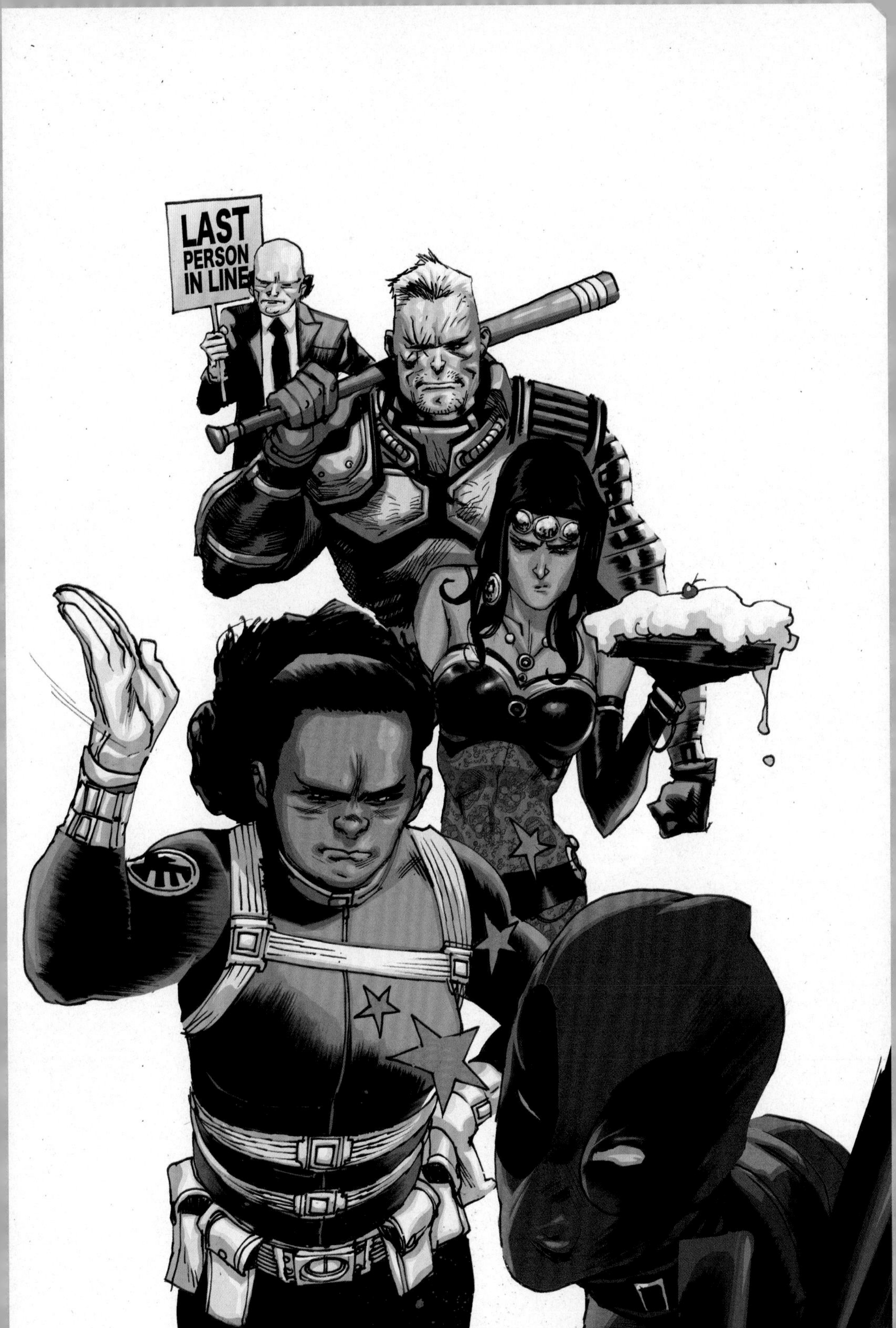
LAST
PERSON
IN LINE

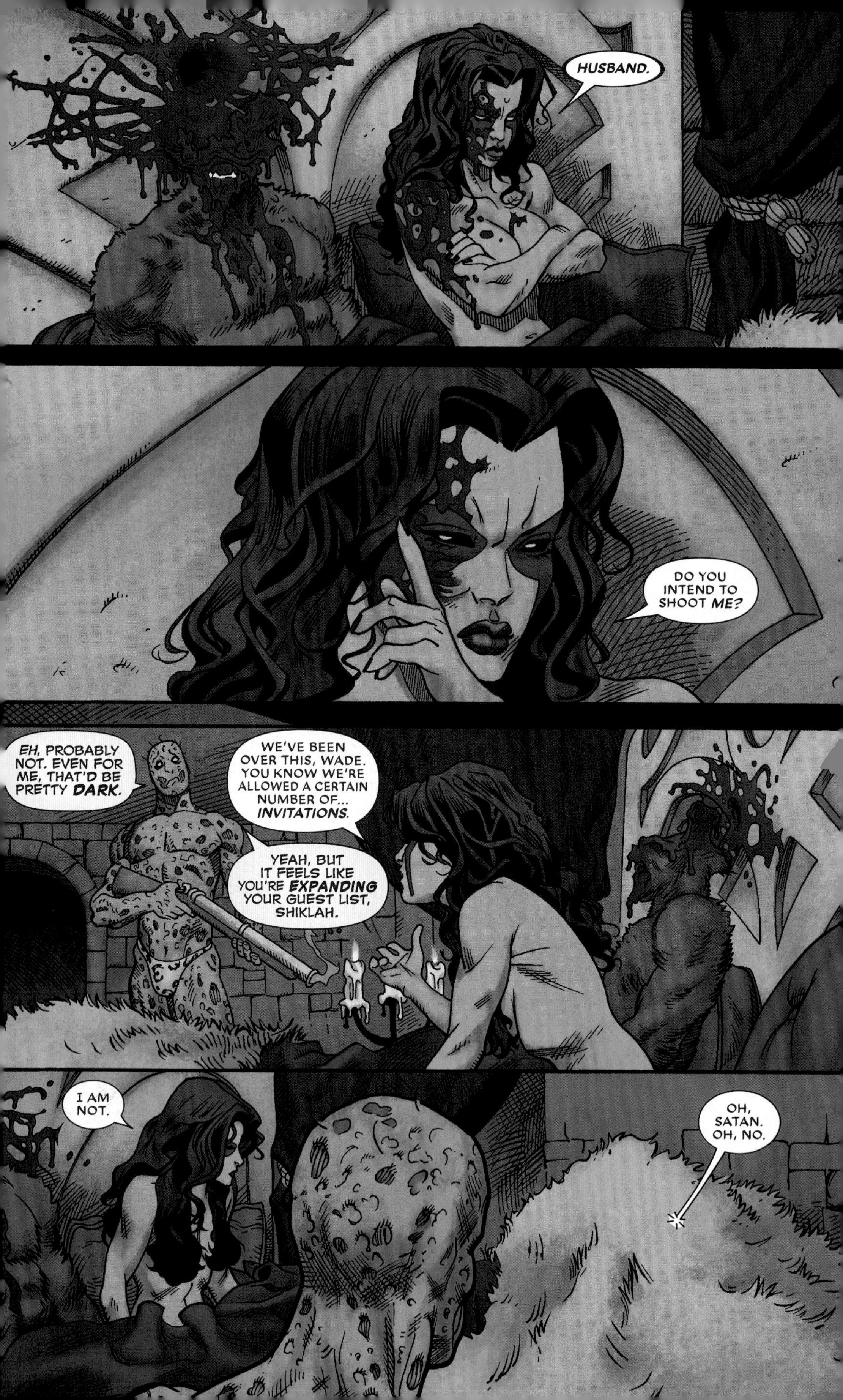
HUSBAND.
DO YOU INTEND TO SHOOT ME?
EH, PROBABLY NOT. EVEN FOR ME, THAT'D BE PRETTY DARK.
WE'VE BEEN OVER THIS, WADE. YOU KNOW WE'RE ALLOWED A CERTAIN NUMBER OF... INVITATIONS.
YEAH, BUT IT FEELS LIKE YOU'RE EXPANDING YOUR GUEST LIST, SHIKLAH.
I AM NOT.
OH, SATAN. OH, NO.

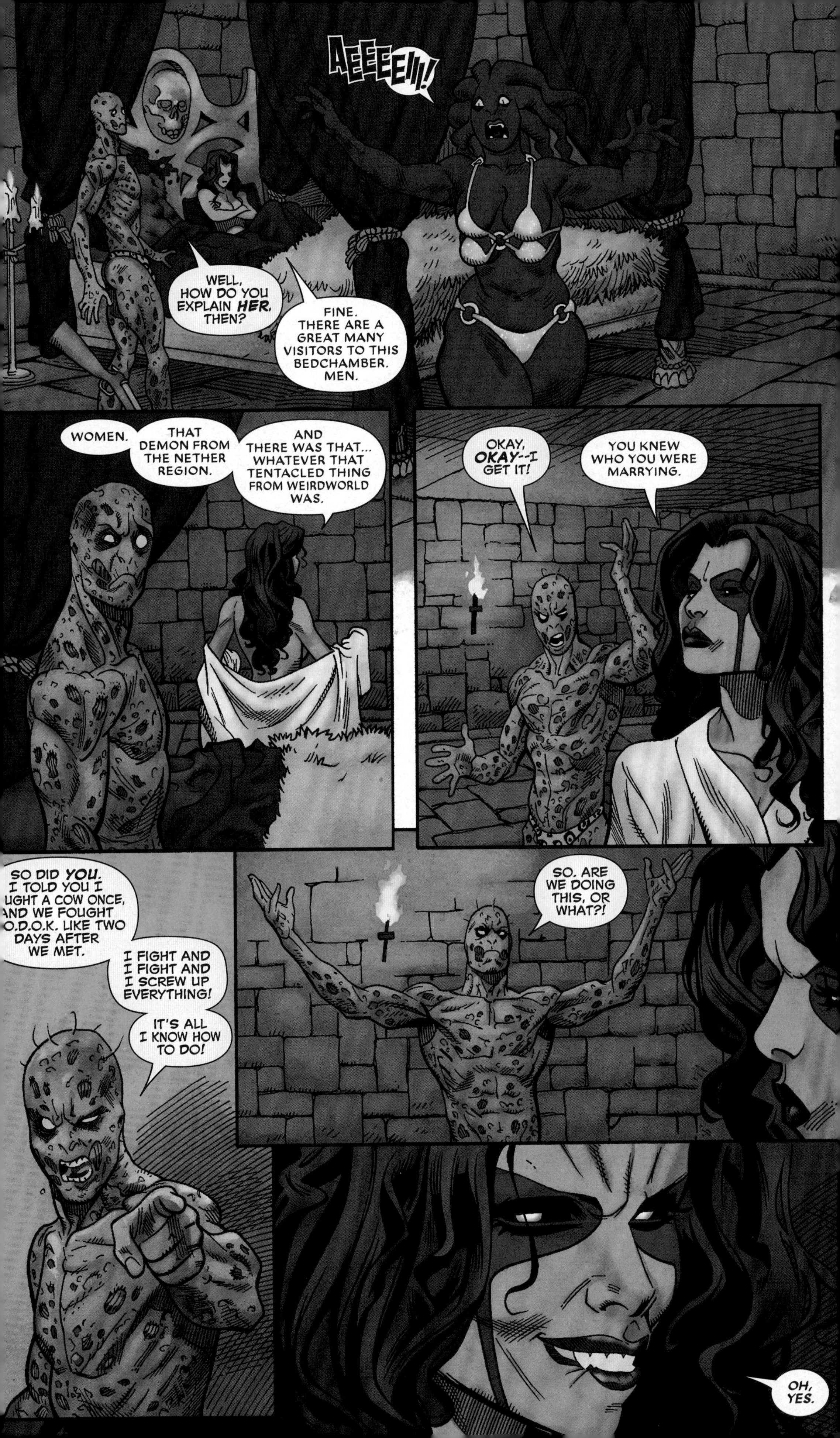
AEEEEIII!
WELL, HOW DO YOU EXPLAIN HER, THEN?
FINE. THERE ARE A GREAT MANY VISITORS TO THIS BEDCHAMBER. MEN.
WOMEN.
THAT DEMON FROM THE NETHER REGION.
AND THERE WAS THAT... WHATEVER THAT TENTACLED THING FROM WEIRDWORLD WAS.
OKAY, OKAY--I GET IT!
YOU KNEW WHO YOU WERE MARRYING.
SO DID YOU. I TOLD YOU I UGHT A COW ONCE, AND WE FOUGHT O.D.O.K. LIKE TWO DAYS AFTER WE MET.
I FIGHT AND I FIGHT AND I SCREW UP EVERYTHING!
IT'S ALL I KNOW HOW TO DO!
SO. ARE WE DOING THIS, OR WHAT?!
OH, YES.

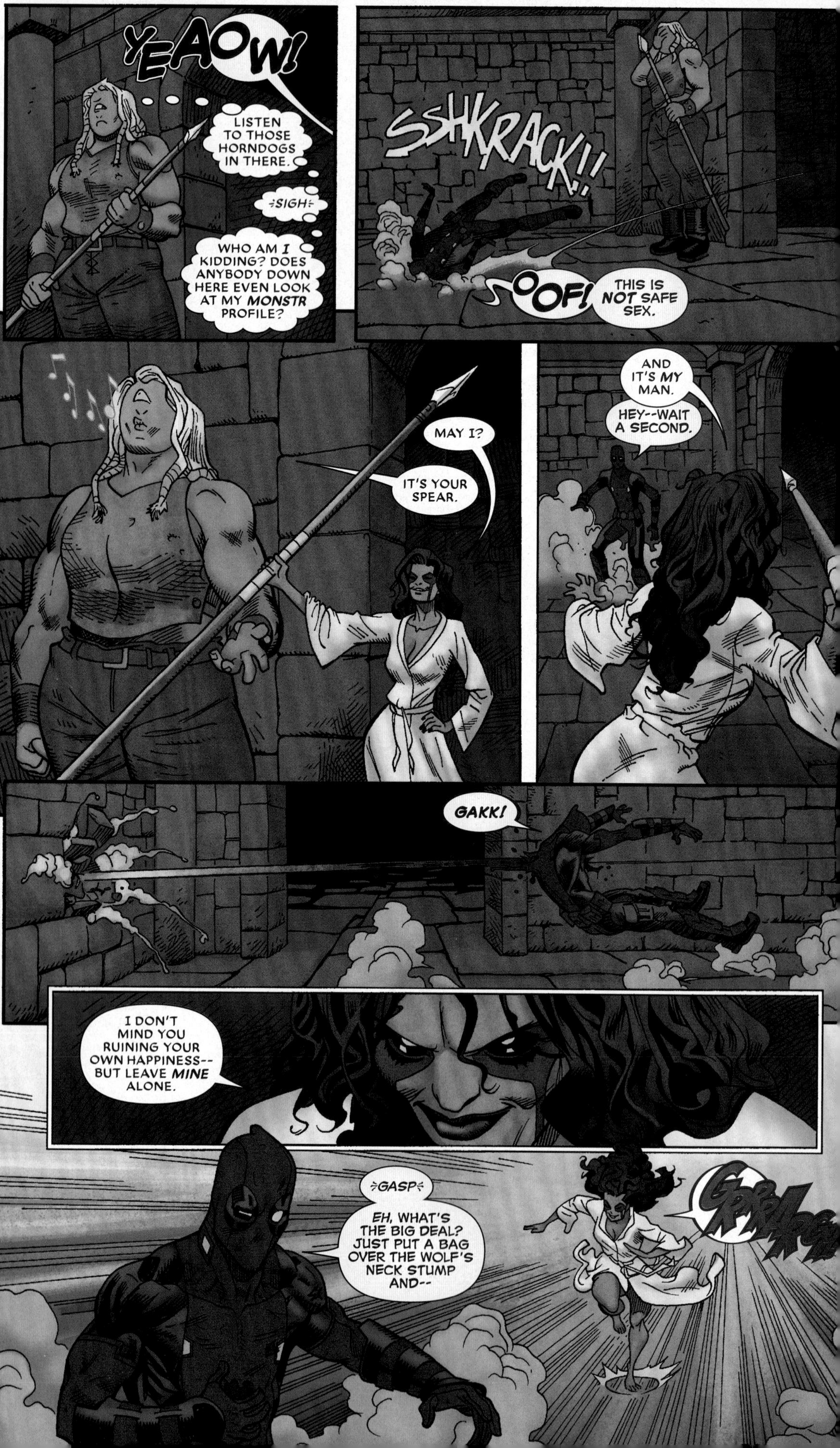
YEAOW!
LISTEN TO THOSE HORNDOGS IN THERE.
⊰SIGH⊱
WHO AM *I* KIDDING? DOES ANYBODY DOWN HERE EVEN LOOK AT MY *MONSTR* PROFILE?
SSHKRACK!!
OOF!
THIS IS *NOT* SAFE SEX.
MAY I?
IT'S YOUR SPEAR.
AND IT'S *MY* MAN.
HEY--WAIT A SECOND.
GAKK!
I DON'T MIND YOU RUINING YOUR OWN HAPPINESS-- BUT LEAVE *MINE* ALONE.
⊰GASP⊱
EH, WHAT'S THE BIG DEAL? JUST PUT A BAG OVER THE WOLF'S NECK STUMP AND--

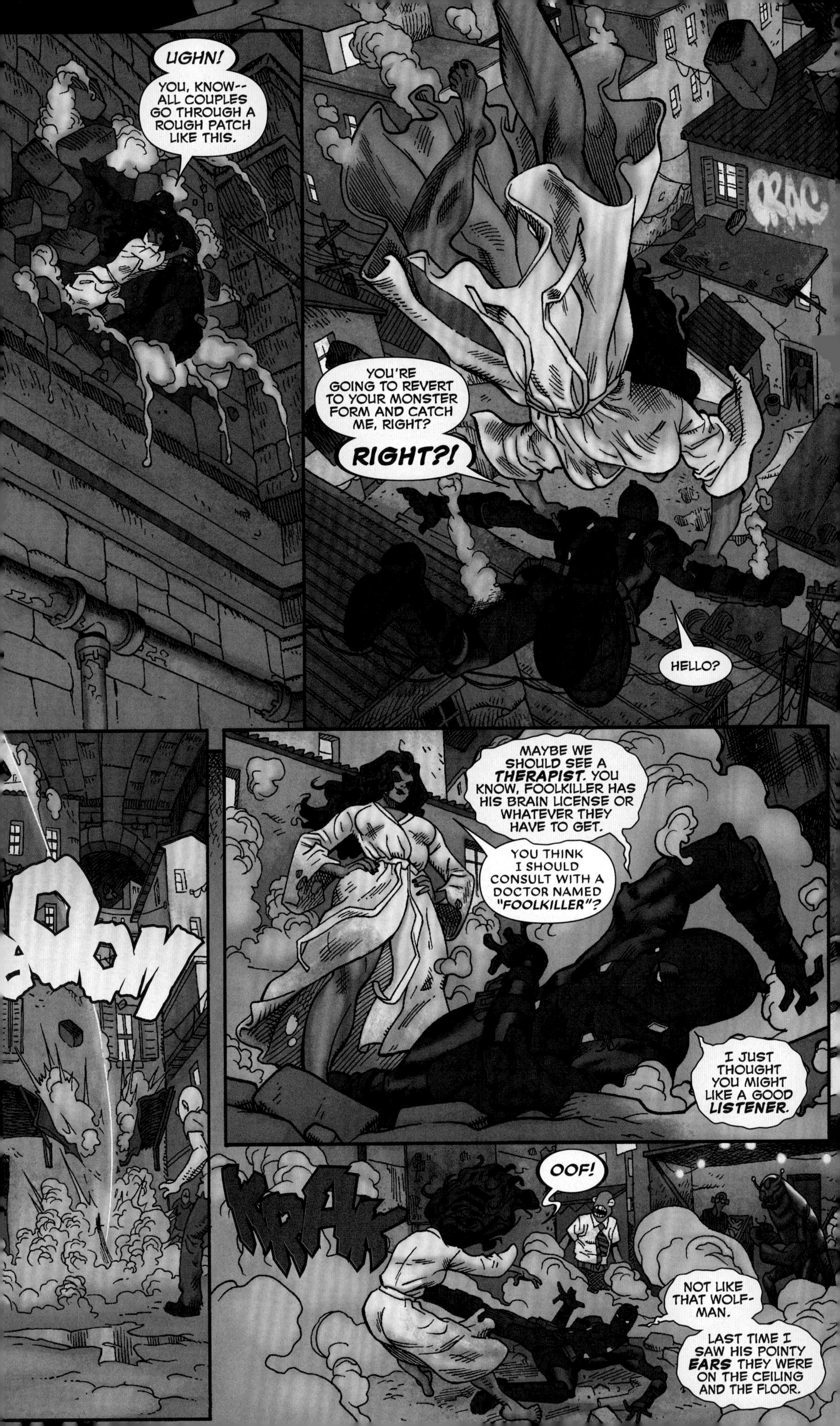

UGHN!
YOU, KNOW-- ALL COUPLES GO THROUGH A ROUGH PATCH LIKE THIS.
YOU'RE GOING TO REVERT TO YOUR MONSTER FORM AND CATCH ME, RIGHT?
RIGHT?!
HELLO?
BOOM
MAYBE WE SHOULD SEE A THERAPIST. YOU KNOW, FOOLKILLER HAS HIS BRAIN LICENSE OR WHATEVER THEY HAVE TO GET.
YOU THINK I SHOULD CONSULT WITH A DOCTOR NAMED "FOOLKILLER"?
I JUST THOUGHT YOU MIGHT LIKE A GOOD LISTENER.
KRAK
OOF!
NOT LIKE THAT WOLF-MAN.
LAST TIME I SAW HIS POINTY EARS THEY WERE ON THE CEILING AND THE FLOOR.

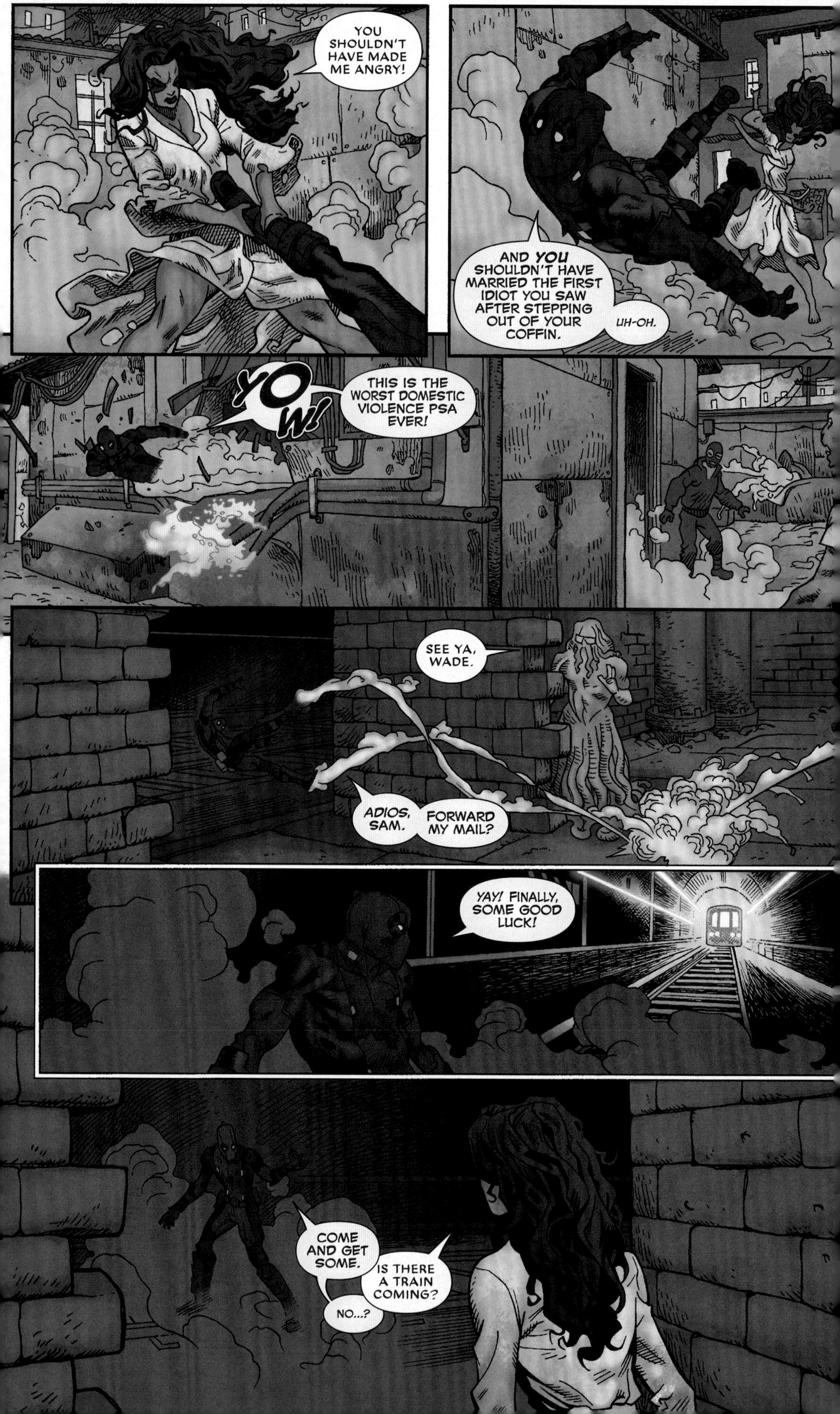
YOU SHOULDN'T HAVE MADE ME ANGRY!
AND YOU SHOULDN'T HAVE MARRIED THE FIRST IDIOT YOU SAW AFTER STEPPING OUT OF YOUR COFFIN.
UH-OH.
YOW!
THIS IS THE WORST DOMESTIC VIOLENCE PSA EVER!
SEE YA, WADE.
ADIOS, SAM.
FORWARD MY MAIL?
YAY! FINALLY, SOME GOOD LUCK!
COME AND GET SOME.
IS THERE A TRAIN COMING?
NO...?

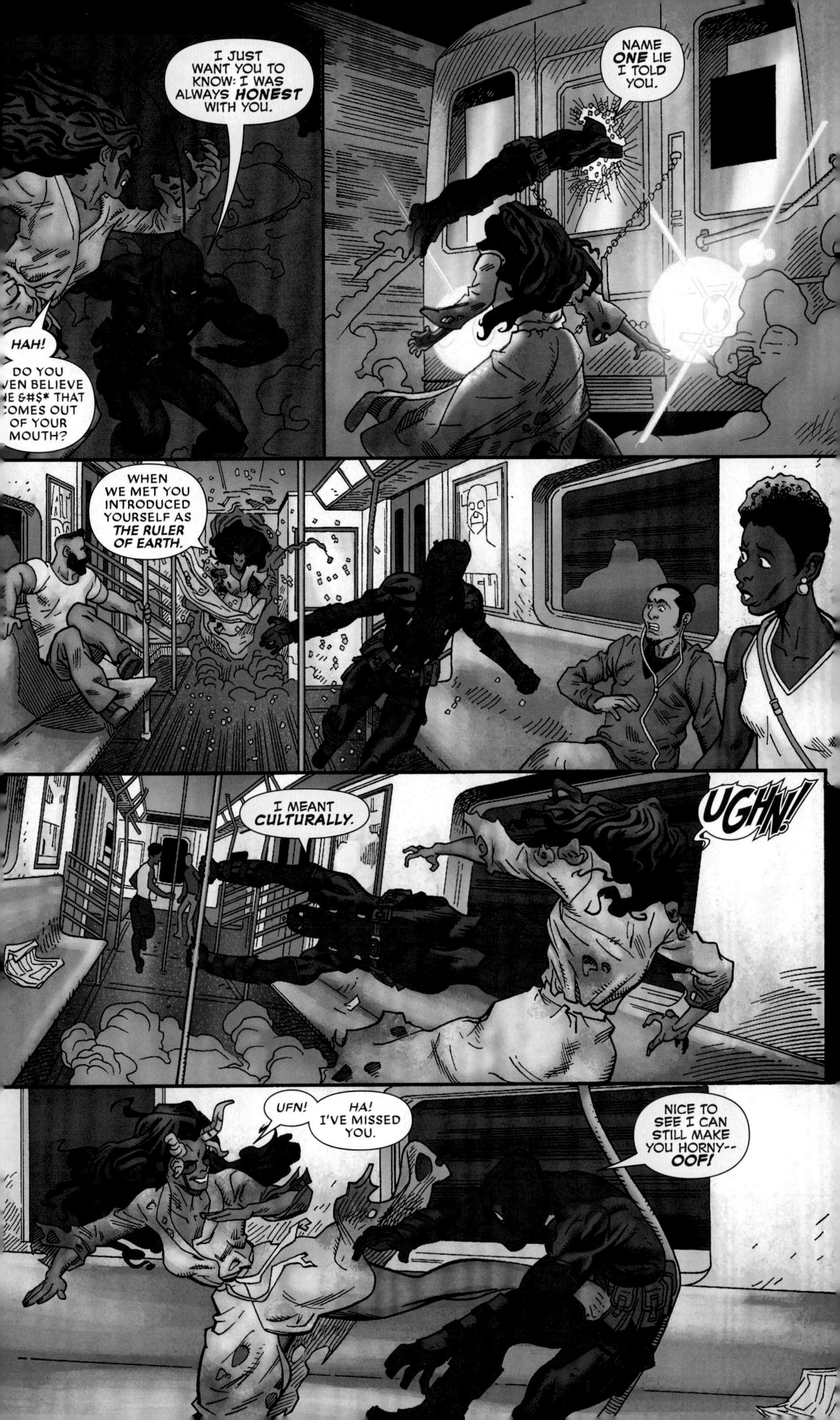
I JUST WANT YOU TO KNOW: I WAS ALWAYS HONEST WITH YOU.
HAH!
DO YOU
VEN BELIEVE
E &#$* THAT
OMES OUT
OF YOUR
MOUTH?
NAME ONE LIE I TOLD YOU.
WHEN WE MET YOU INTRODUCED YOURSELF AS THE RULER OF EARTH.
I MEANT CULTURALLY.
UGHN!
UFN!
HA! I'VE MISSED YOU.
NICE TO SEE I CAN STILL MAKE YOU HORNY-- OOF!

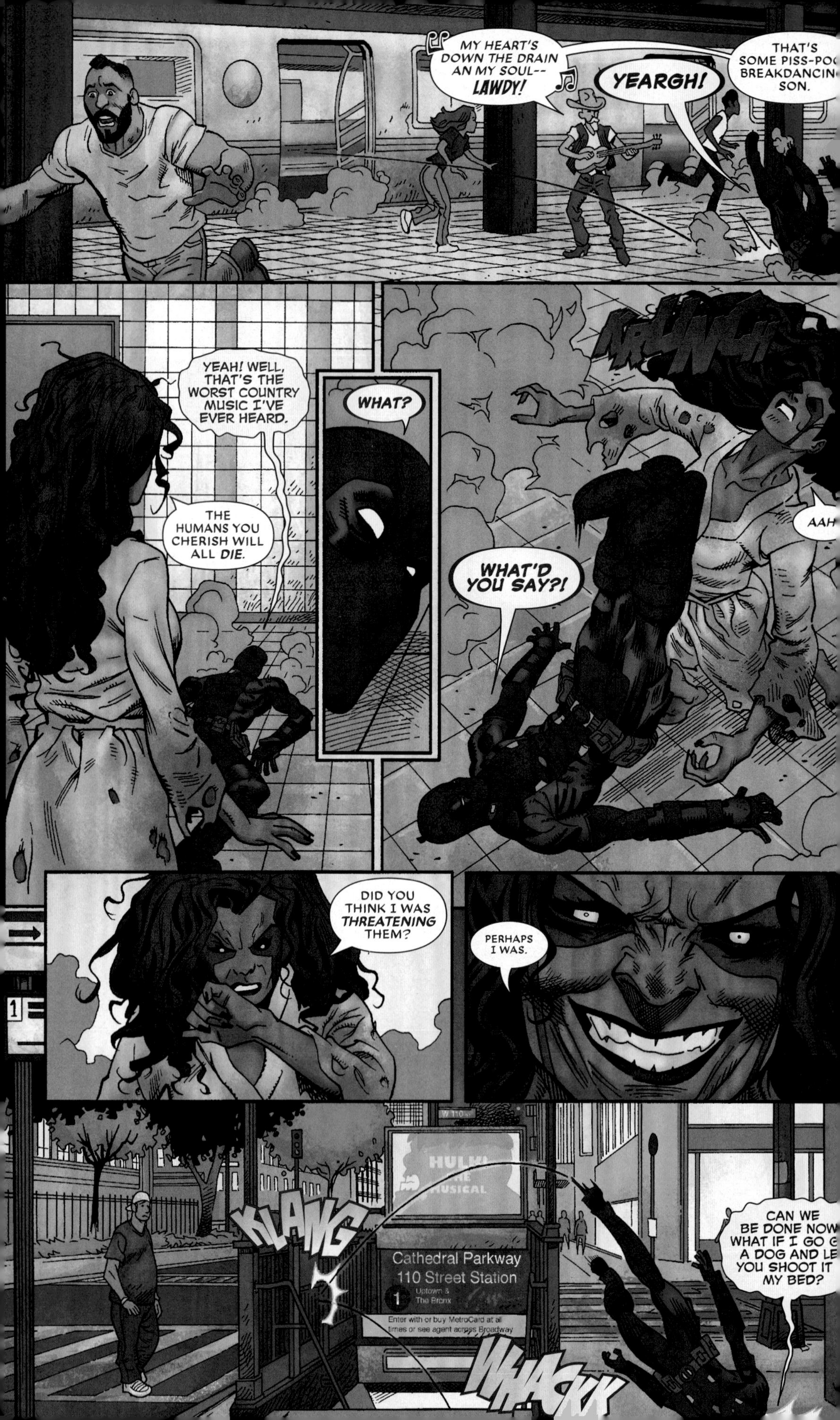
MY HEART'S DOWN THE DRAIN AN MY SOUL-- LAWDY!
YEARGH!
THAT'S SOME PISS-PO BREAKDANCIN SON.
YEAH! WELL, THAT'S THE WORST COUNTRY MUSIC I'VE EVER HEARD.
THE HUMANS YOU CHERISH WILL ALL DIE.
WHAT?
KRUNCH
WHAT'D YOU SAY?!
AAH
DID YOU THINK I WAS THREATENING THEM?
PERHAPS I WAS.
HULK! THE MUSICAL
KLANG
Cathedral Parkway
110 Street Station
1 Uptown & The Bronx
Enter with or buy MetroCard at all times or see agent across Broadway
CAN WE BE DONE NOW WHAT IF I GO G A DOG AND LE YOU SHOOT IT MY BED?
WHACKK

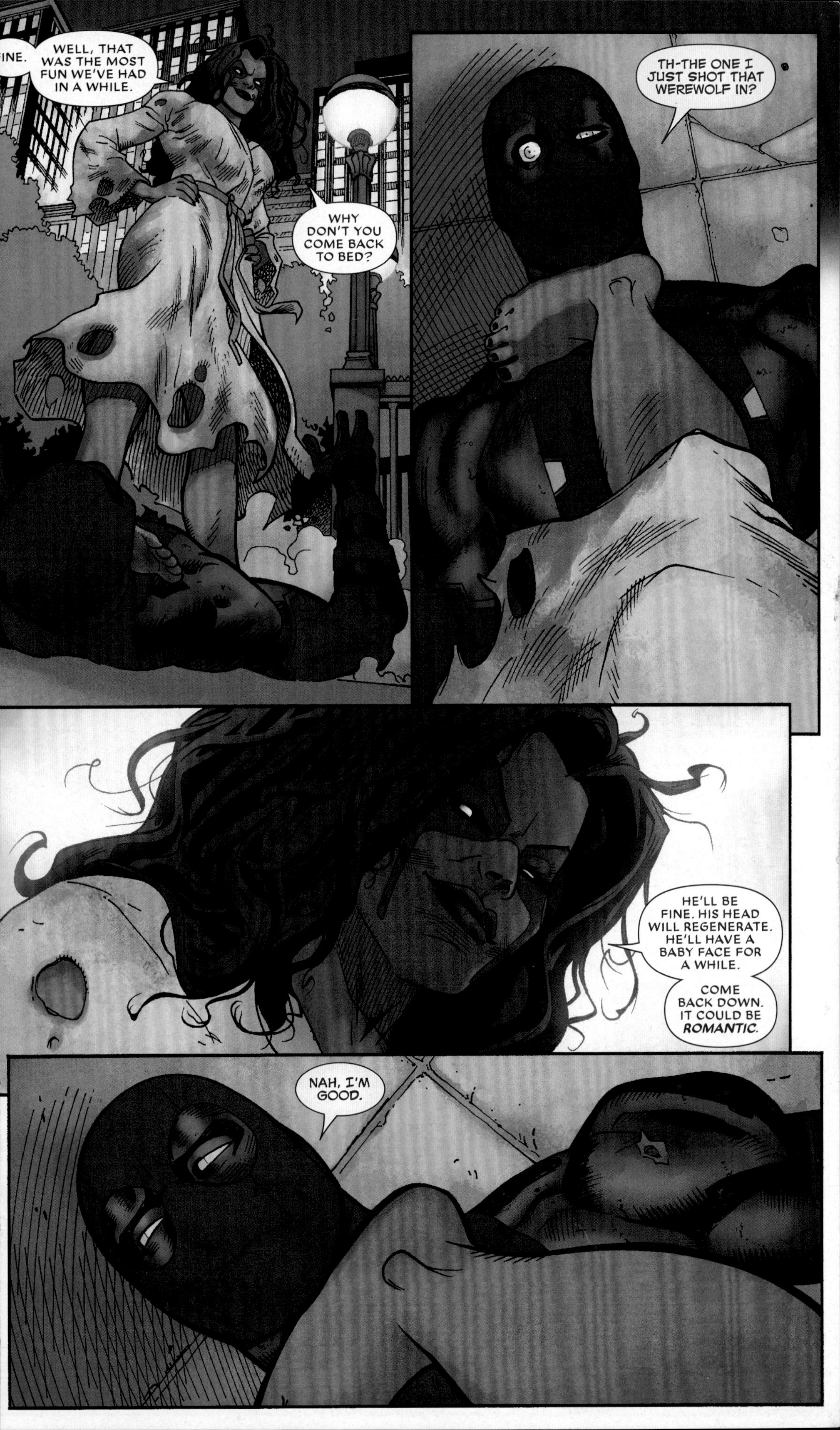
FINE.
WELL, THAT WAS THE MOST FUN WE'VE HAD IN A WHILE.
WHY DON'T YOU COME BACK TO BED?
TH-THE ONE I JUST SHOT THAT WEREWOLF IN?
HE'LL BE FINE. HIS HEAD WILL REGENERATE. HE'LL HAVE A BABY FACE FOR A WHILE.
COME BACK DOWN. IT COULD BE *ROMANTIC*.
NAH, I'M GOOD.

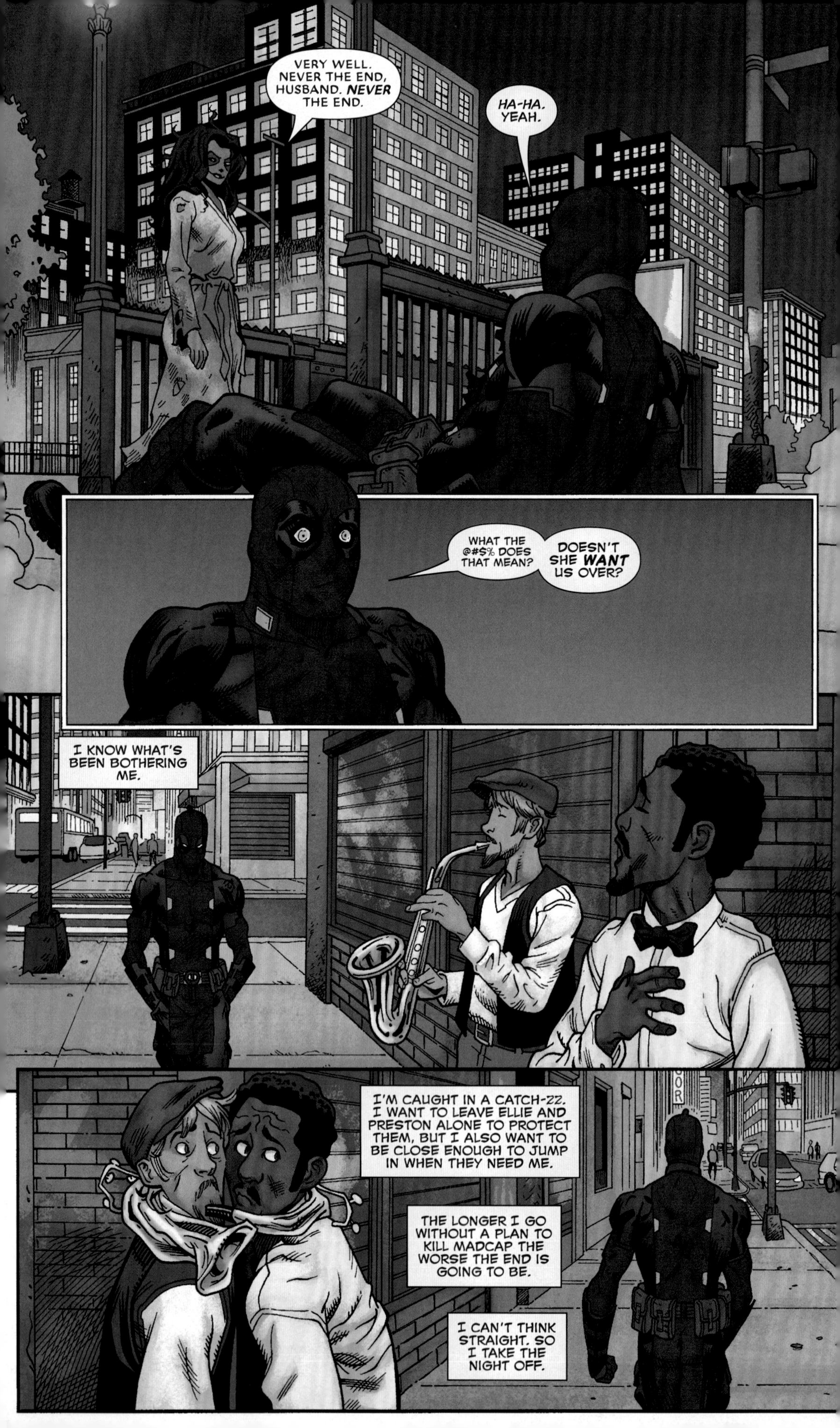
VERY WELL. NEVER THE END, HUSBAND. ***NEVER*** THE END.
HA-HA. YEAH.
WHAT THE @#$% DOES THAT MEAN?
DOESN'T SHE ***WANT*** US OVER?
I KNOW WHAT'S BEEN BOTHERING ME.
I'M CAUGHT IN A CATCH-22. I WANT TO LEAVE ELLIE AND PRESTON ALONE TO PROTECT THEM, BUT I ALSO WANT TO BE CLOSE ENOUGH TO JUMP IN WHEN THEY NEED ME.
THE LONGER I GO WITHOUT A PLAN TO KILL MADCAP THE WORSE THE END IS GOING TO BE.
I CAN'T THINK STRAIGHT. SO I TAKE THE NIGHT OFF.

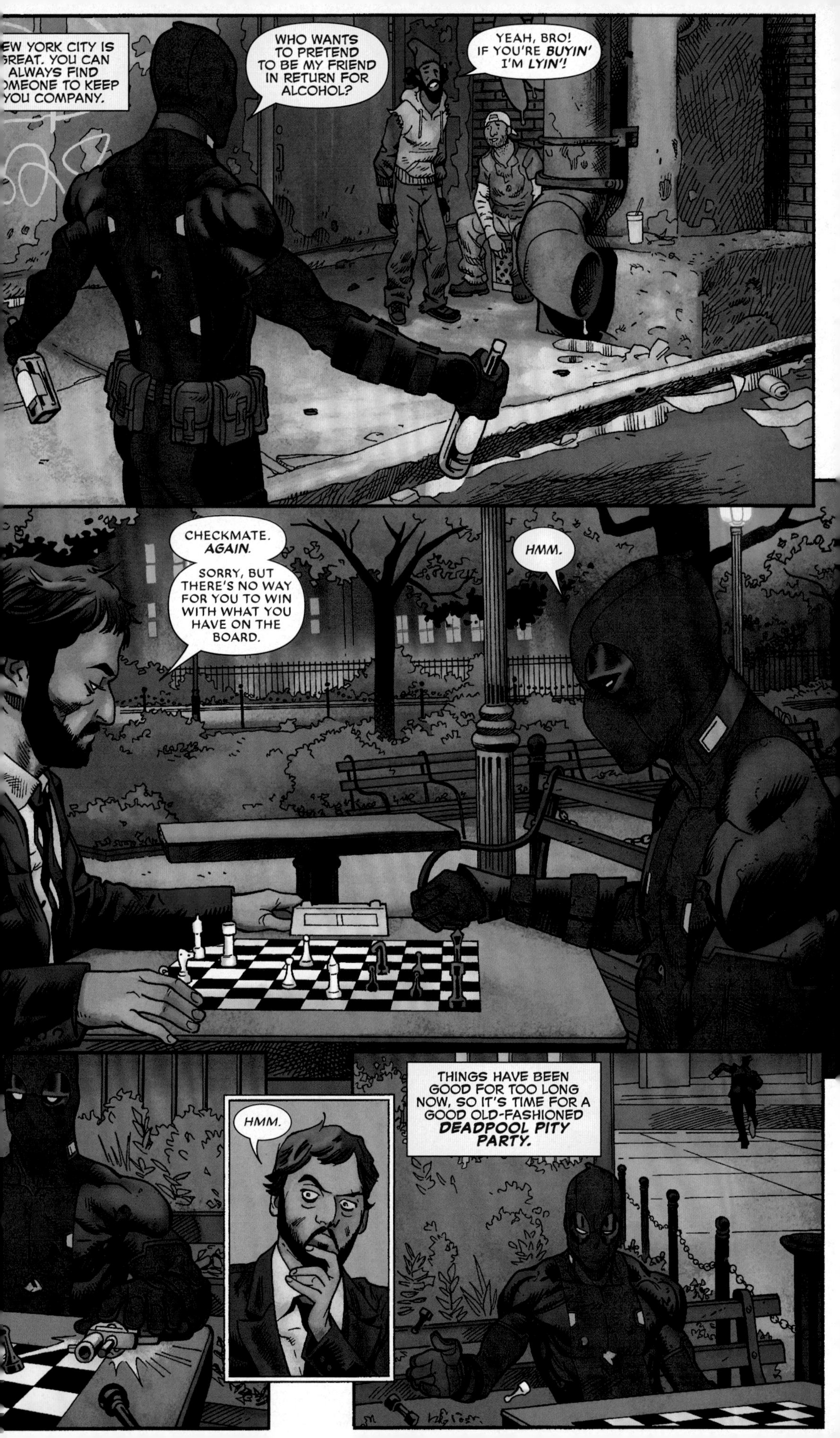
EW YORK CITY IS GREAT. YOU CAN ALWAYS FIND OMEONE TO KEEP YOU COMPANY.
WHO WANTS TO PRETEND TO BE MY FRIEND IN RETURN FOR ALCOHOL?
YEAH, BRO! IF YOU'RE BUYIN' I'M LYIN'!
CHECKMATE. AGAIN.
SORRY, BUT THERE'S NO WAY FOR YOU TO WIN WITH WHAT YOU HAVE ON THE BOARD.
HMM.
HMM.
THINGS HAVE BEEN GOOD FOR TOO LONG NOW, SO IT'S TIME FOR A GOOD OLD-FASHIONED DEADPOOL PITY PARTY.

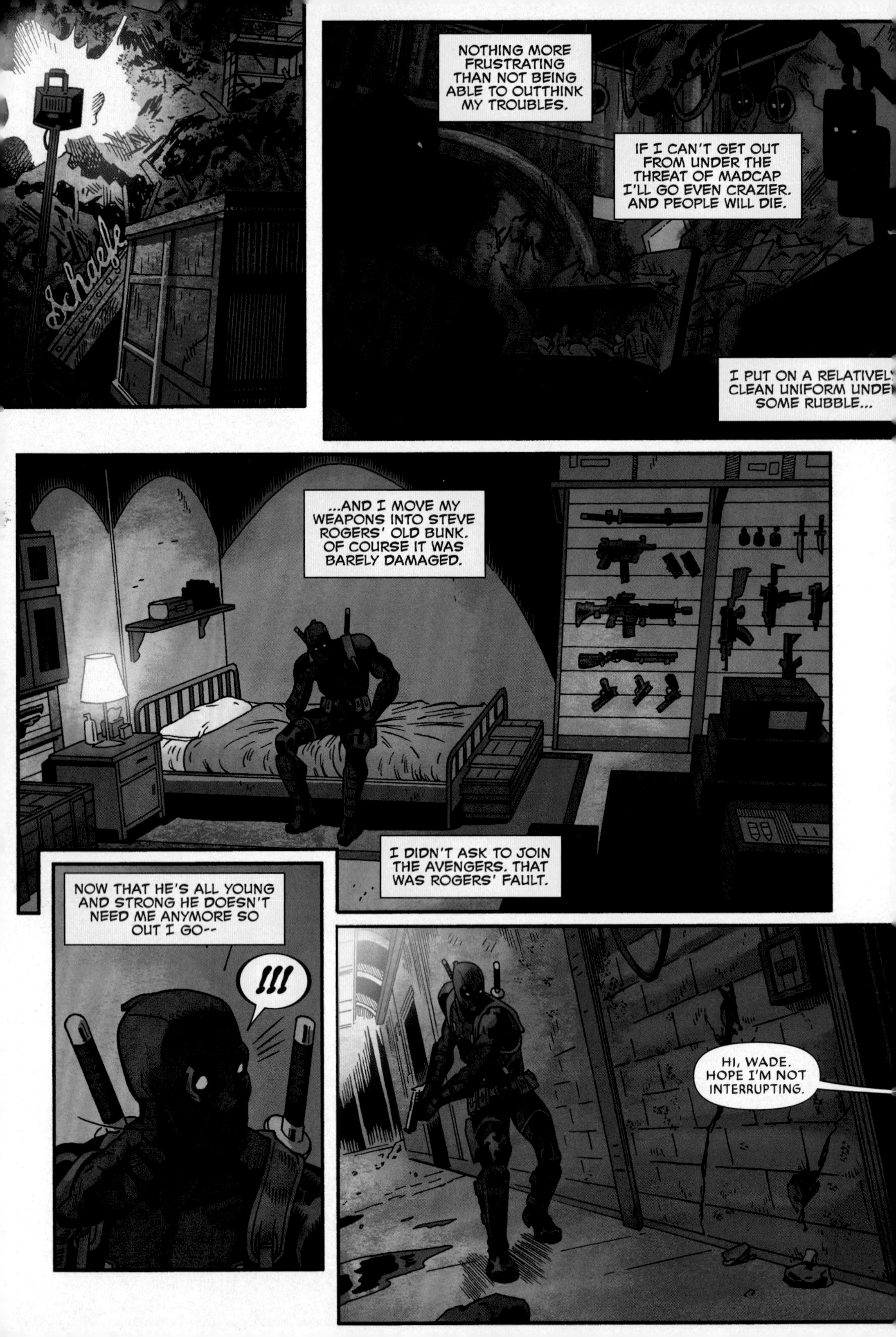
NOTHING MORE FRUSTRATING THAN NOT BEING ABLE TO OUTTHINK MY TROUBLES.
IF I CAN'T GET OUT FROM UNDER THE THREAT OF MADCAP I'LL GO EVEN CRAZIER. AND PEOPLE WILL DIE.
I PUT ON A RELATIVELY CLEAN UNIFORM UNDER SOME RUBBLE...
...AND I MOVE MY WEAPONS INTO STEVE ROGERS' OLD BUNK. OF COURSE IT WAS BARELY DAMAGED.
I DIDN'T ASK TO JOIN THE AVENGERS. THAT WAS ROGERS' FAULT.
NOW THAT HE'S ALL YOUNG AND STRONG HE DOESN'T NEED ME ANYMORE SO OUT I GO--
!!!
HI, WADE. HOPE I'M NOT INTERRUPTING.

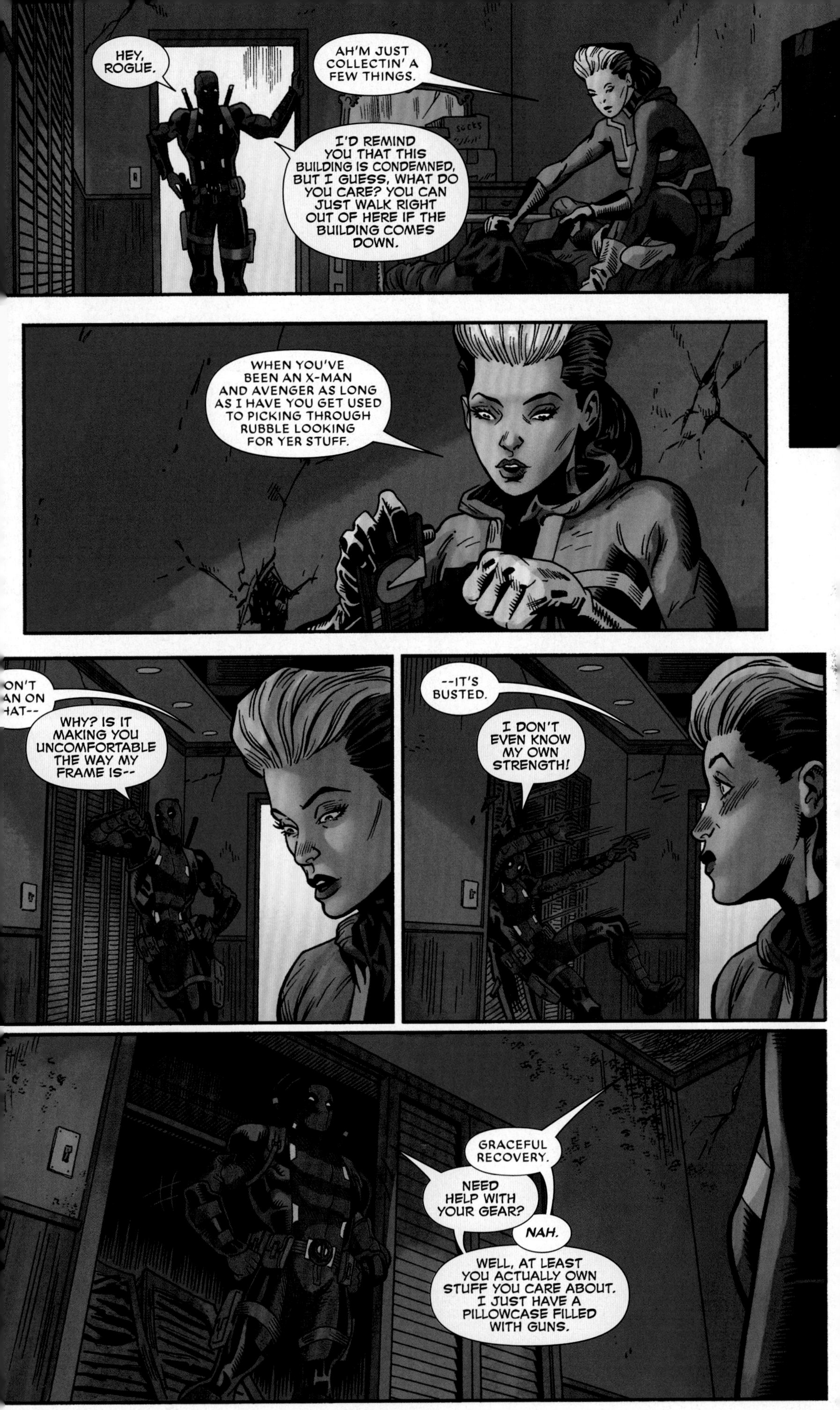

HEY, ROGUE.
AH'M JUST COLLECTIN' A FEW THINGS.
I'D REMIND YOU THAT THIS BUILDING IS CONDEMNED, BUT I GUESS, WHAT DO YOU CARE? YOU CAN JUST WALK RIGHT OUT OF HERE IF THE BUILDING COMES DOWN.
WHEN YOU'VE BEEN AN X-MAN AND AVENGER AS LONG AS I HAVE YOU GET USED TO PICKING THROUGH RUBBLE LOOKING FOR YER STUFF.
ON'T AN ON HAT--
WHY? IS IT MAKING YOU UNCOMFORTABLE THE WAY MY FRAME IS--
--IT'S BUSTED.
I DON'T EVEN KNOW MY OWN STRENGTH!
GRACEFUL RECOVERY.
NEED HELP WITH YOUR GEAR?
NAH.
WELL, AT LEAST YOU ACTUALLY OWN STUFF YOU CARE ABOUT. I JUST HAVE A PILLOWCASE FILLED WITH GUNS.

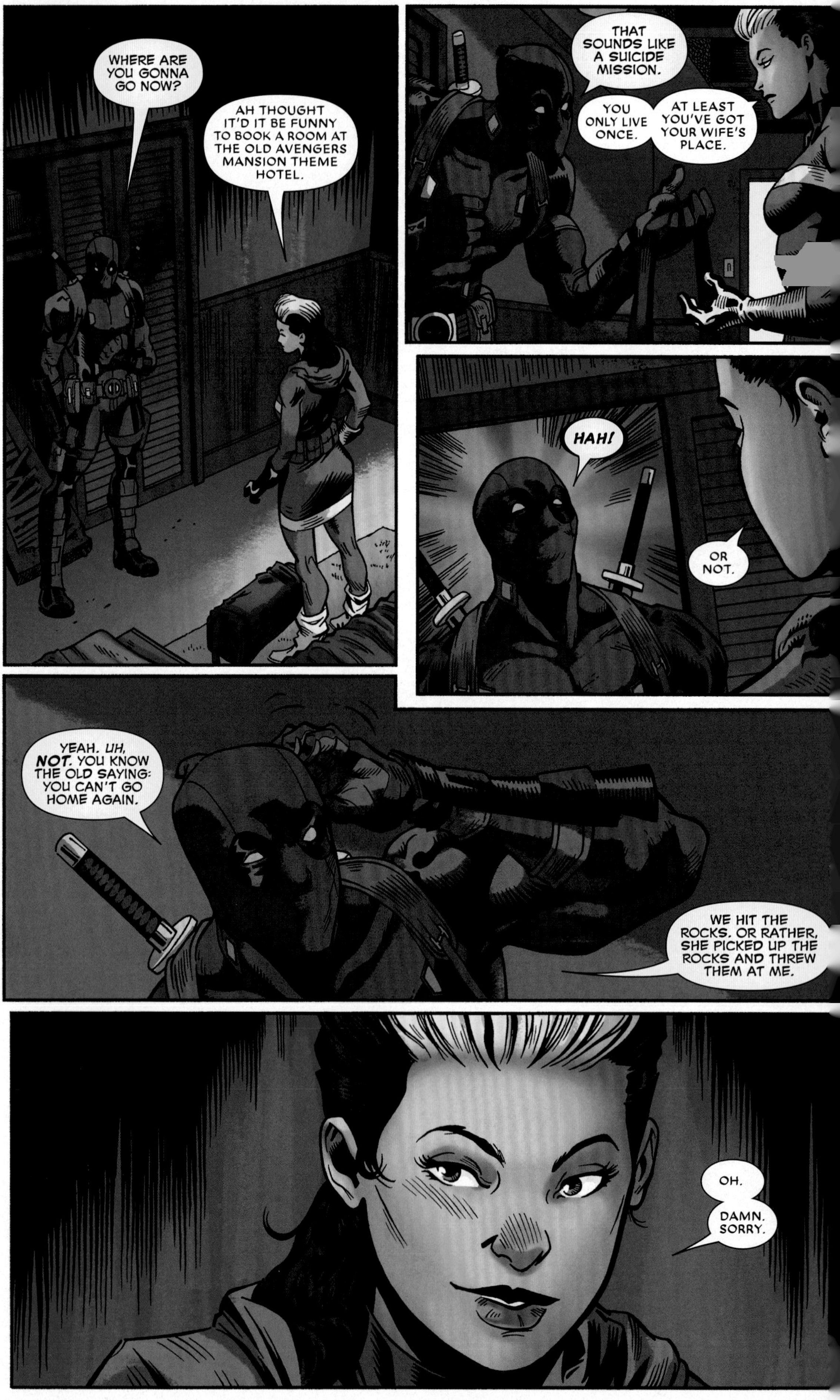
WHERE ARE YOU GONNA GO NOW?
AH THOUGHT IT'D IT BE FUNNY TO BOOK A ROOM AT THE OLD AVENGERS MANSION THEME HOTEL.
THAT SOUNDS LIKE A SUICIDE MISSION.
YOU ONLY LIVE ONCE.
AT LEAST YOU'VE GOT YOUR WIFE'S PLACE.
HAH!
OR NOT.
YEAH. *UH,* ***NOT.*** YOU KNOW THE OLD SAYING: YOU CAN'T GO HOME AGAIN.
WE HIT THE ROCKS. OR RATHER, SHE PICKED UP THE ROCKS AND THREW THEM AT ME.
OH.
DAMN. SORRY.

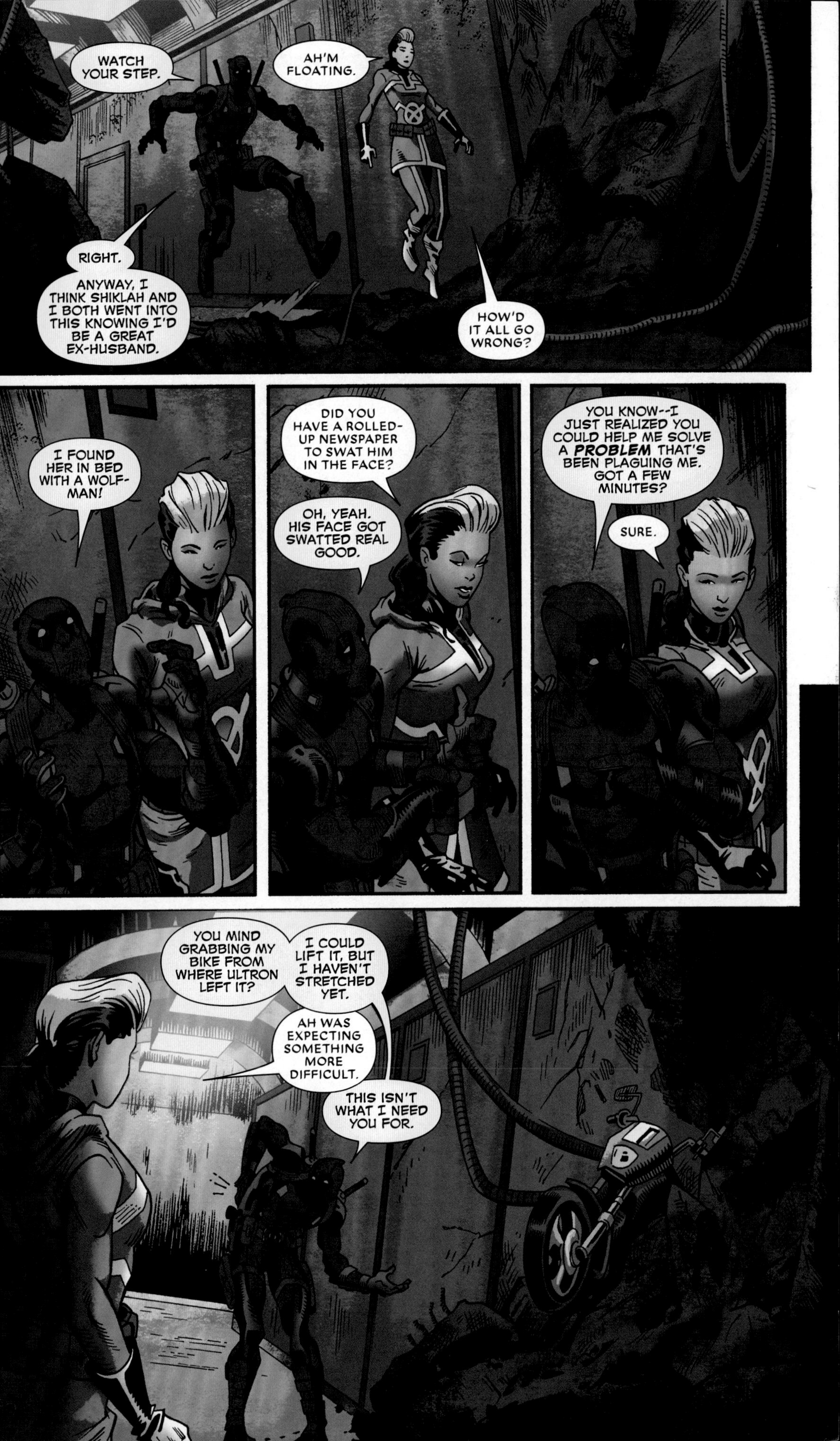
WATCH YOUR STEP.
AH'M FLOATING.
RIGHT.
ANYWAY, I THINK SHIKLAH AND I BOTH WENT INTO THIS KNOWING I'D BE A GREAT EX-HUSBAND.
HOW'D IT ALL GO WRONG?
I FOUND HER IN BED WITH A WOLF-MAN!
DID YOU HAVE A ROLLED-UP NEWSPAPER TO SWAT HIM IN THE FACE?
OH, YEAH. HIS FACE GOT SWATTED REAL GOOD.
YOU KNOW--I JUST REALIZED YOU COULD HELP ME SOLVE A PROBLEM THAT'S BEEN PLAGUING ME. GOT A FEW MINUTES?
SURE.
YOU MIND GRABBING MY BIKE FROM WHERE ULTRON LEFT IT?
I COULD LIFT IT, BUT I HAVEN'T STRETCHED YET.
AH WAS EXPECTING SOMETHING MORE DIFFICULT.
THIS ISN'T WHAT I NEED YOU FOR.

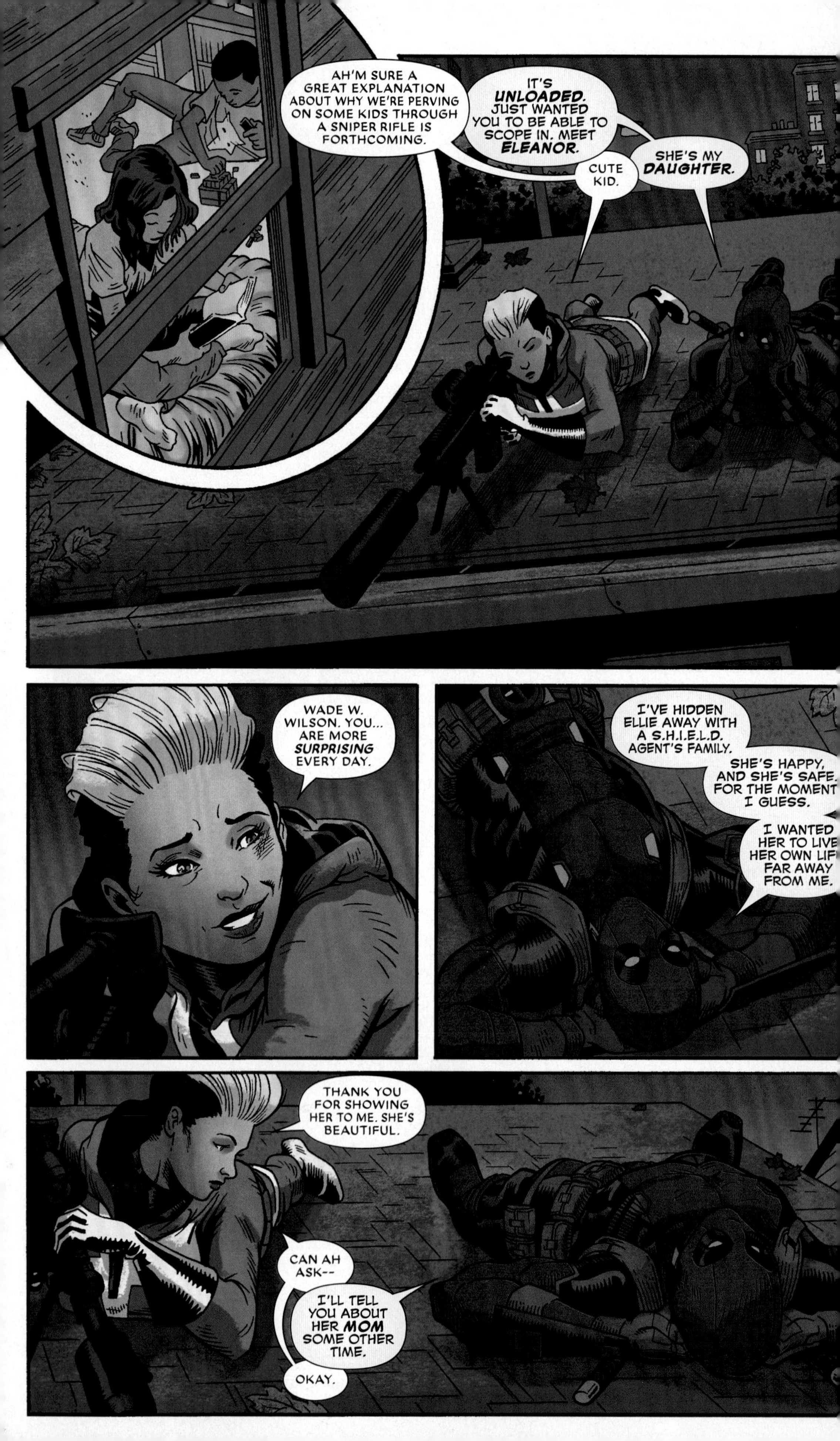
AH'M SURE A GREAT EXPLANATION ABOUT WHY WE'RE PERVING ON SOME KIDS THROUGH A SNIPER RIFLE IS FORTHCOMING.
IT'S UNLOADED. JUST WANTED YOU TO BE ABLE TO SCOPE IN. MEET ELEANOR.
CUTE KID.
SHE'S MY DAUGHTER.
WADE W. WILSON. YOU... ARE MORE SURPRISING EVERY DAY.
I'VE HIDDEN ELLIE AWAY WITH A S.H.I.E.L.D. AGENT'S FAMILY.
SHE'S HAPPY, AND SHE'S SAFE. FOR THE MOMENT I GUESS.
I WANTED HER TO LIVE HER OWN LIF FAR AWAY FROM ME.
THANK YOU FOR SHOWING HER TO ME. SHE'S BEAUTIFUL.
CAN AH ASK--
I'LL TELL YOU ABOUT HER MOM SOME OTHER TIME.
OKAY.

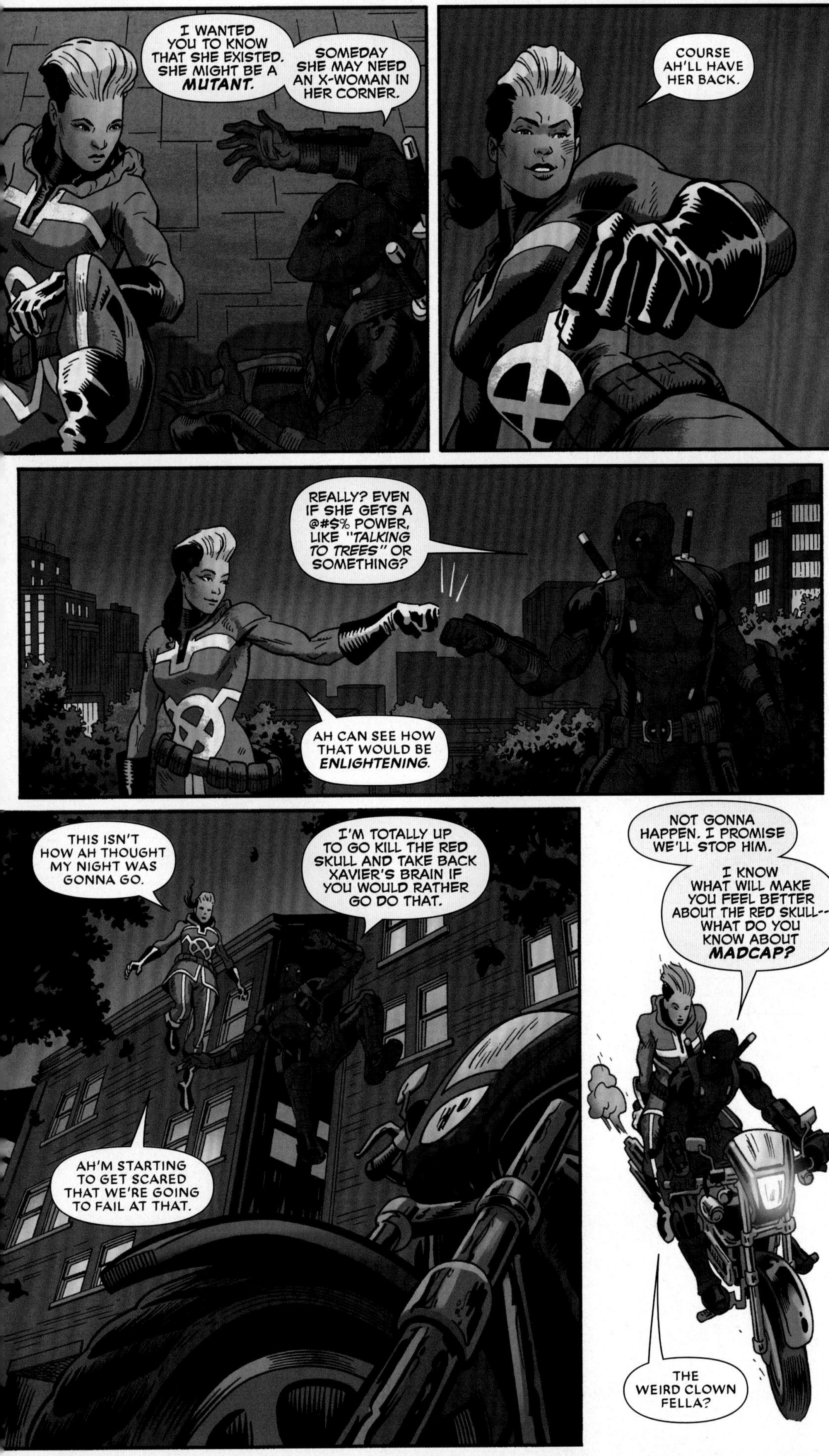
I WANTED YOU TO KNOW THAT SHE EXISTED. SHE MIGHT BE A *MUTANT*.
SOMEDAY SHE MAY NEED AN X-WOMAN IN HER CORNER.
COURSE AH'LL HAVE HER BACK.
REALLY? EVEN IF SHE GETS A @#$% POWER, LIKE *"TALKING TO TREES"* OR SOMETHING?
AH CAN SEE HOW THAT WOULD BE *ENLIGHTENING*.
THIS ISN'T HOW AH THOUGHT MY NIGHT WAS GONNA GO.
I'M TOTALLY UP TO GO KILL THE RED SKULL AND TAKE BACK XAVIER'S BRAIN IF YOU WOULD RATHER GO DO THAT.
AH'M STARTING TO GET SCARED THAT WE'RE GOING TO FAIL AT THAT.
NOT GONNA HAPPEN. I PROMISE WE'LL STOP HIM.
I KNOW WHAT WILL MAKE YOU FEEL BETTER ABOUT THE RED SKULL-- WHAT DO YOU KNOW ABOUT ***MADCAP?***
THE WEIRD CLOWN FELLA?

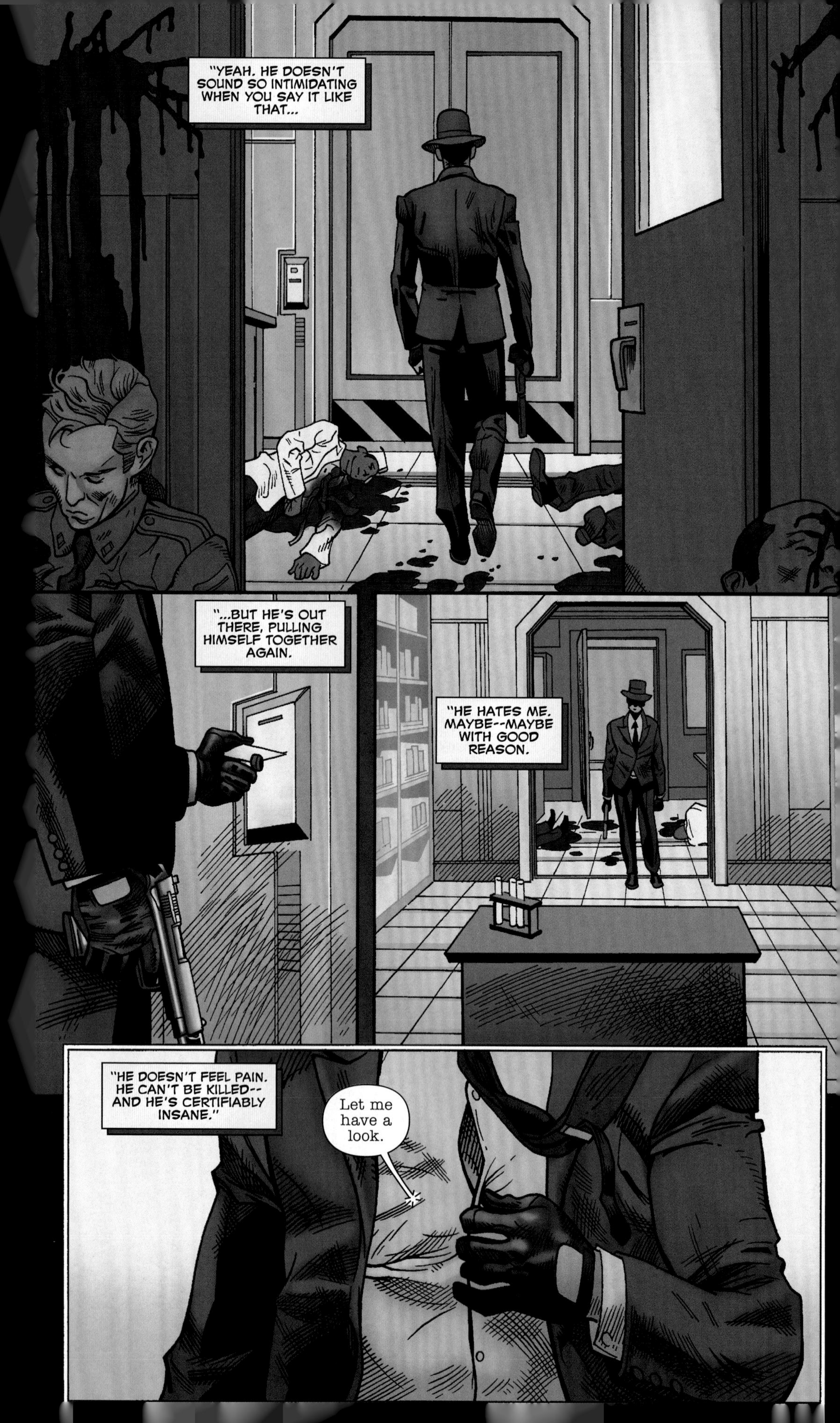
"YEAH. HE DOESN'T SOUND SO INTIMIDATING WHEN YOU SAY IT LIKE THAT...
"...BUT HE'S OUT THERE, PULLING HIMSELF TOGETHER AGAIN.
"HE HATES ME. MAYBE--MAYBE WITH GOOD REASON.
"HE DOESN'T FEEL PAIN. HE CAN'T BE KILLED-- AND HE'S CERTIFIABLY INSANE."
Let me have a look.

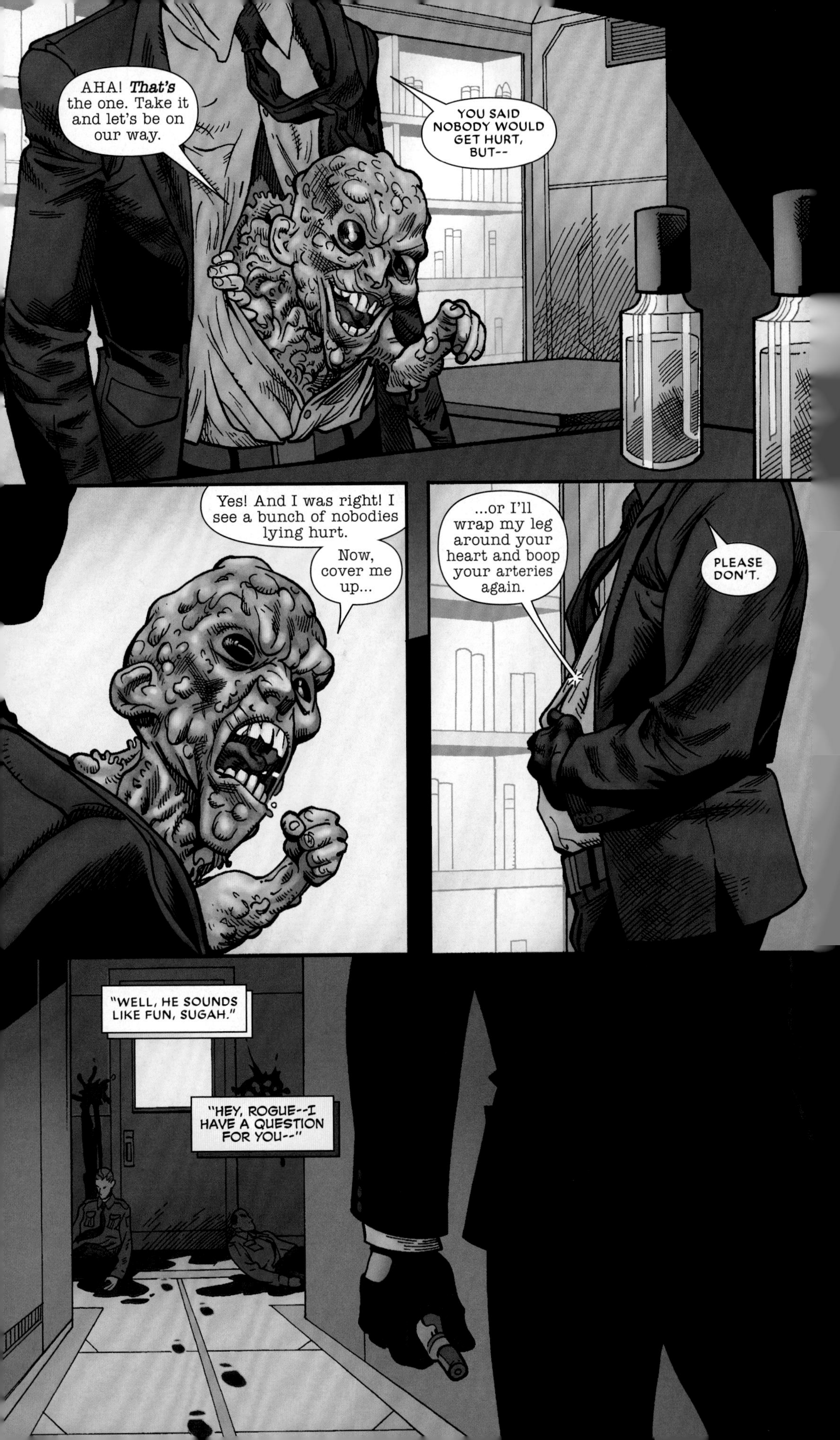
AHA! *That's* the one. Take it and let's be on our way.
YOU SAID NOBODY WOULD GET HURT, BUT--
Yes! And I was right! I see a bunch of nobodies lying hurt.
Now, cover me up...
...or I'll wrap my leg around your heart and boop your arteries again.
PLEASE DON'T.
"WELL, HE SOUNDS LIKE FUN, SUGAH."
"HEY, ROGUE--I HAVE A QUESTION FOR YOU--"

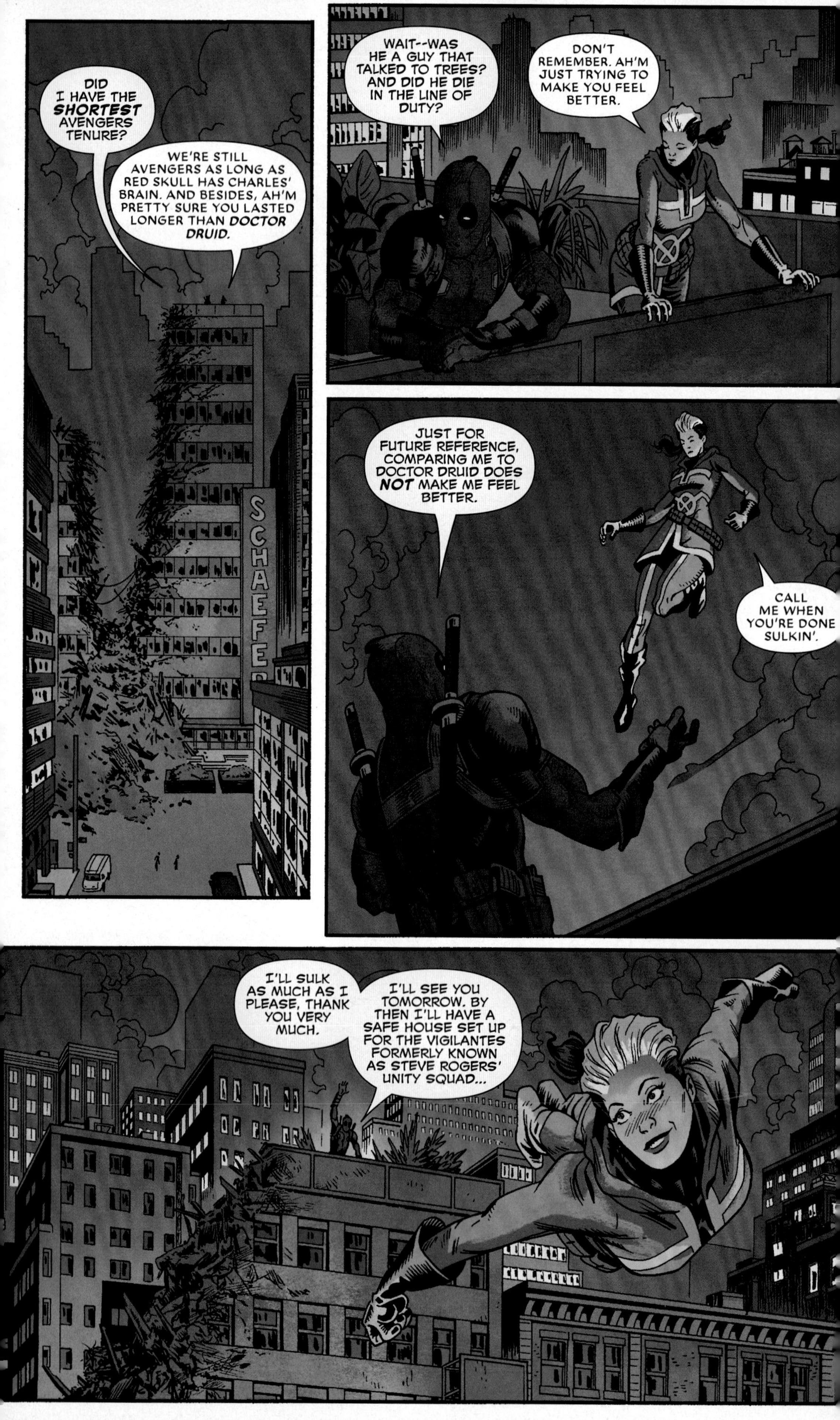
DID I HAVE THE SHORTEST AVENGERS TENURE?
WE'RE STILL AVENGERS AS LONG AS RED SKULL HAS CHARLES' BRAIN. AND BESIDES, AH'M PRETTY SURE YOU LASTED LONGER THAN DOCTOR DRUID.
SCHAEFE
WAIT--WAS HE A GUY THAT TALKED TO TREES? AND DID HE DIE IN THE LINE OF DUTY?
DON'T REMEMBER. AH'M JUST TRYING TO MAKE YOU FEEL BETTER.
JUST FOR FUTURE REFERENCE, COMPARING ME TO DOCTOR DRUID DOES NOT MAKE ME FEEL BETTER.
CALL ME WHEN YOU'RE DONE SULKIN'.
I'LL SULK AS MUCH AS I PLEASE, THANK YOU VERY MUCH.
I'LL SEE YOU TOMORROW. BY THEN I'LL HAVE A SAFE HOUSE SET UP FOR THE VIGILANTES FORMERLY KNOWN AS STEVE ROGERS' UNITY SQUAD...

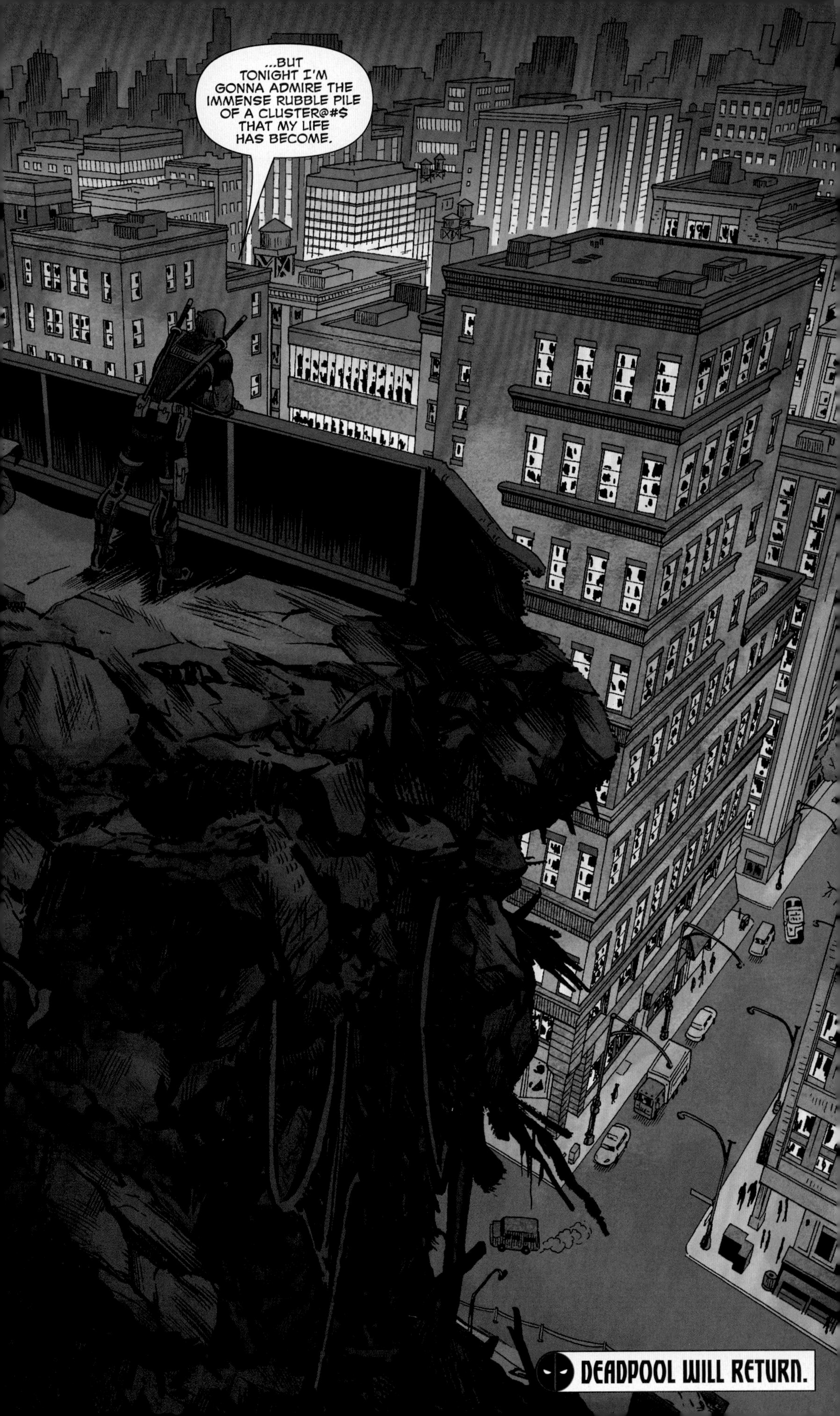
...BUT TONIGHT I'M GONNA ADMIRE THE IMMENSE RUBBLE PILE OF A CLUSTER@#$ THAT MY LIFE HAS BECOME.
DEADPOOL WILL RETURN.

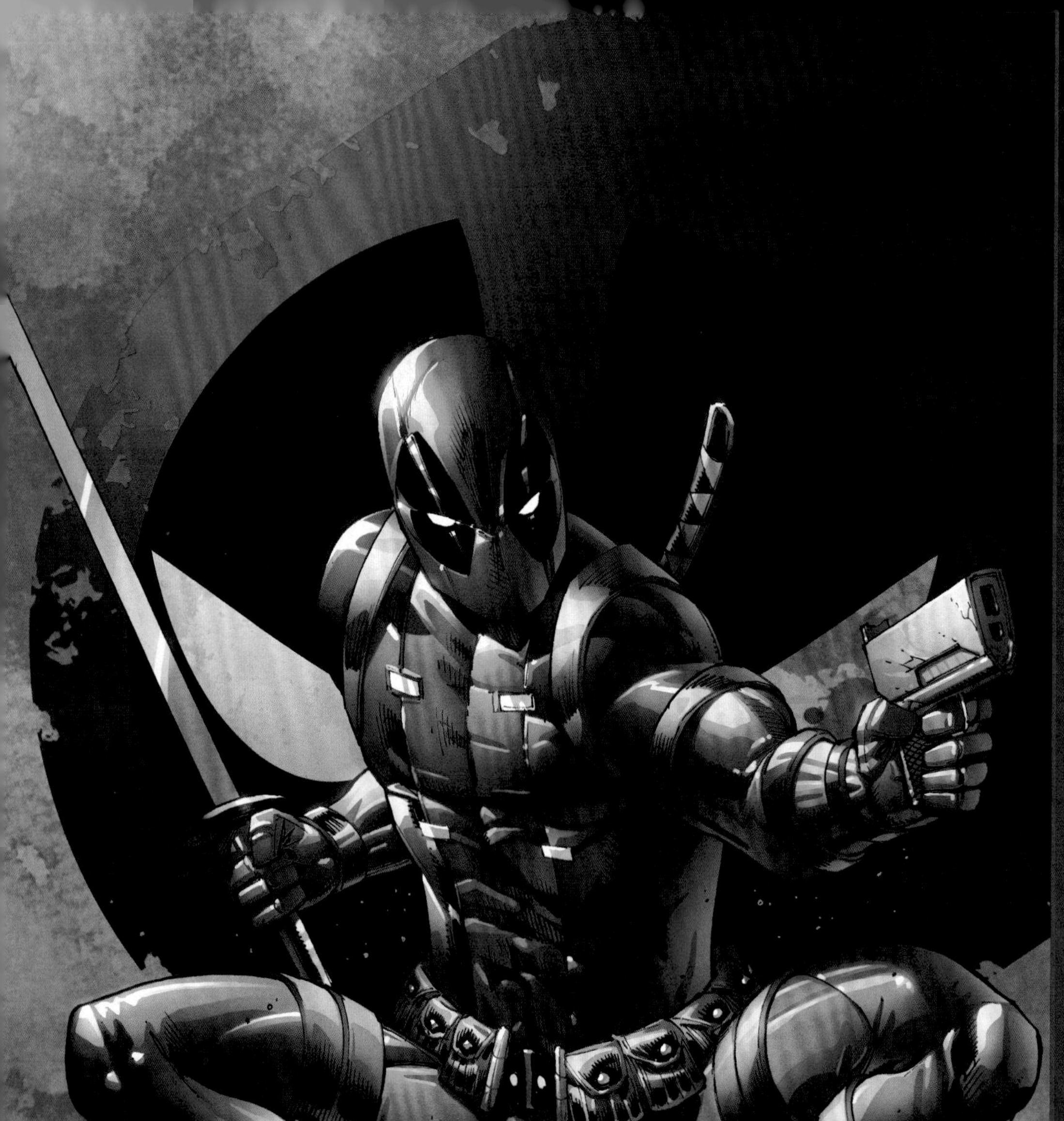
LIEFELD
ABURTOV

#18 variant by ROB LIEFELD & JESUS ABURTOV

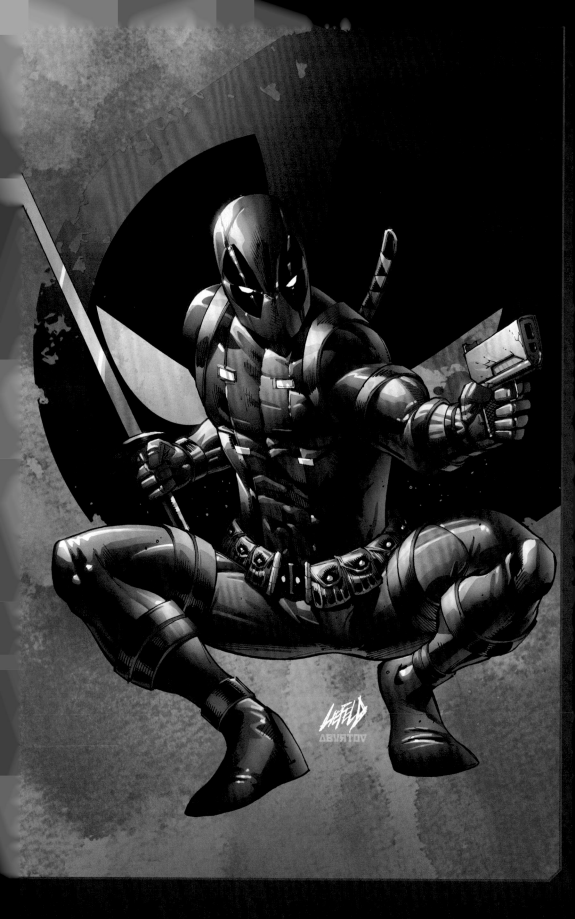

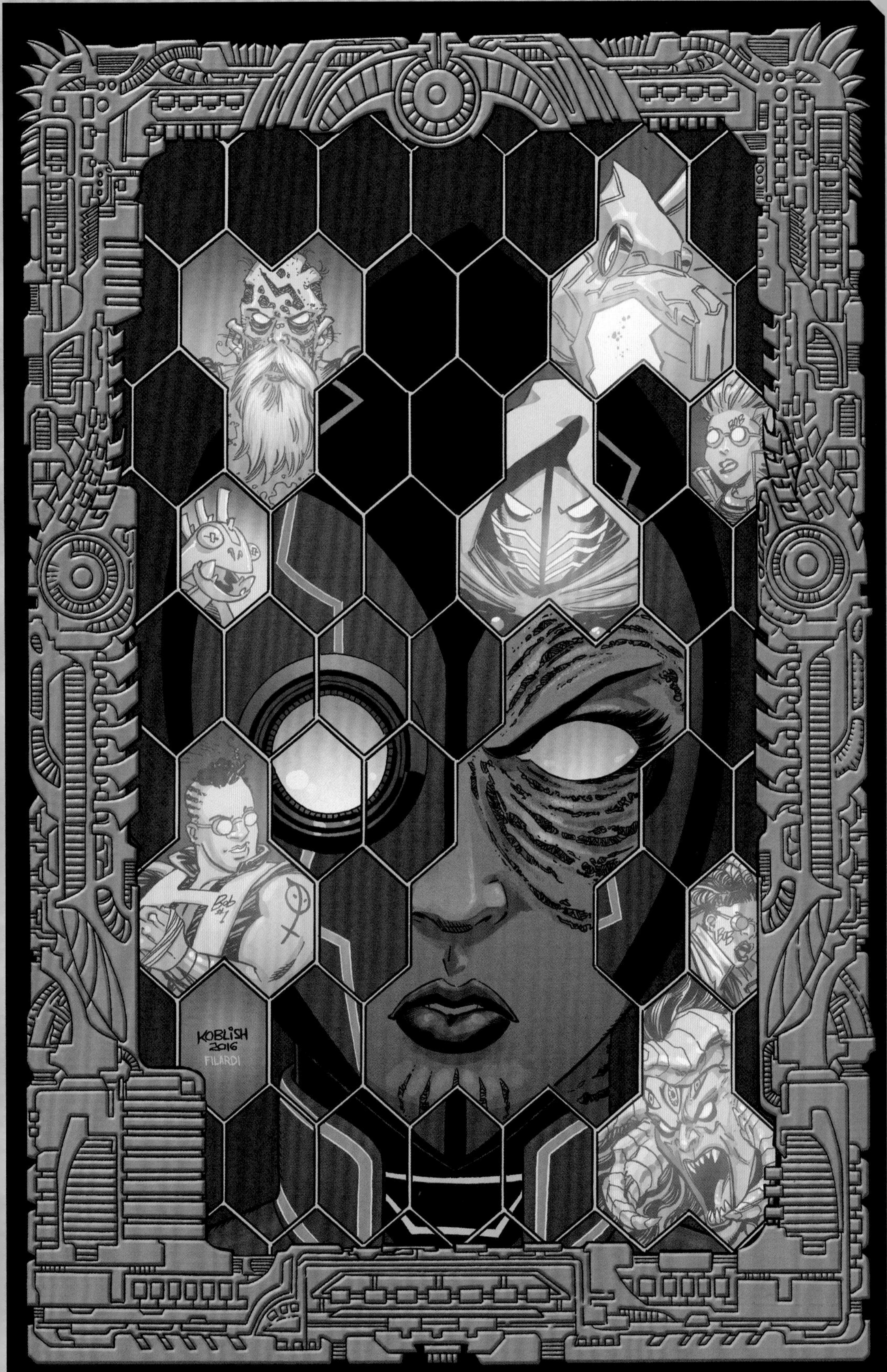
KOBLISH
2016
FILARDI

POSSIBLY THE MOST SKILLED MERCENARY OF THE CENTURY, AND DEFINITELY T
MOST DANGEROUS, WARDA WILSON WREAKS HAVOK ACROSS THE WORLD OF 20
REBELLING AGAINST SOCIETY AND DOING THINGS HER OWN WAY. DAUGHTER OF
FAST-TALKING MERCENARY WITH A HEALING FACTOR AND A DEMONIC SUCCUB
QUEEN, WARDA HAS NEVER FIT IN ANYWHERE...SO SHE MAKES HER HOME ON T
OUTSIDE, LIVING BY HER OWN RULES. CALL HER THE MERC WITH THE MOUTH...CA
HER THE REGENERATIN' DEGENERATE...CALL HER...

DEADPOOL

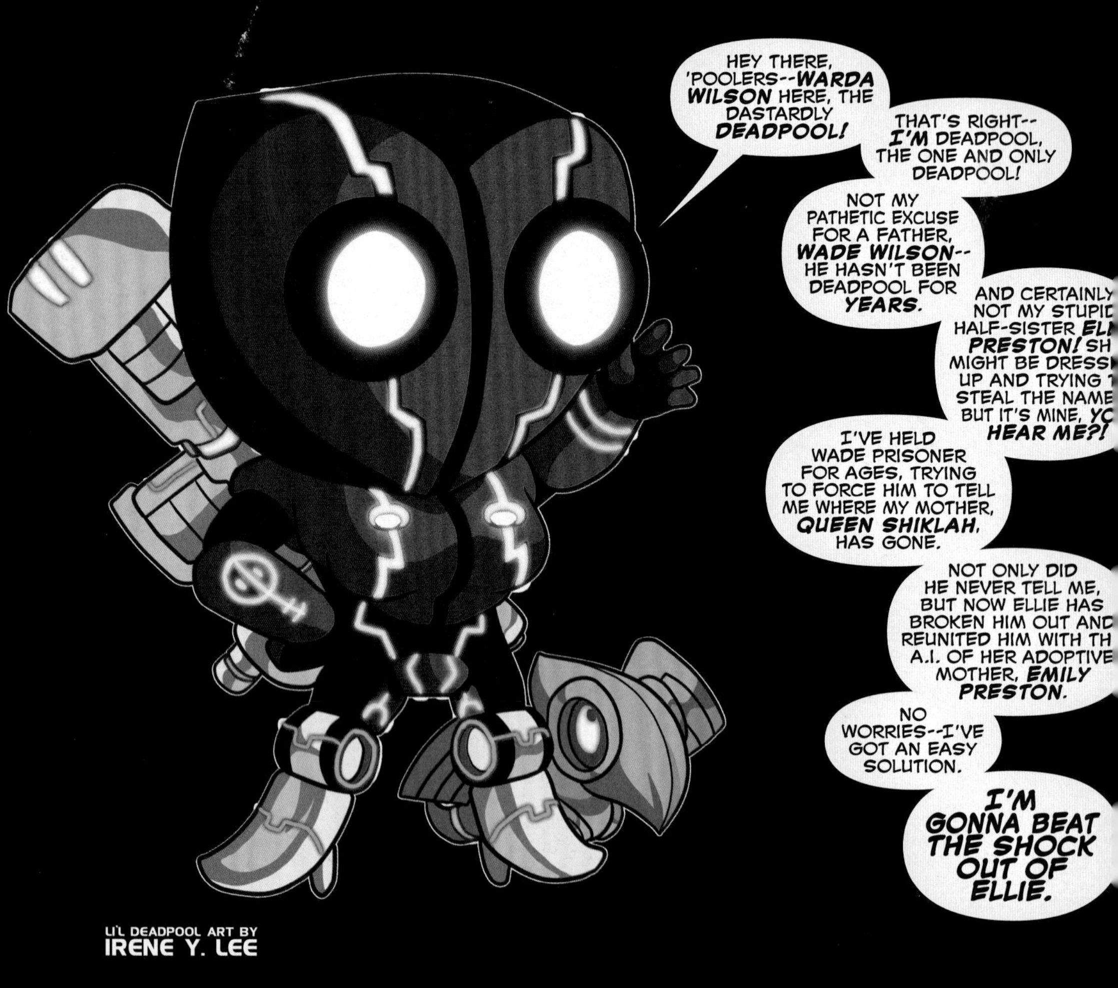
HEY THERE, 'POOLERS--**WARDA WILSON** HERE, THE DASTARDLY **DEADPOOL!**
THAT'S RIGHT-- ***I'M*** DEADPOOL, THE ONE AND ONLY DEADPOOL!
NOT MY PATHETIC EXCUSE FOR A FATHER, **WADE WILSON**-- HE HASN'T BEEN DEADPOOL FOR **YEARS**.
AND CERTAINLY NOT MY STUPID HALF-SISTER **EL PRESTON!** SH MIGHT BE DRESS UP AND TRYING STEAL THE NAME BUT IT'S MINE, Y **HEAR ME?!**
I'VE HELD WADE PRISONER FOR AGES, TRYING TO FORCE HIM TO TELL ME WHERE MY MOTHER, **QUEEN SHIKLAH**, HAS GONE.
NOT ONLY DID HE NEVER TELL ME, BUT NOW ELLIE HAS BROKEN HIM OUT AND REUNITED HIM WITH TH A.I. OF HER ADOPTIVE MOTHER, **EMILY PRESTON**.
NO WORRIES--I'VE GOT AN EASY SOLUTION.
I'M GONNA BEAT THE SHOCK OUT OF ELLIE.

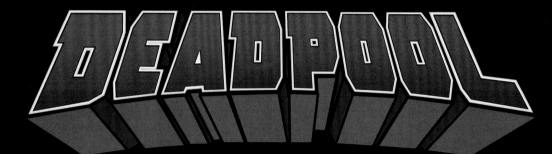

LI'L DEADPOOL ART BY
IRENE Y. LEE

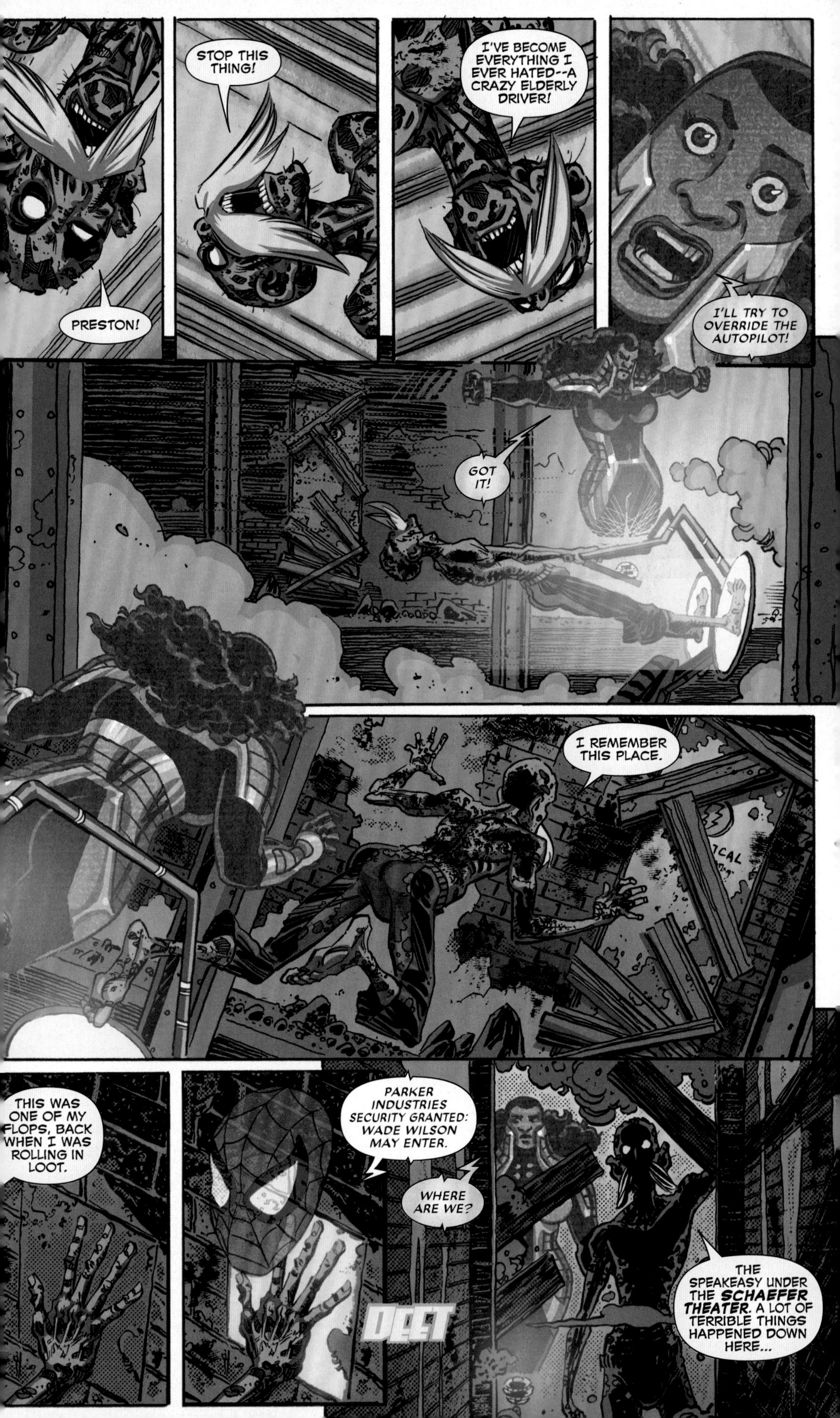
PRESTON!
STOP THIS THING!
I'VE BECOME EVERYTHING I EVER HATED--A CRAZY ELDERLY DRIVER!
I'LL TRY TO OVERRIDE THE AUTOPILOT!
GOT IT!
I REMEMBER THIS PLACE.
THIS WAS ONE OF MY FLOPS, BACK WHEN I WAS ROLLING IN LOOT.
PARKER INDUSTRIES SECURITY GRANTED: WADE WILSON MAY ENTER.
DEET
WHERE ARE WE?
THE SPEAKEASY UNDER THE SCHAEFER THEATER. A LOT OF TERRIBLE THINGS HAPPENED DOWN HERE...

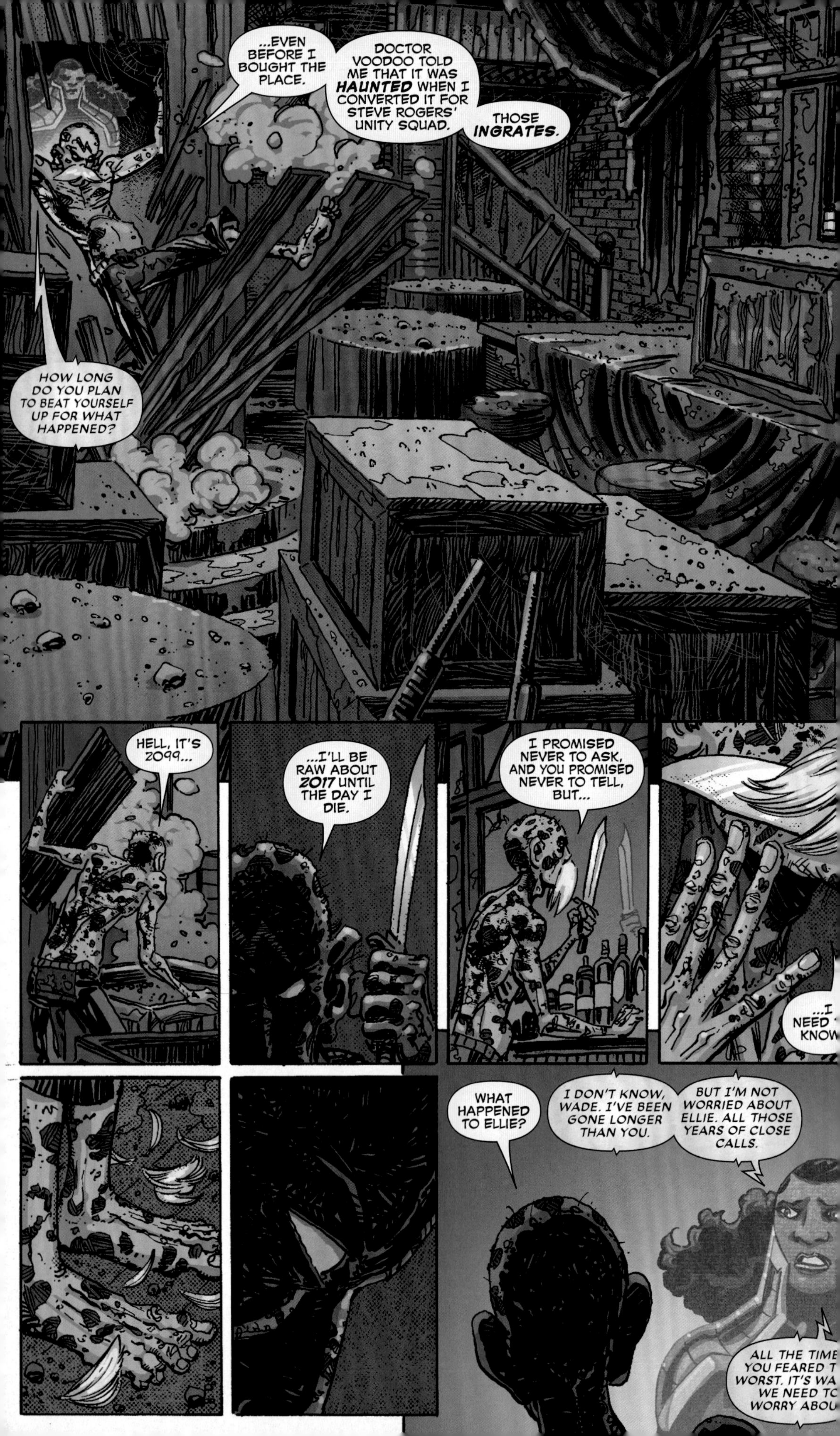

...EVEN BEFORE I BOUGHT THE PLACE.
DOCTOR VOODOO TOLD ME THAT IT WAS HAUNTED WHEN I CONVERTED IT FOR STEVE ROGERS' UNITY SQUAD.
THOSE INGRATES.
HOW LONG DO YOU PLAN TO BEAT YOURSELF UP FOR WHAT HAPPENED?
HELL, IT'S 2099...
...I'LL BE RAW ABOUT 2017 UNTIL THE DAY I DIE.
I PROMISED NEVER TO ASK, AND YOU PROMISED NEVER TO TELL, BUT...
...I NEED KNOW
WHAT HAPPENED TO ELLIE?
I DON'T KNOW, WADE. I'VE BEEN GONE LONGER THAN YOU.
BUT I'M NOT WORRIED ABOUT ELLIE. ALL THOSE YEARS OF CLOSE CALLS.
ALL THE TIME YOU FEARED T WORST. IT'S WA WE NEED TO WORRY ABOU

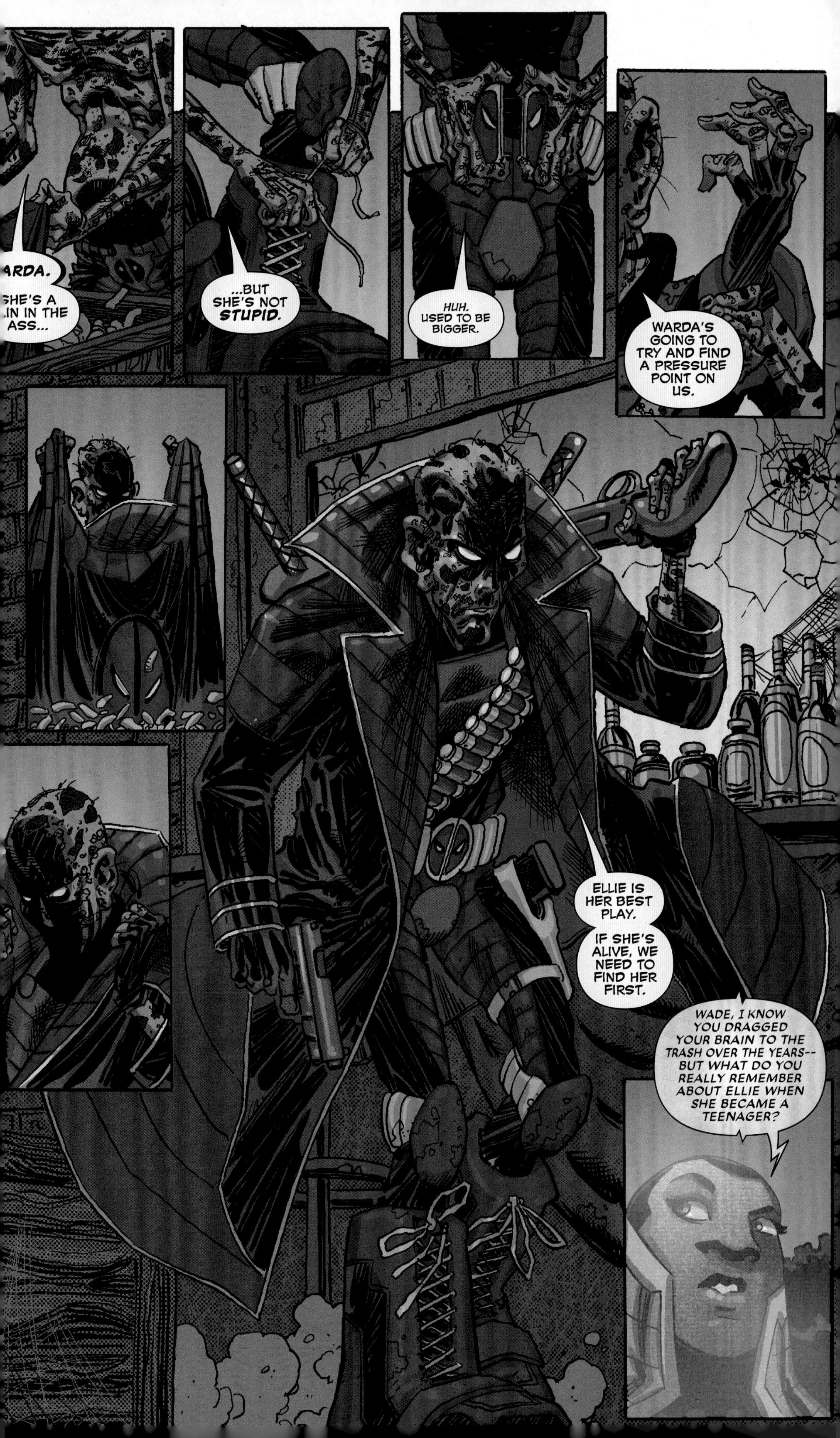
ARDA.
HE'S A
IN IN THE
ASS...
...BUT SHE'S NOT STUPID.
HUH. USED TO BE BIGGER.
WARDA'S GOING TO TRY AND FIND A PRESSURE POINT ON US.
ELLIE IS HER BEST PLAY.
IF SHE'S ALIVE, WE NEED TO FIND HER FIRST.
WADE, I KNOW YOU DRAGGED YOUR BRAIN TO THE TRASH OVER THE YEARS-- BUT WHAT DO YOU REALLY REMEMBER ABOUT ELLIE WHEN SHE BECAME A TEENAGER?

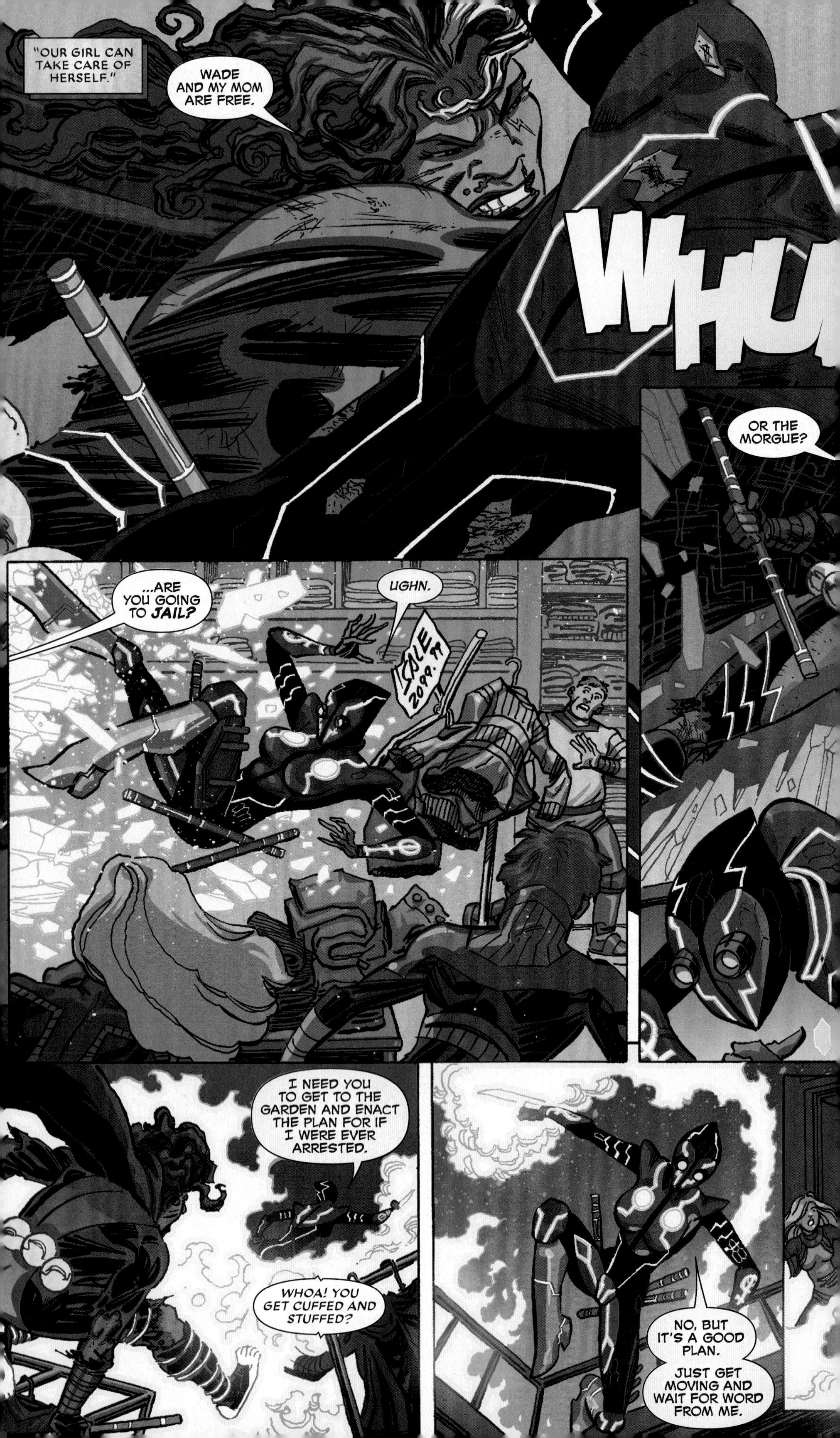
"OUR GIRL CAN TAKE CARE OF HERSELF."
WADE AND MY MOM ARE FREE.
WHU
OR THE MORGUE?
...ARE YOU GOING TO JAIL?
UGHN.
SALE 2099.99
I NEED YOU TO GET TO THE GARDEN AND ENACT THE PLAN FOR IF I WERE EVER ARRESTED.
WHOA! YOU GET CUFFED AND STUFFED?
NO, BUT IT'S A GOOD PLAN.
JUST GET MOVING AND WAIT FOR WORD FROM ME.

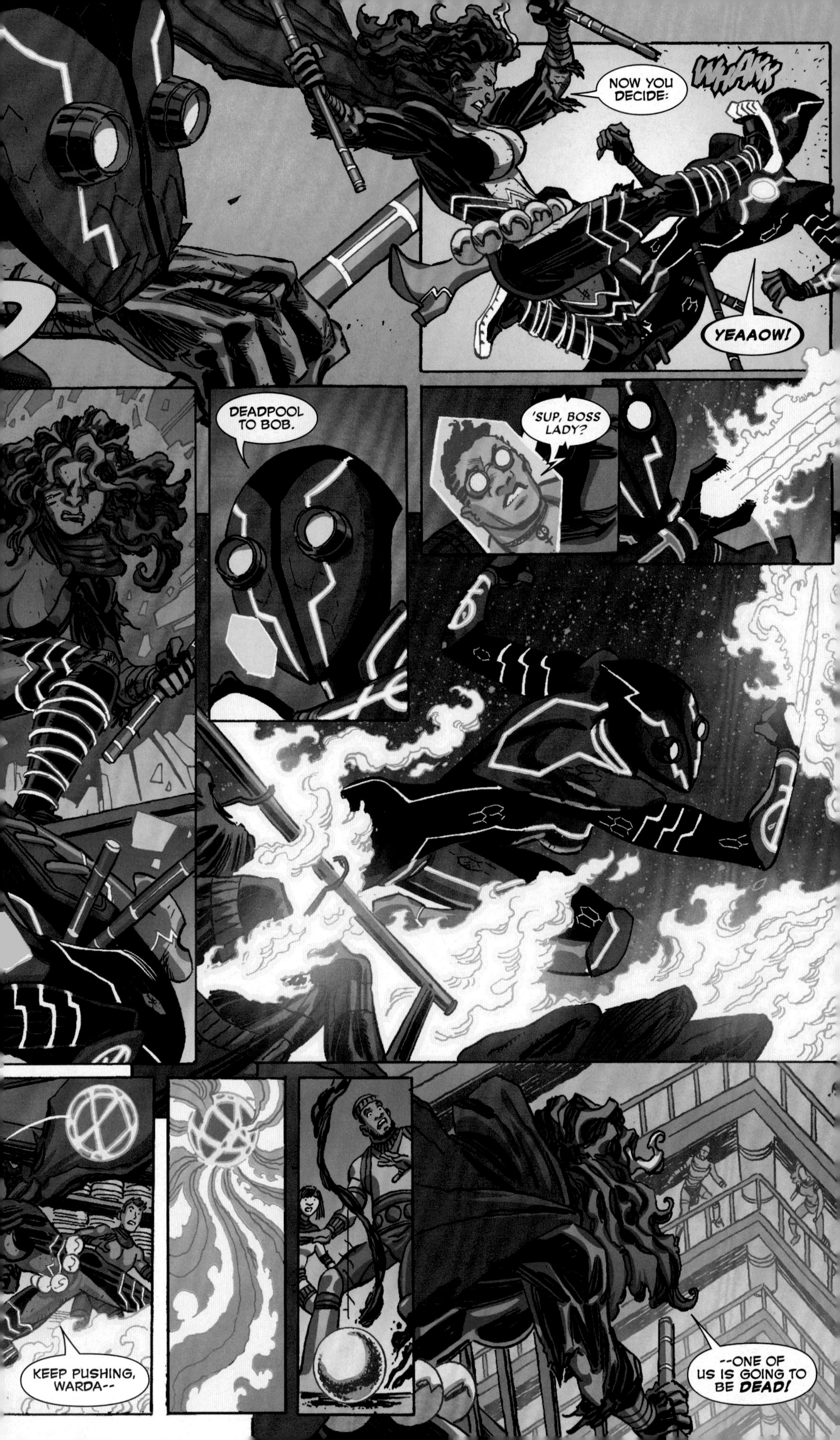
NOW YOU DECIDE:
WHAKK
YEAAOW!
DEADPOOL TO BOB.
'SUP, BOSS LADY?
KEEP PUSHING, WARDA--
--ONE OF US IS GOING TO BE DEAD!

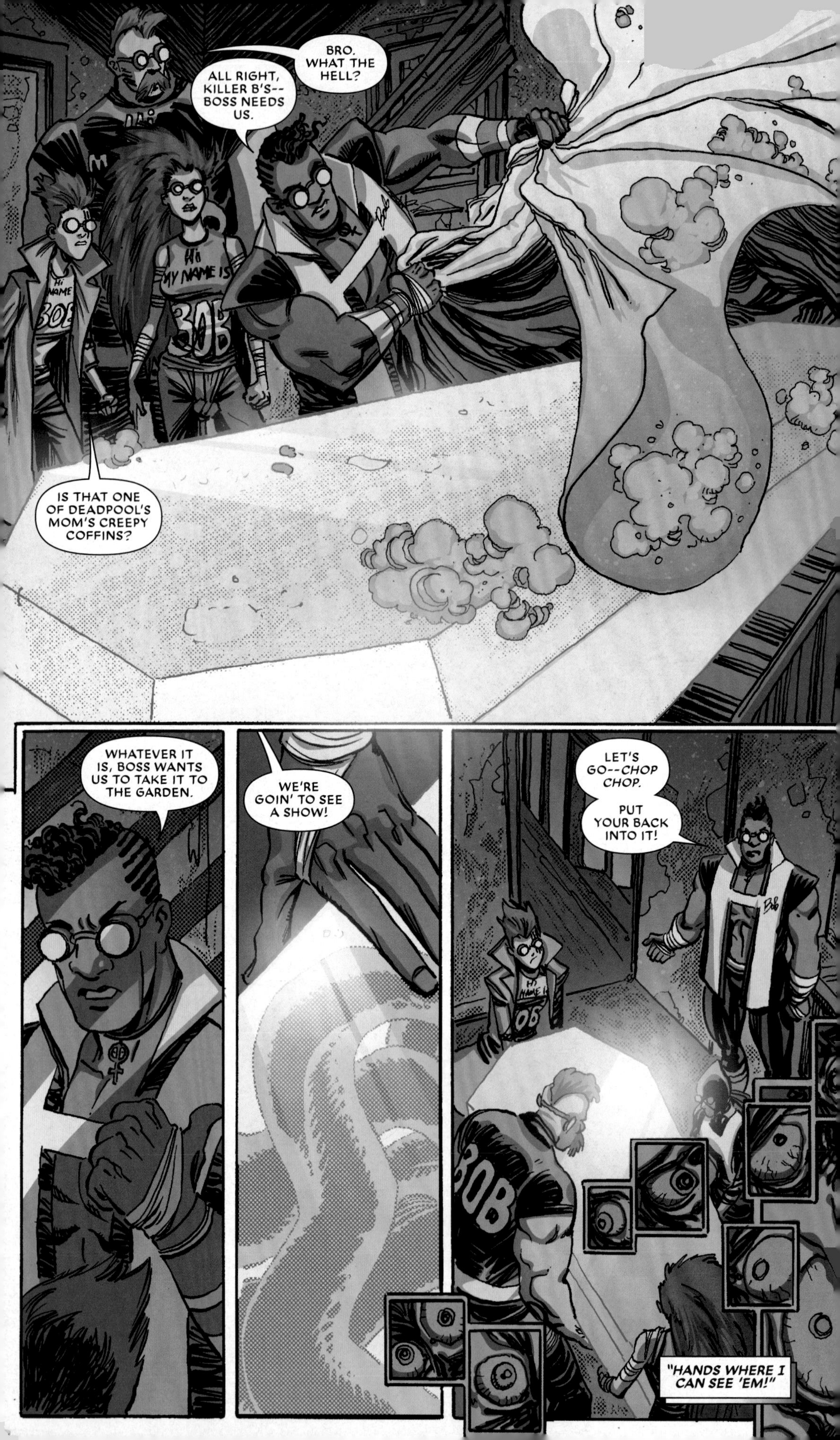
BRO. WHAT THE HELL?
ALL RIGHT, KILLER B'S-- BOSS NEEDS US.
IS THAT ONE OF DEADPOOL'S MOM'S CREEPY COFFINS?
WHATEVER IT IS, BOSS WANTS US TO TAKE IT TO THE GARDEN.
WE'RE GOIN' TO SEE A SHOW!
LET'S GO--CHOP CHOP.
PUT YOUR BACK INTO IT!
"HANDS WHERE I CAN SEE 'EM!"

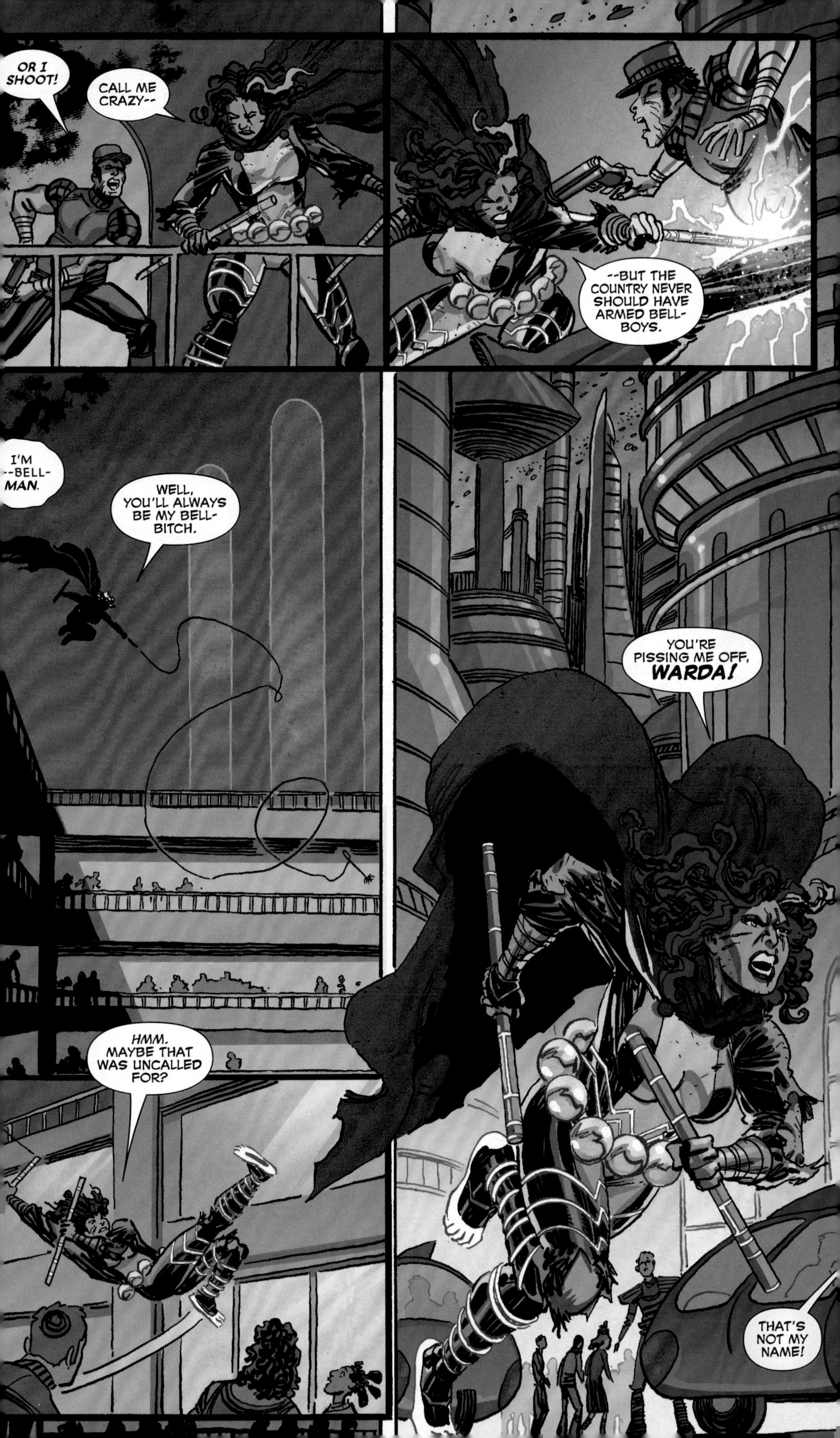
OR I SHOOT!
CALL ME CRAZY--
--BUT THE COUNTRY NEVER SHOULD HAVE ARMED BELL-BOYS.
I'M --BELL-MAN.
WELL, YOU'LL ALWAYS BE MY BELL-BITCH.
HMM. MAYBE THAT WAS UNCALLED FOR?
YOU'RE PISSING ME OFF, WARDA!
THAT'S NOT MY NAME!

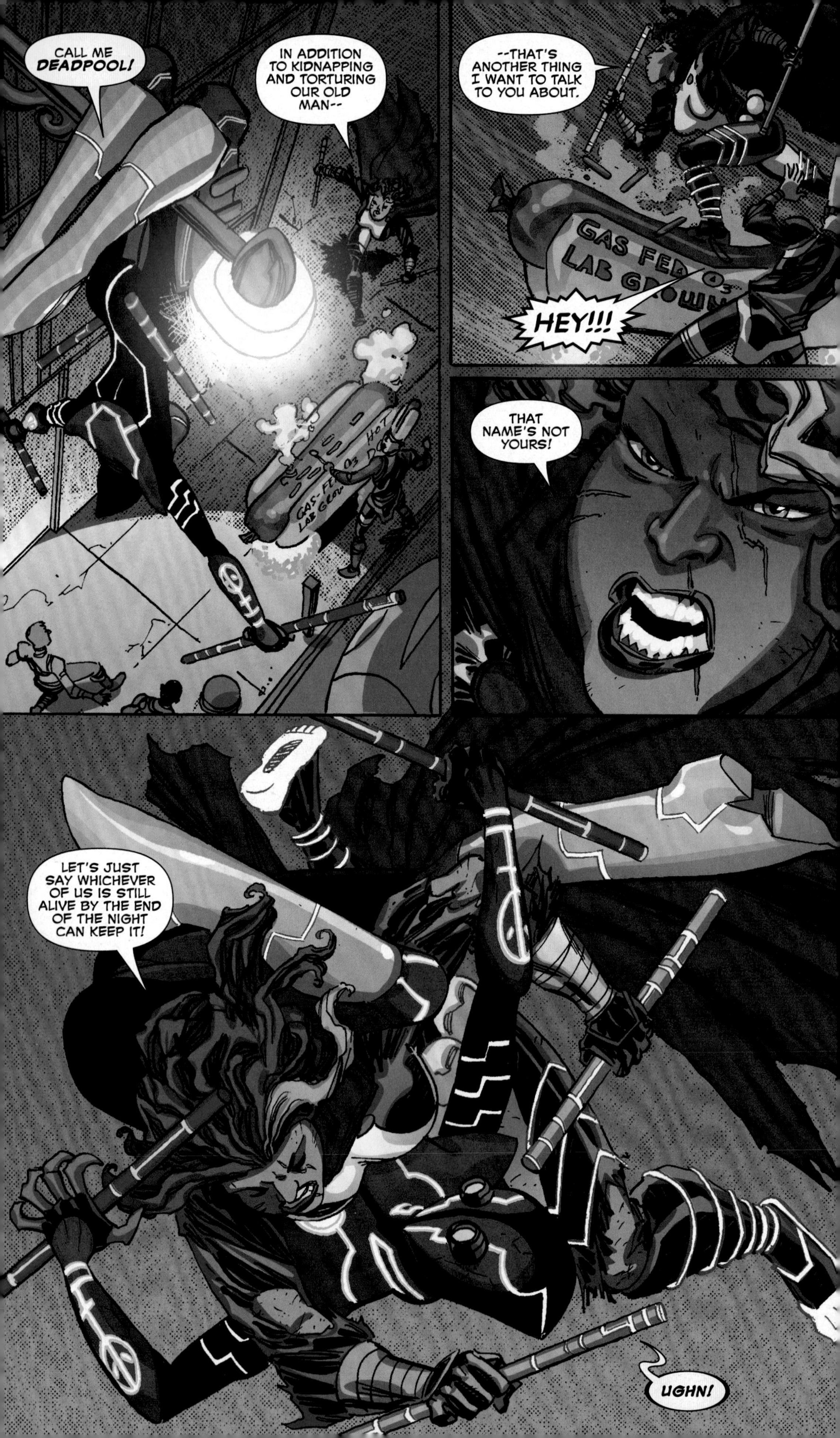
CALL ME DEADPOOL!
IN ADDITION TO KIDNAPPING AND TORTURING OUR OLD MAN--
--THAT'S ANOTHER THING I WANT TO TALK TO YOU ABOUT.
GAS FEB 03 LAB GROWN
HEY!!!
THAT NAME'S NOT YOURS!
LET'S JUST SAY WHICHEVER OF US IS STILL ALIVE BY THE END OF THE NIGHT CAN KEEP IT!
UGHN!

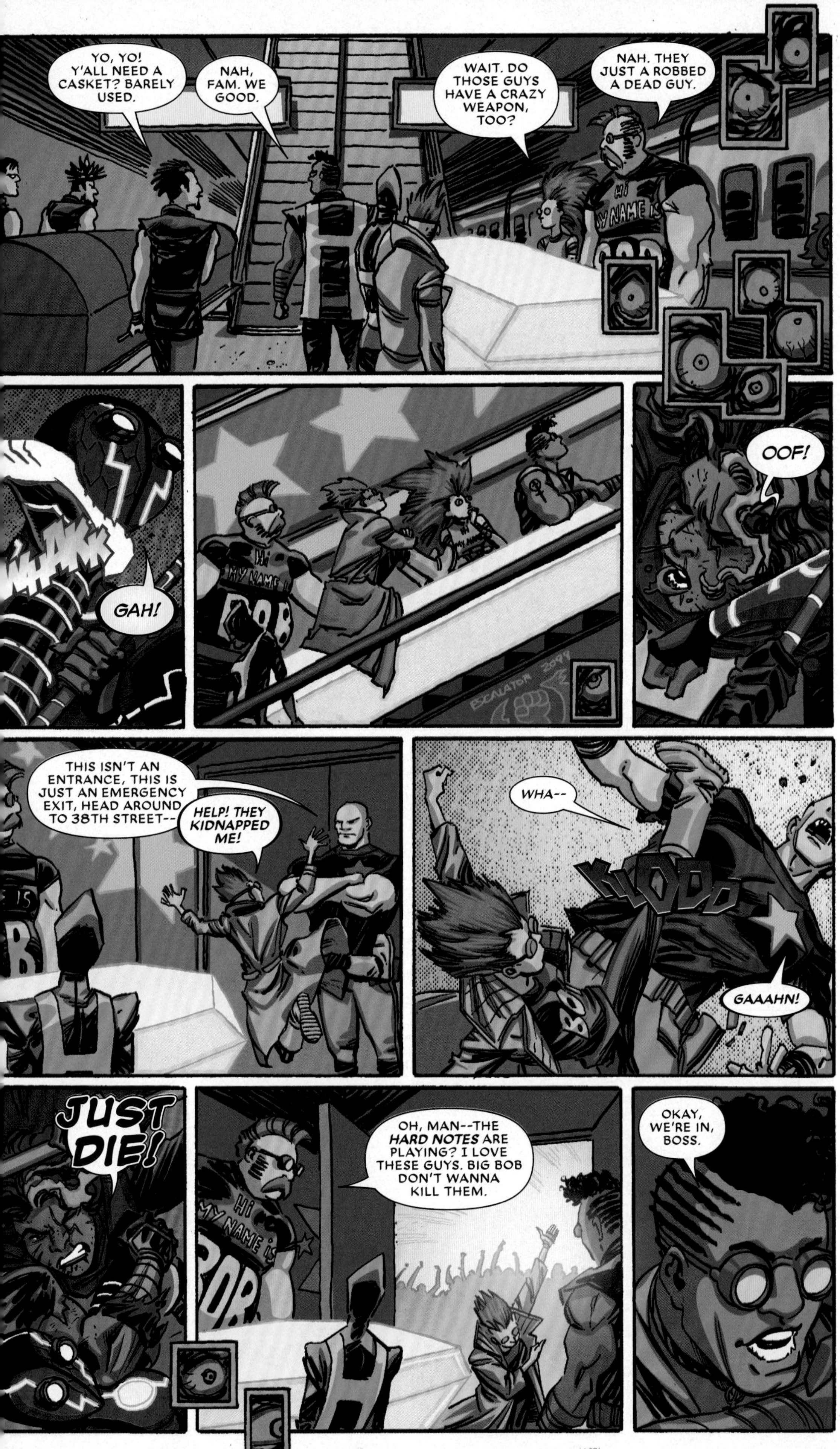
YO, YO! Y'ALL NEED A CASKET? BARELY USED.
NAH, FAM. WE GOOD.
WAIT. DO THOSE GUYS HAVE A CRAZY WEAPON, TOO?
NAH. THEY JUST A ROBBED A DEAD GUY.
HI MY NAME IS BOB
GAH!
ESCALATOR 2099
OOF!
THIS ISN'T AN ENTRANCE, THIS IS JUST AN EMERGENCY EXIT, HEAD AROUND TO 38TH STREET--
HELP! THEY KIDNAPPED ME!
WHA--
KLODD
GAAAHN!
JUST DIE!
OH, MAN--THE *HARD NOTES* ARE PLAYING? I LOVE THESE GUYS. BIG BOB DON'T WANNA KILL THEM.
OKAY, WE'RE IN, BOSS.

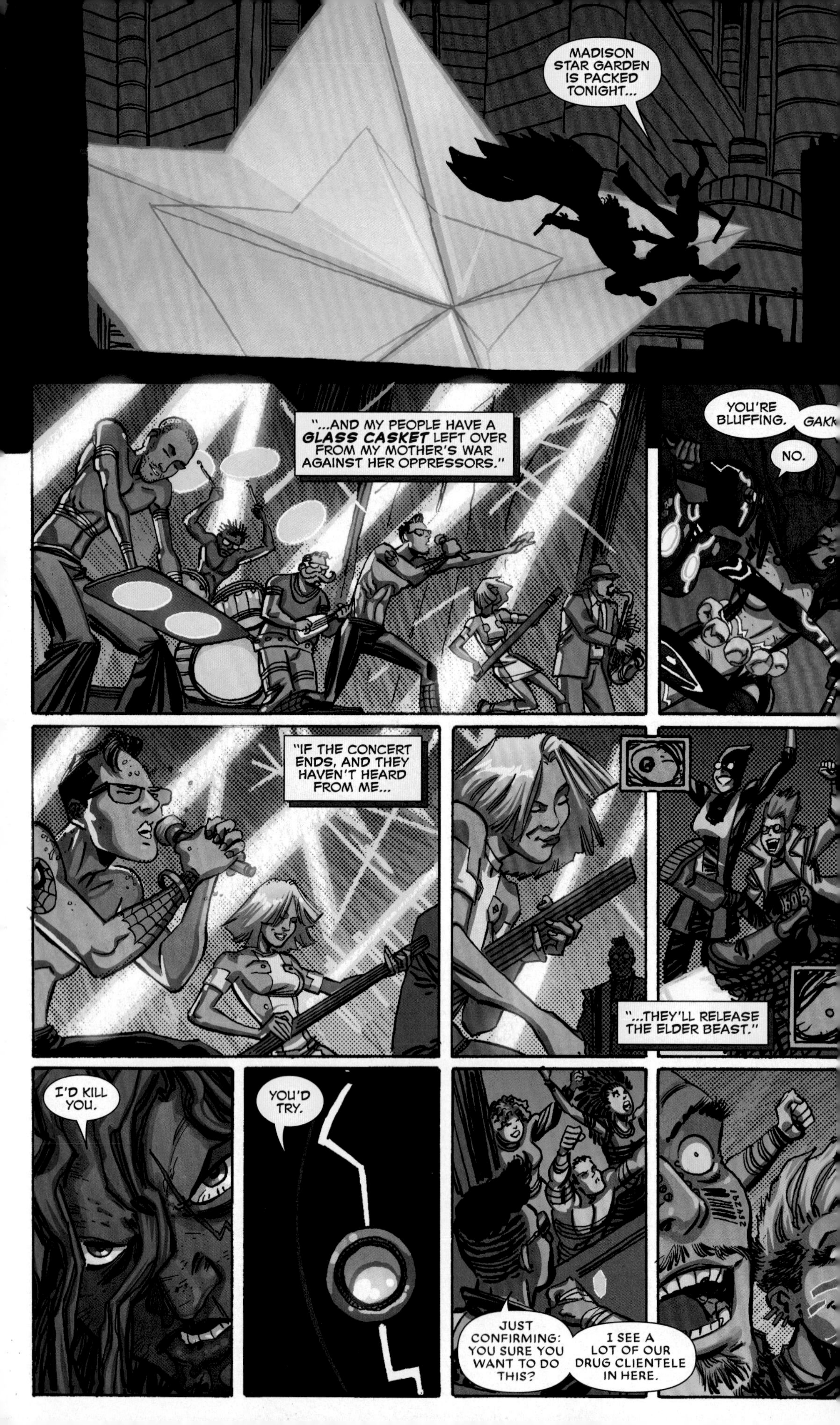
MADISON STAR GARDEN IS PACKED TONIGHT...
"...AND MY PEOPLE HAVE A GLASS CASKET LEFT OVER FROM MY MOTHER'S WAR AGAINST HER OPPRESSORS."
YOU'RE BLUFFING.
GAKK
NO.
"IF THE CONCERT ENDS, AND THEY HAVEN'T HEARD FROM ME...
"...THEY'LL RELEASE THE ELDER BEAST."
I'D KILL YOU.
YOU'D TRY.
JUST CONFIRMING: YOU SURE YOU WANT TO DO THIS?
I SEE A LOT OF OUR DRUG CLIENTELE IN HERE.

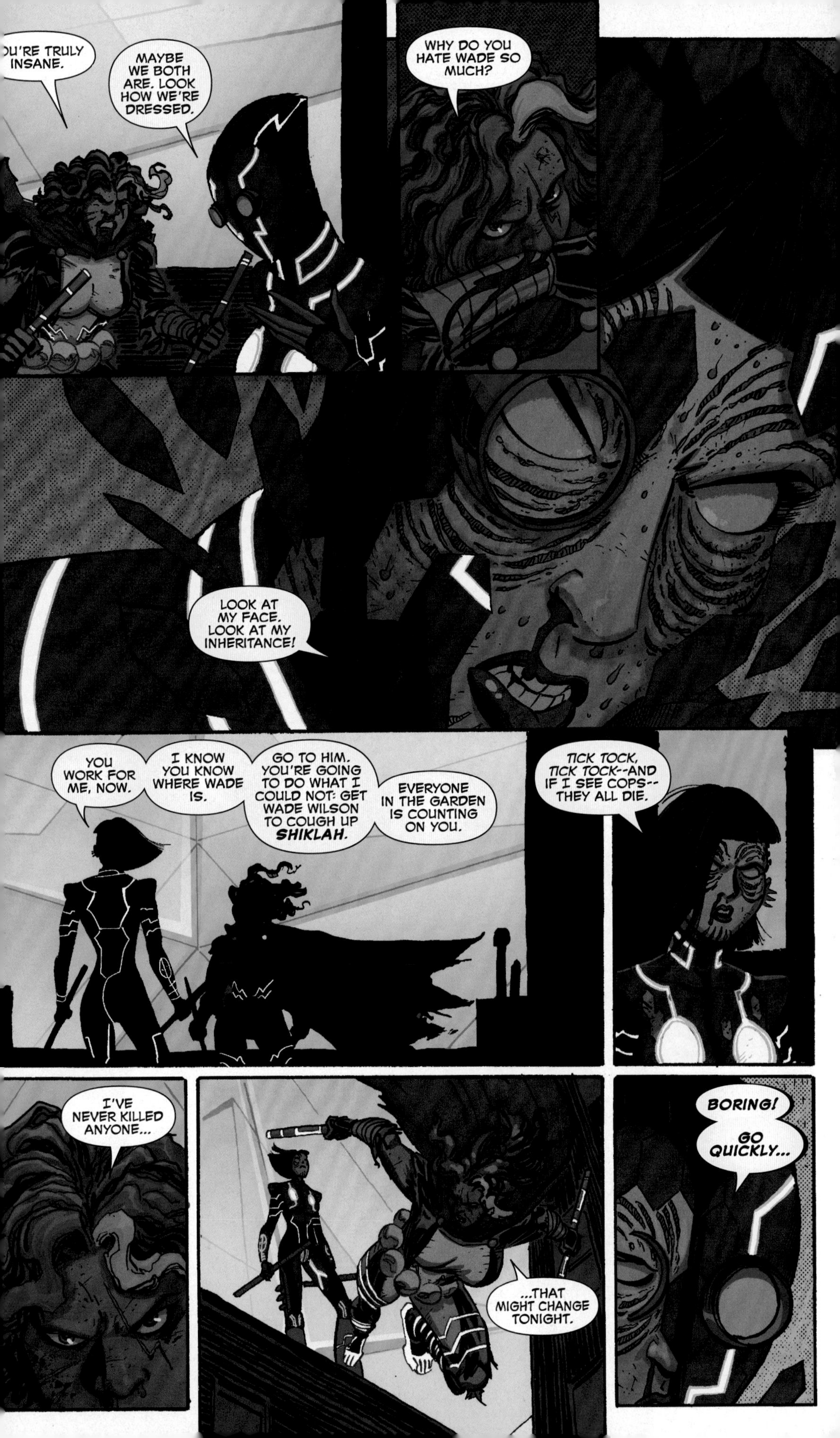
U'RE TRULY INSANE.
MAYBE WE BOTH ARE. LOOK HOW WE'RE DRESSED.
WHY DO YOU HATE WADE SO MUCH?
LOOK AT MY FACE. LOOK AT MY INHERITANCE!
YOU WORK FOR ME, NOW.
I KNOW YOU KNOW WHERE WADE IS.
GO TO HIM. YOU'RE GOING TO DO WHAT I COULD NOT: GET WADE WILSON TO COUGH UP SHIKLAH.
EVERYONE IN THE GARDEN IS COUNTING ON YOU.
TICK TOCK, TICK TOCK--AND IF I SEE COPS--THEY ALL DIE.
I'VE NEVER KILLED ANYONE...
...THAT MIGHT CHANGE TONIGHT.
BORING!
GO QUICKLY...

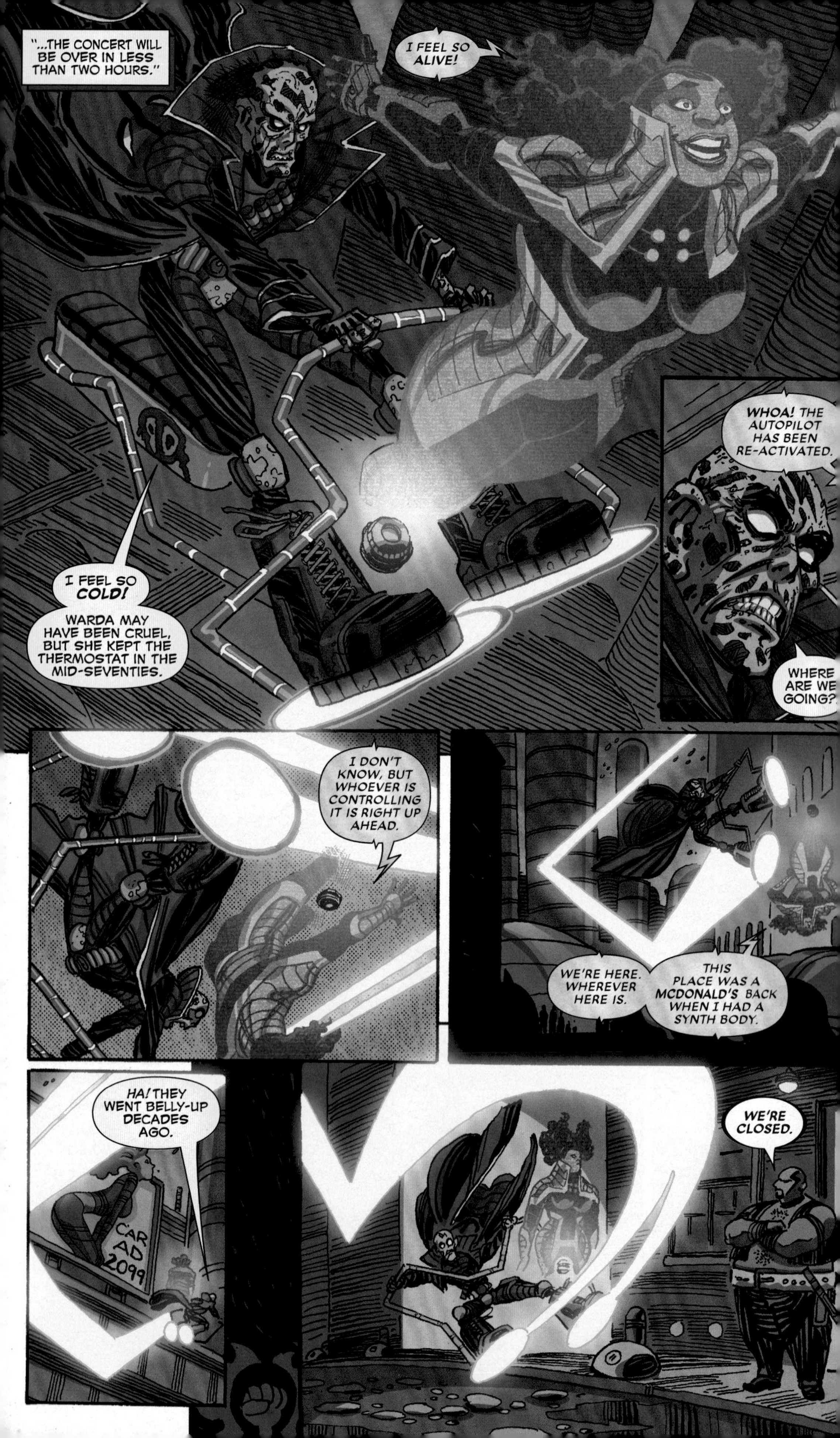
"...THE CONCERT WILL BE OVER IN LESS THAN TWO HOURS."
I FEEL SO ALIVE!
I FEEL SO COLD!
WARDA MAY HAVE BEEN CRUEL, BUT SHE KEPT THE THERMOSTAT IN THE MID-SEVENTIES.
WHOA! THE AUTOPILOT HAS BEEN RE-ACTIVATED.
WHERE ARE WE GOING?
I DON'T KNOW, BUT WHOEVER IS CONTROLLING IT IS RIGHT UP AHEAD.
WE'RE HERE. WHEREVER HERE IS.
THIS PLACE WAS A MCDONALD'S BACK WHEN I HAD A SYNTH BODY.
HA! THEY WENT BELLY-UP DECADES AGO.
CAR AD 2099
WE'RE CLOSED.

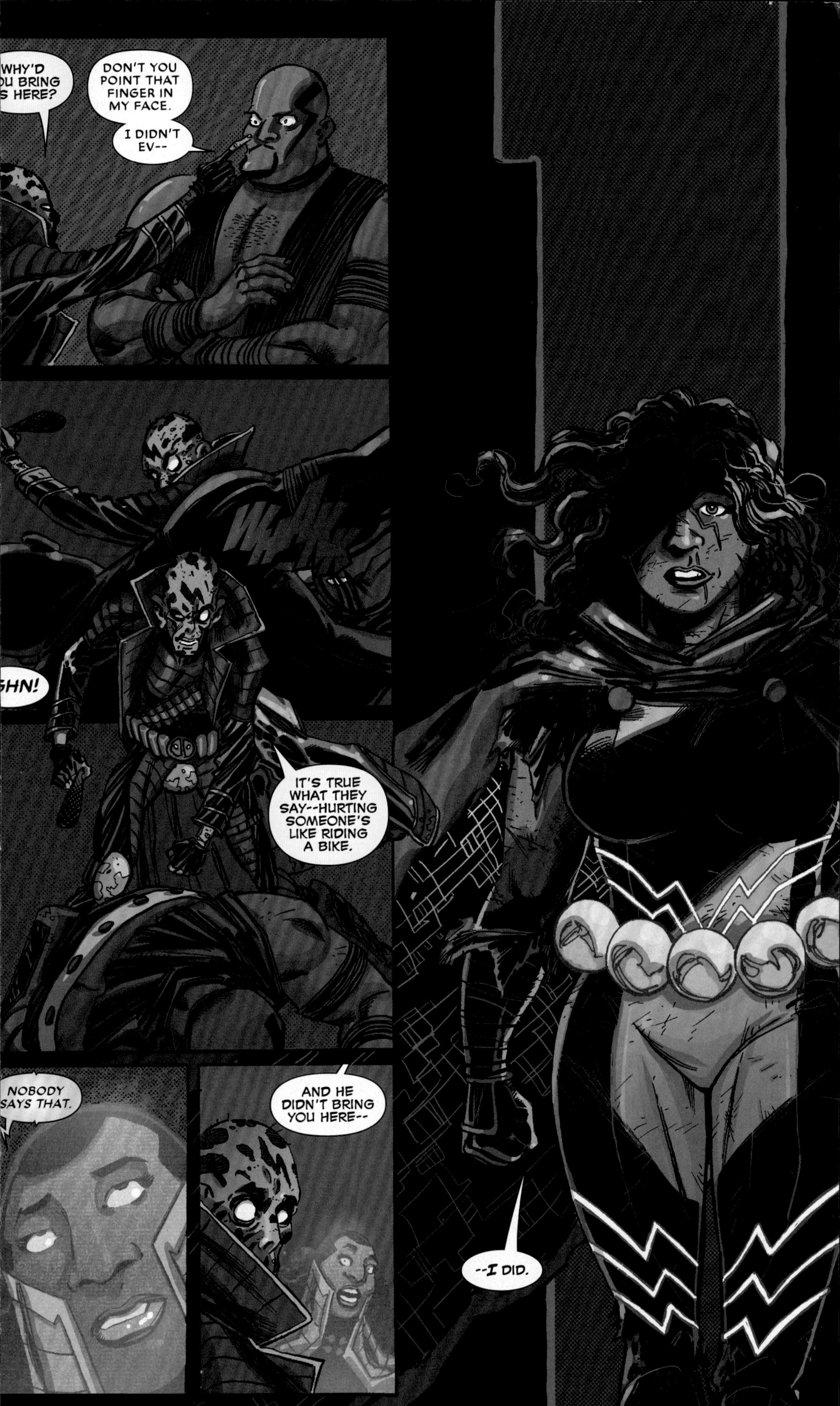
WHY'D
OU BRING
S HERE?
DON'T YOU POINT THAT FINGER IN MY FACE.
I DIDN'T EV--
GHN!
IT'S TRUE WHAT THEY SAY--HURTING SOMEONE'S LIKE RIDING A BIKE.
NOBODY
SAYS THAT.
AND HE DIDN'T BRING YOU HERE--
--I DID.

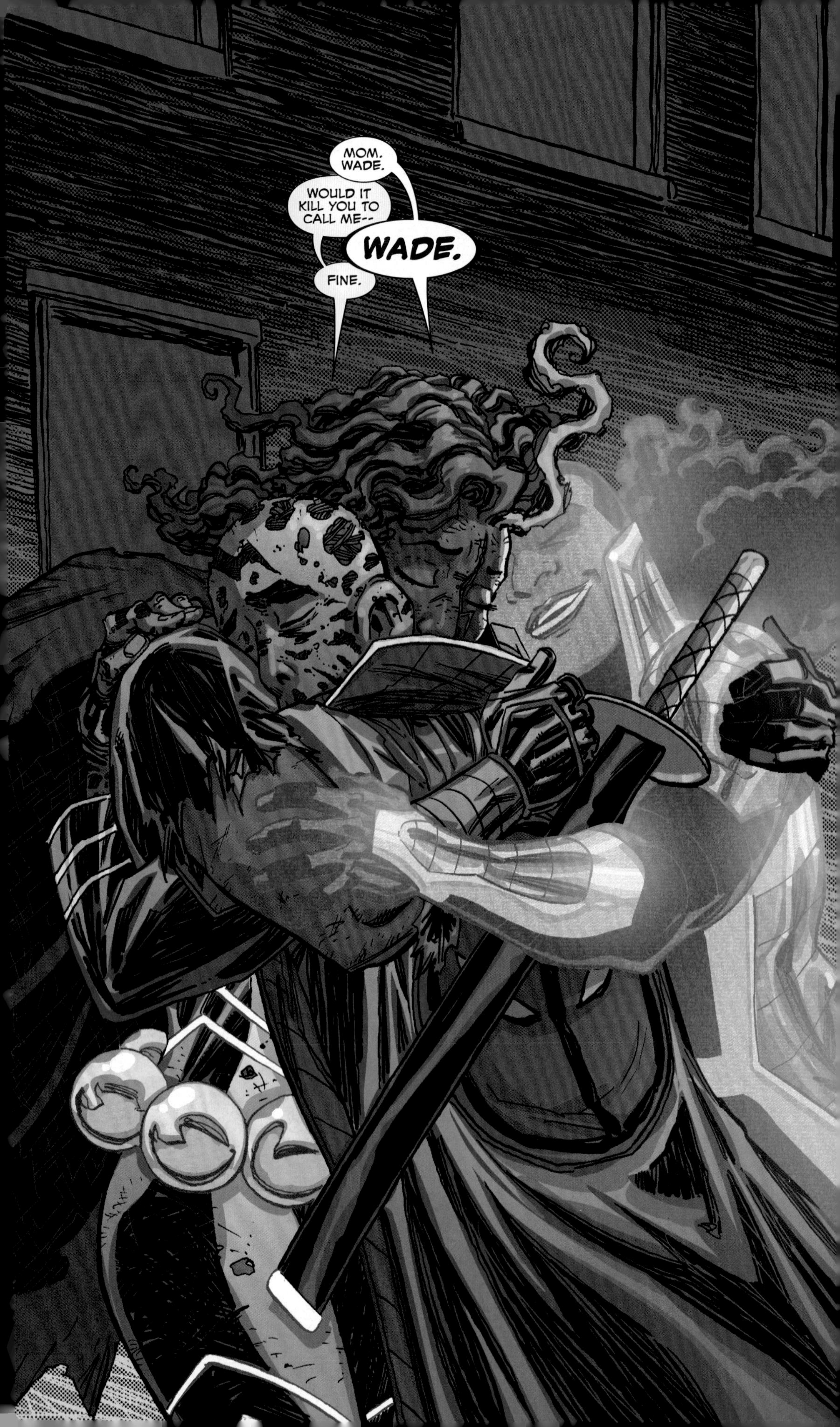
MOM. WADE.
WOULD IT KILL YOU TO CALL ME--
WADE.
FINE.

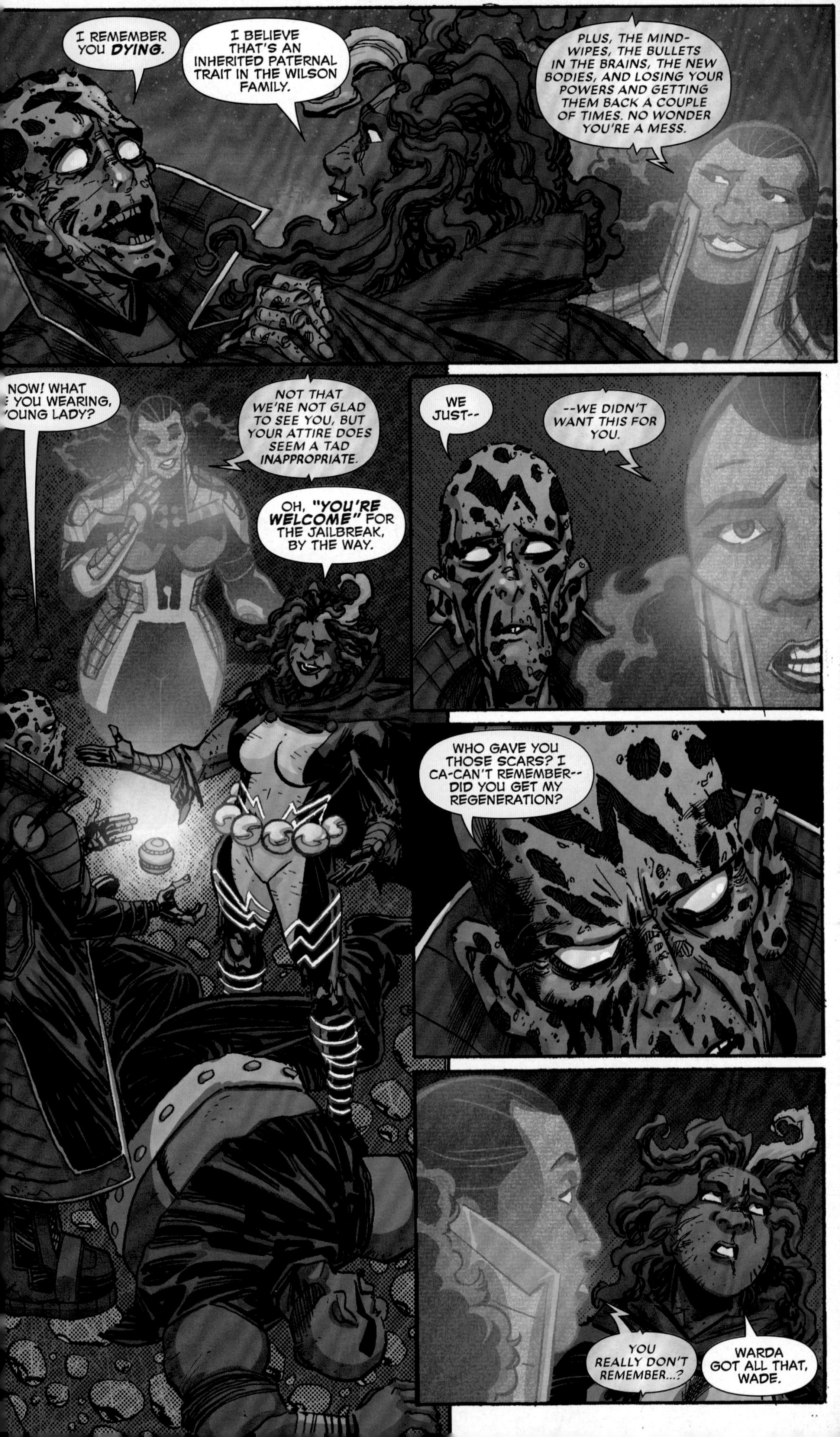

I REMEMBER YOU DYING.
I BELIEVE THAT'S AN INHERITED PATERNAL TRAIT IN THE WILSON FAMILY.
PLUS, THE MIND-WIPES, THE BULLETS IN THE BRAINS, THE NEW BODIES, AND LOSING YOUR POWERS AND GETTING THEM BACK A COUPLE OF TIMES. NO WONDER YOU'RE A MESS.
NOW! WHAT E YOU WEARING, YOUNG LADY?
NOT THAT WE'RE NOT GLAD TO SEE YOU, BUT YOUR ATTIRE DOES SEEM A TAD INAPPROPRIATE.
OH, "YOU'RE WELCOME" FOR THE JAILBREAK, BY THE WAY.
WE JUST--
--WE DIDN'T WANT THIS FOR YOU.
WHO GAVE YOU THOSE SCARS? I CA-CAN'T REMEMBER-- DID YOU GET MY REGENERATION?
YOU REALLY DON'T REMEMBER...?
WARDA GOT ALL THAT, WADE.

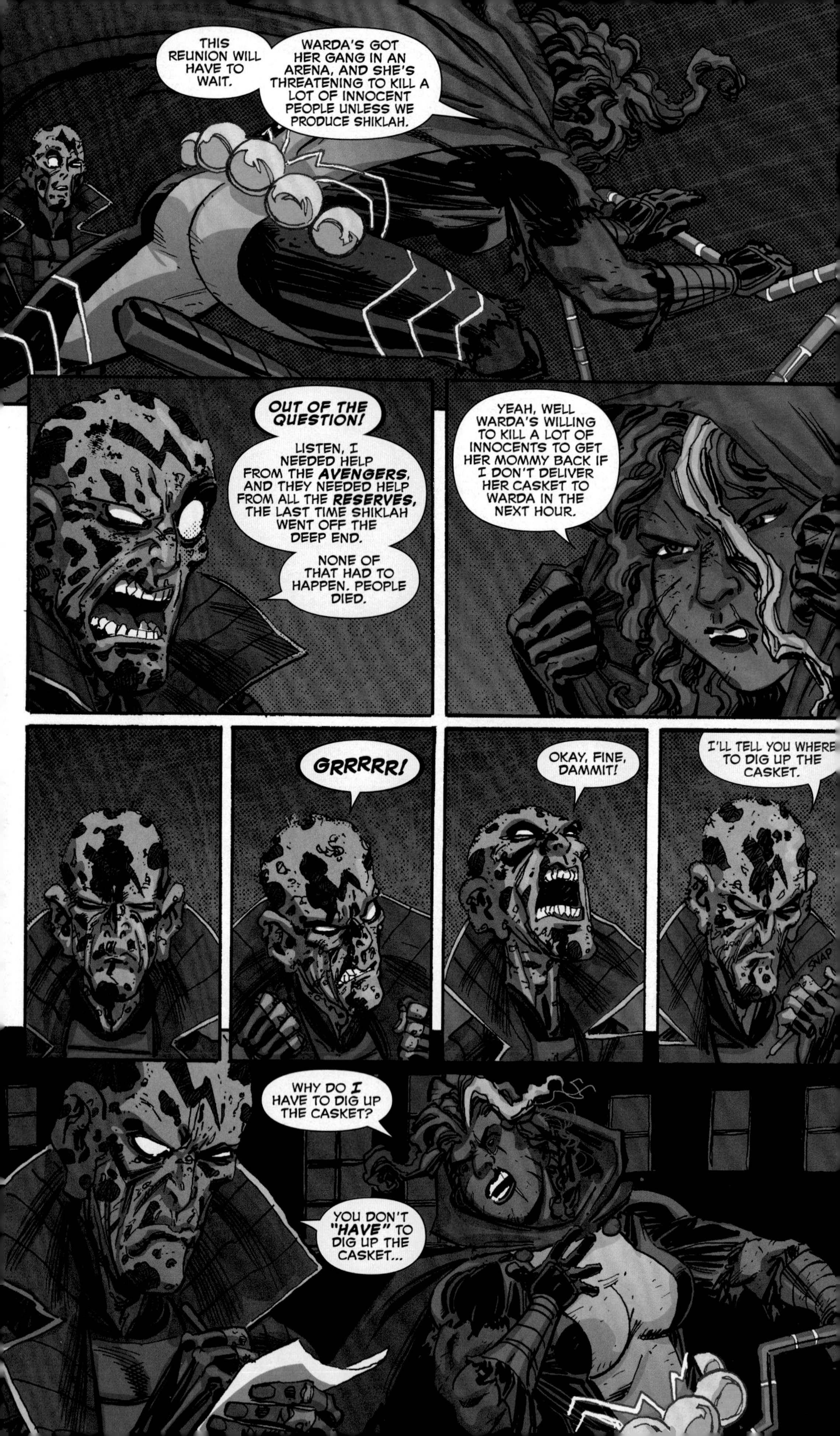
THIS REUNION WILL HAVE TO WAIT.
WARDA'S GOT HER GANG IN AN ARENA, AND SHE'S THREATENING TO KILL A LOT OF INNOCENT PEOPLE UNLESS WE PRODUCE SHIKLAH.
OUT OF THE QUESTION!
LISTEN, I NEEDED HELP FROM THE AVENGERS, AND THEY NEEDED HELP FROM ALL THE RESERVES, THE LAST TIME SHIKLAH WENT OFF THE DEEP END.
NONE OF THAT HAD TO HAPPEN. PEOPLE DIED.
YEAH, WELL WARDA'S WILLING TO KILL A LOT OF INNOCENTS TO GET HER MOMMY BACK IF I DON'T DELIVER HER CASKET TO WARDA IN THE NEXT HOUR.
GRRRRR!
OKAY, FINE, DAMMIT!
I'LL TELL YOU WHERE TO DIG UP THE CASKET.
SNAP
WHY DO I HAVE TO DIG UP THE CASKET?
YOU DON'T "HAVE" TO DIG UP THE CASKET...

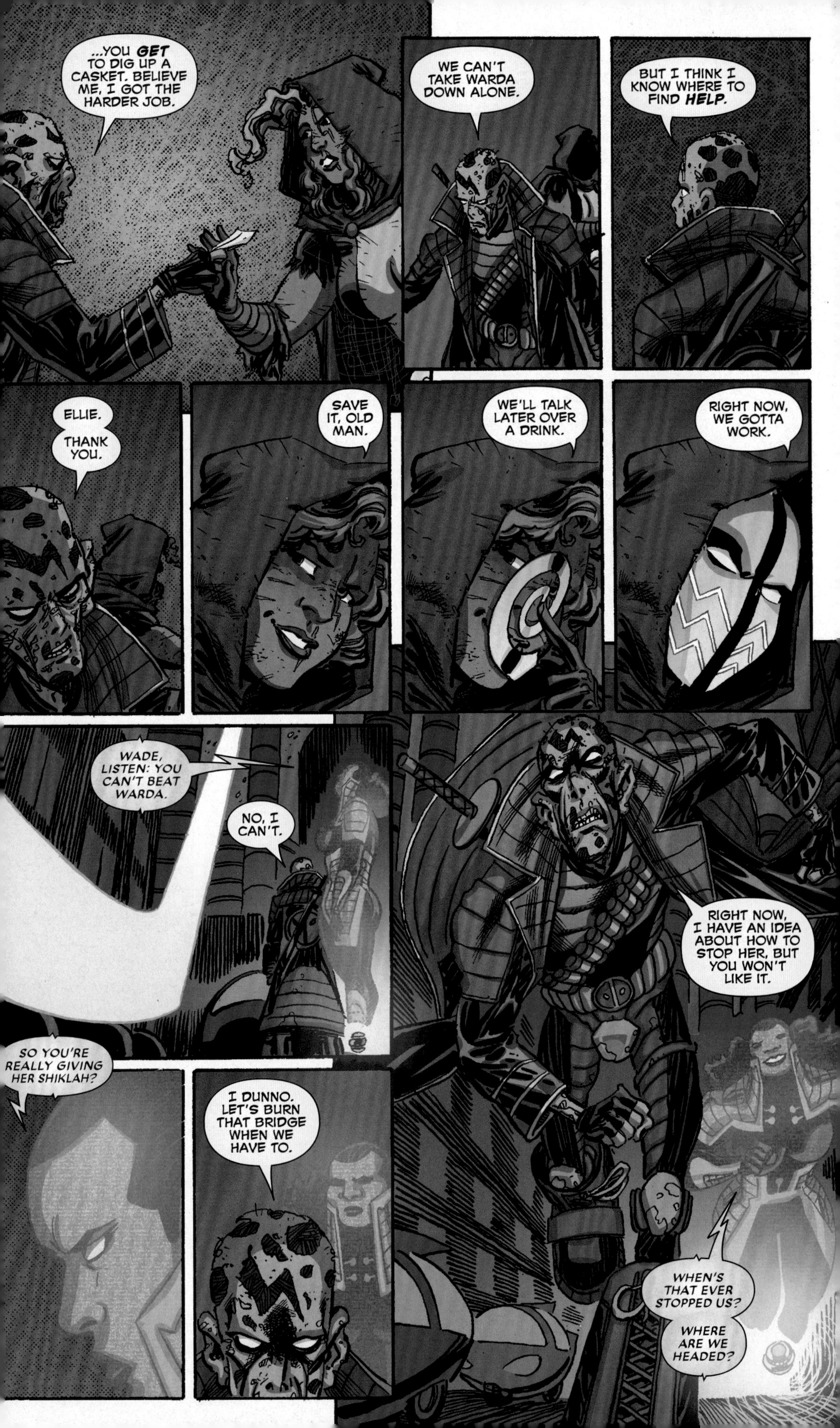
...YOU GET TO DIG UP A CASKET. BELIEVE ME, I GOT THE HARDER JOB.
WE CAN'T TAKE WARDA DOWN ALONE.
BUT I THINK I KNOW WHERE TO FIND HELP.
ELLIE.
THANK YOU.
SAVE IT, OLD MAN.
WE'LL TALK LATER OVER A DRINK.
RIGHT NOW, WE GOTTA WORK.
WADE, LISTEN: YOU CAN'T BEAT WARDA.
NO, I CAN'T.
RIGHT NOW, I HAVE AN IDEA ABOUT HOW TO STOP HER, BUT YOU WON'T LIKE IT.
SO YOU'RE REALLY GIVING HER SHIKLAH?
I DUNNO. LET'S BURN THAT BRIDGE WHEN WE HAVE TO.
WHEN'S THAT EVER STOPPED US?
WHERE ARE WE HEADED?

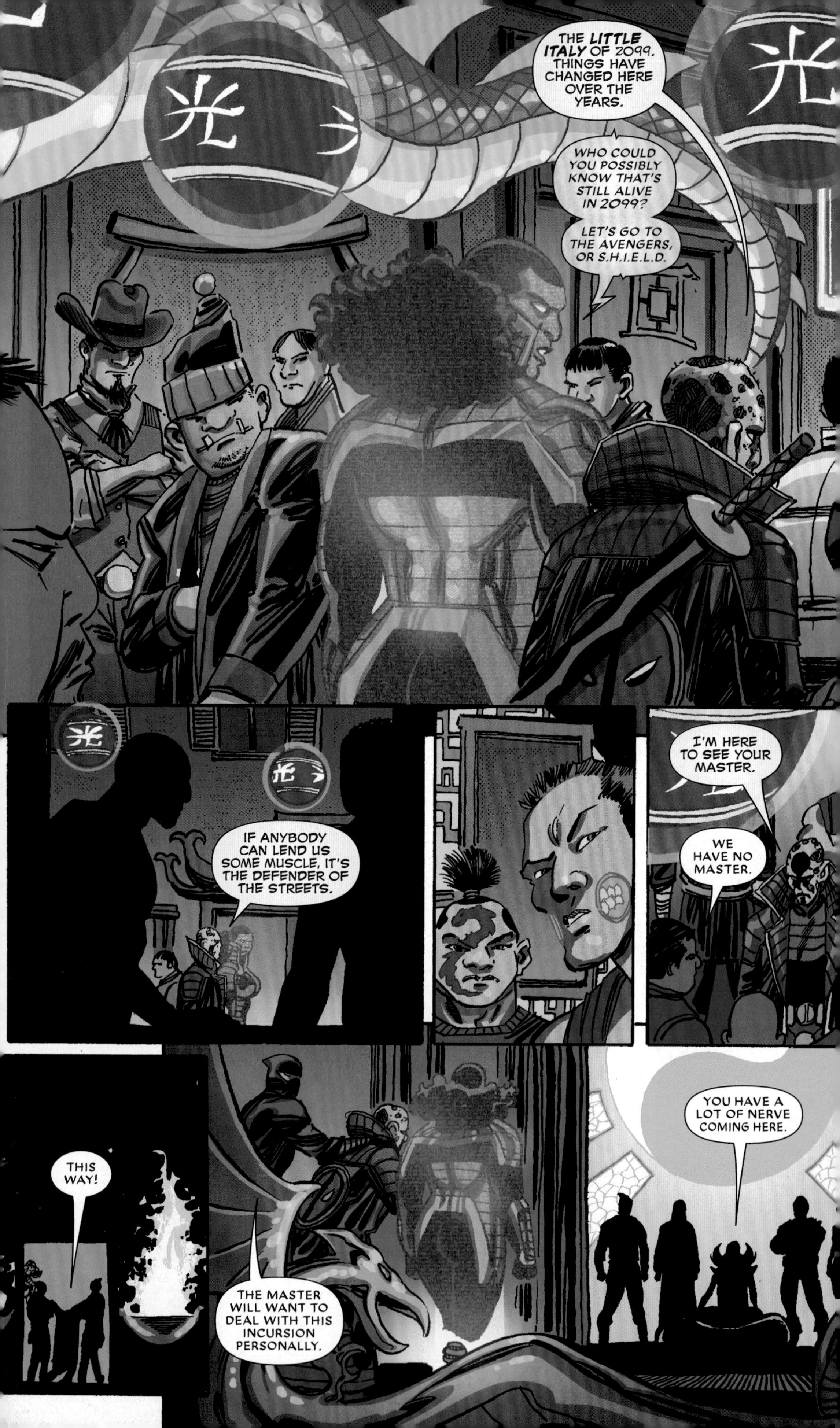
THE LITTLE ITALY OF 2099. THINGS HAVE CHANGED HERE OVER THE YEARS.
WHO COULD YOU POSSIBLY KNOW THAT'S STILL ALIVE IN 2099?
LET'S GO TO THE AVENGERS, OR S.H.I.E.L.D.
IF ANYBODY CAN LEND US SOME MUSCLE, IT'S THE DEFENDER OF THE STREETS.
I'M HERE TO SEE YOUR MASTER.
WE HAVE NO MASTER.
THIS WAY!
THE MASTER WILL WANT TO DEAL WITH THIS INCURSION PERSONALLY.
YOU HAVE A LOT OF NERVE COMING HERE.

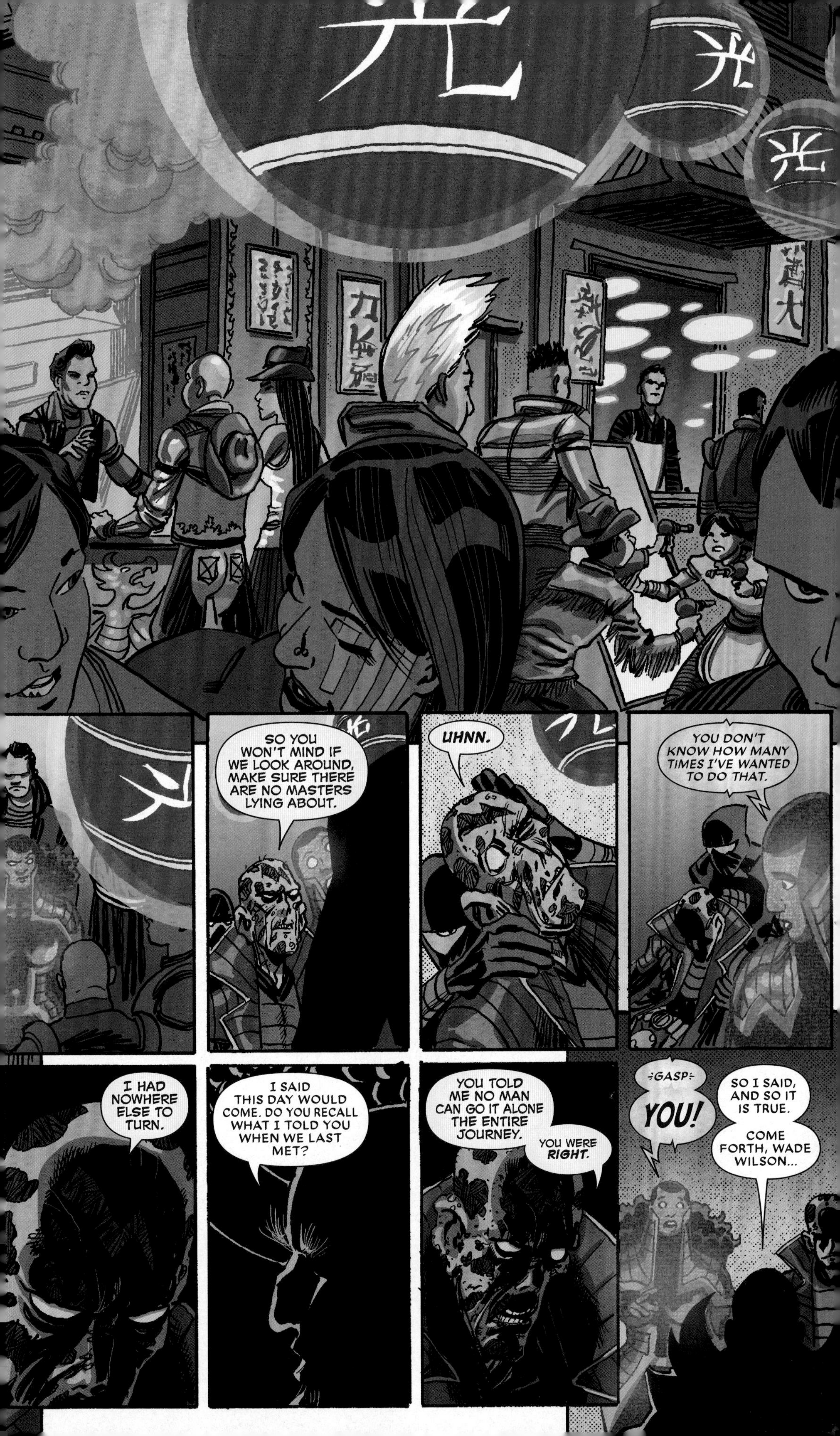

SO YOU WON'T MIND IF WE LOOK AROUND, MAKE SURE THERE ARE NO MASTERS LYING ABOUT.
UHNN.
YOU DON'T KNOW HOW MANY TIMES I'VE WANTED TO DO THAT.
I HAD NOWHERE ELSE TO TURN.
I SAID THIS DAY WOULD COME. DO YOU RECALL WHAT I TOLD YOU WHEN WE LAST MET?
YOU TOLD ME NO MAN CAN GO IT ALONE THE ENTIRE JOURNEY.
YOU WERE RIGHT.
GASP
YOU!
SO I SAID, AND SO IT IS TRUE.
COME FORTH, WADE WILSON...

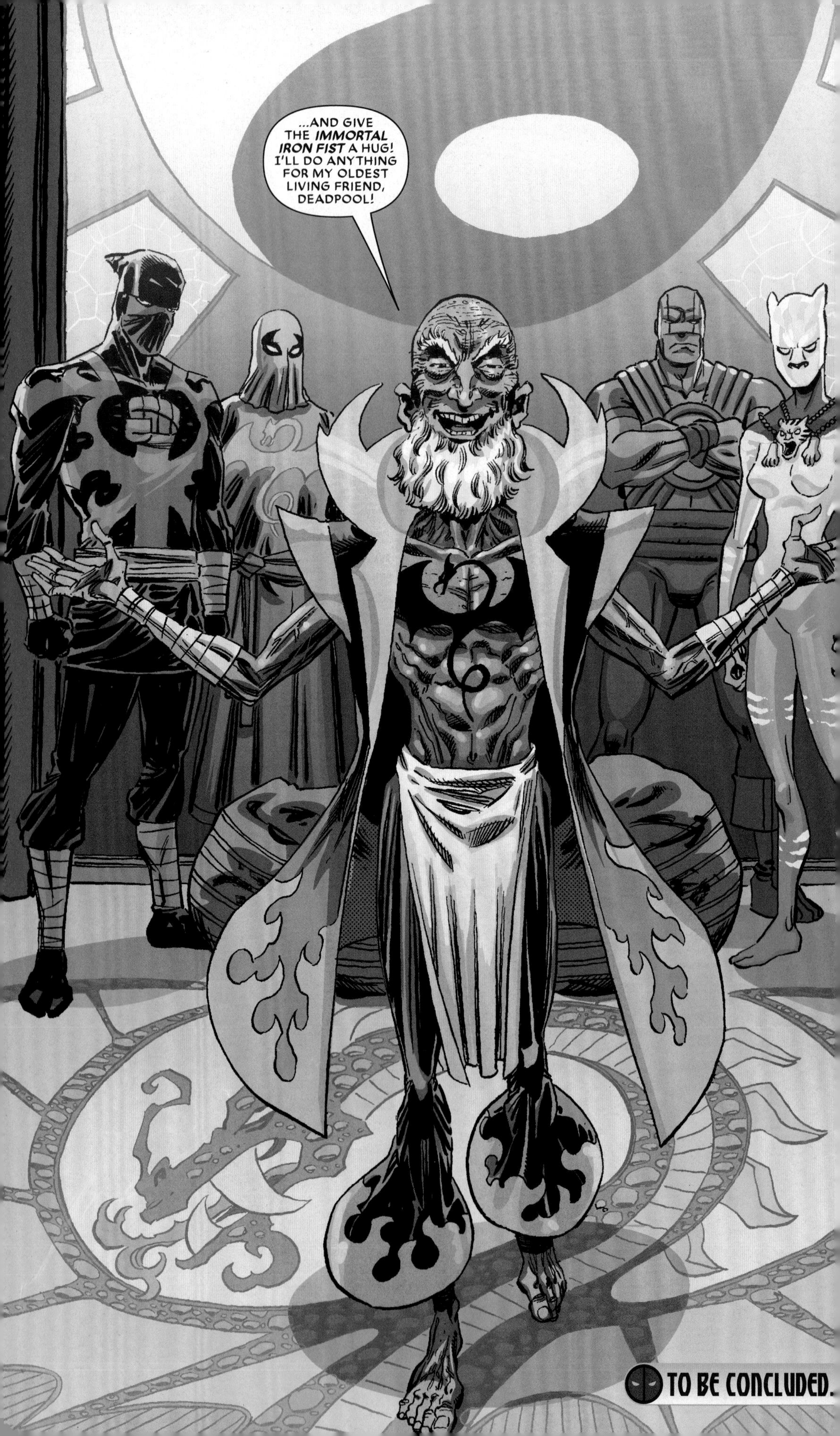
...AND GIVE THE *IMMORTAL IRON FIST* A HUG! I'LL DO ANYTHING FOR MY OLDEST LIVING FRIEND, DEADPOOL!
TO BE CONCLUDED.

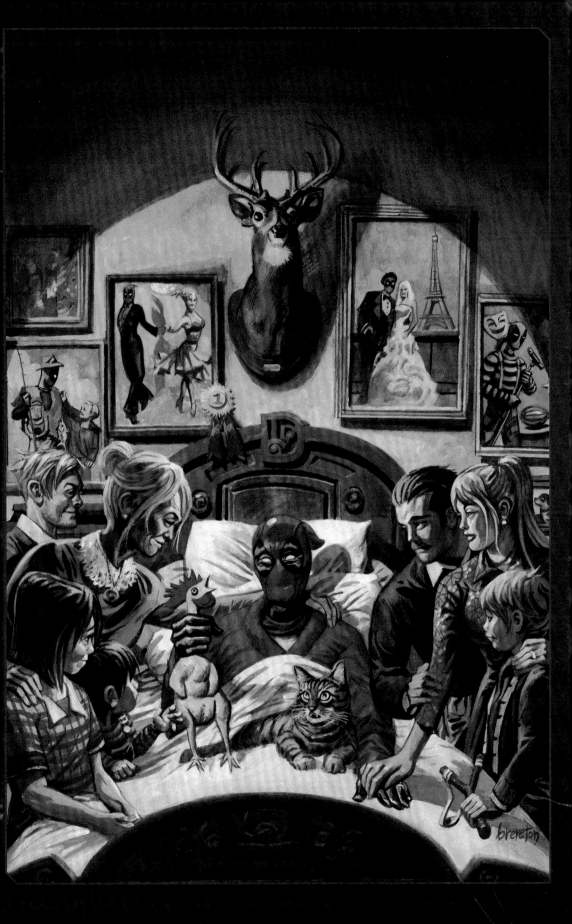

#15 Death of X variant by DAN BRERETON

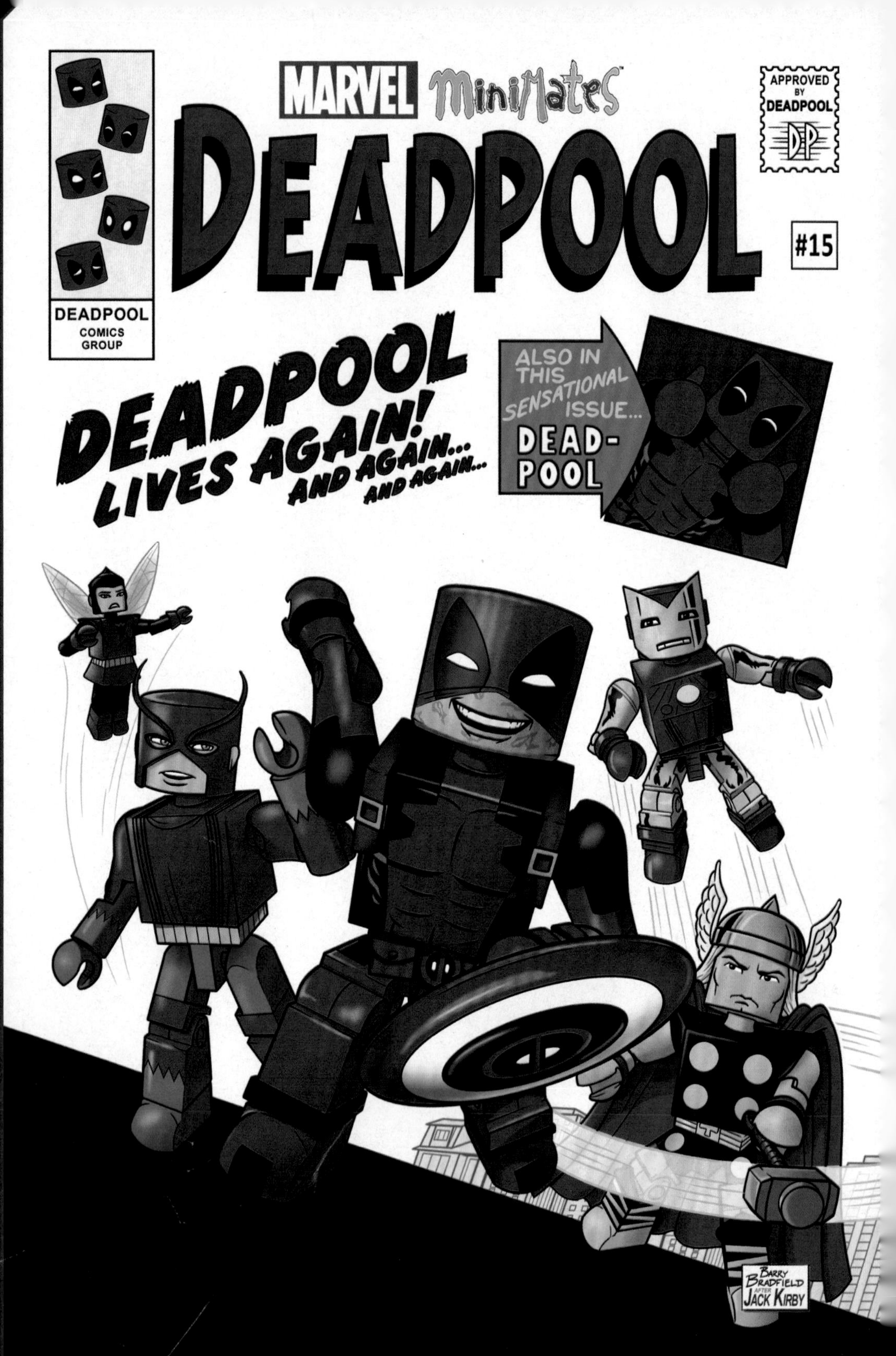
MARVEL MiniMates
DEADPOOL
APPROVED BY DEADPOOL
#15
DEADPOOL COMICS GROUP
DEADPOOL LIVES AGAIN! AND AGAIN... AND AGAIN...
ALSO IN THIS SENSATIONAL ISSUE... DEAD-POOL
BARRY BRADFIELD AFTER JACK KIRBY

#15 MiniMates variant by BARRY BRADFIELD

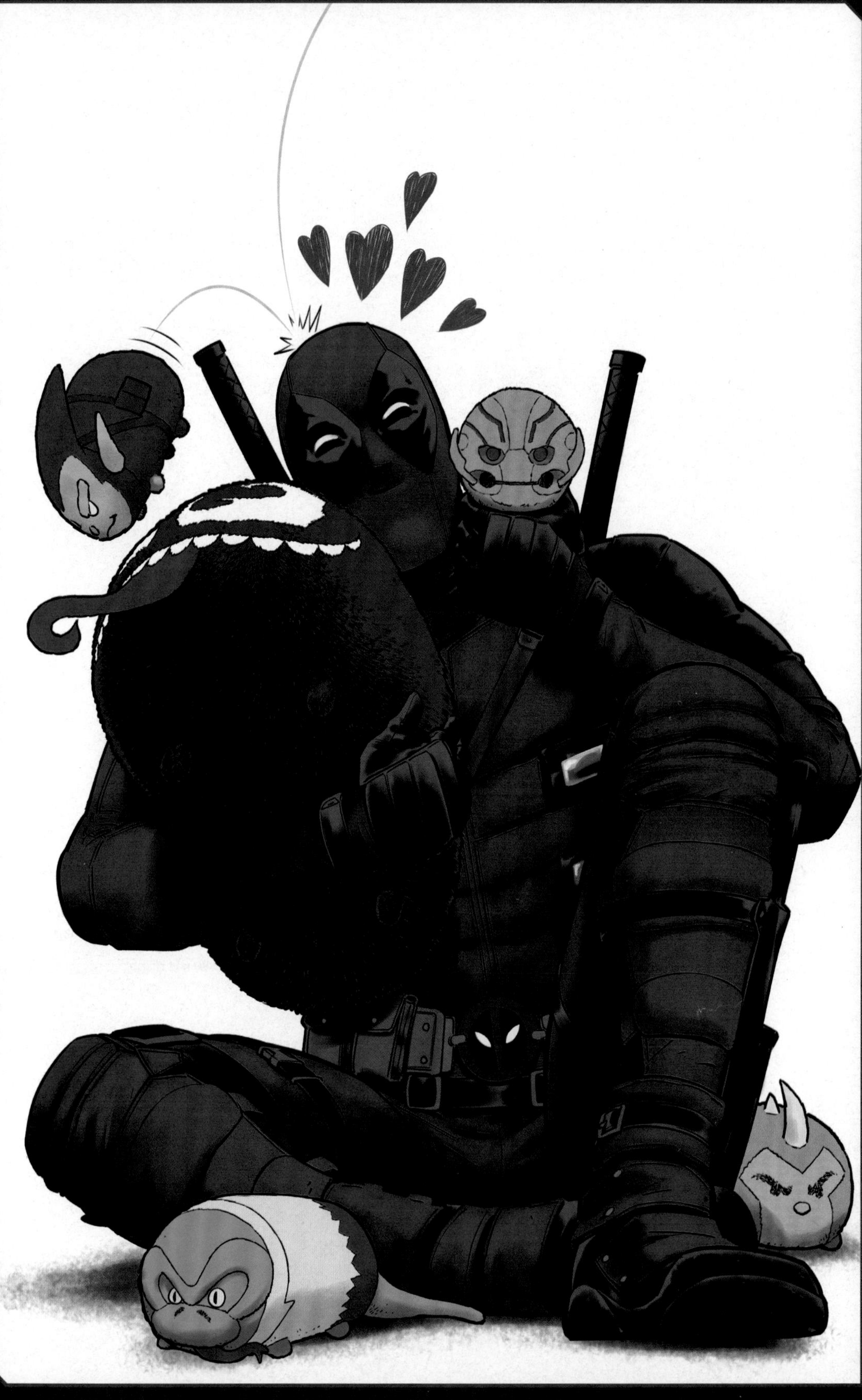

#17 Marvel Tsum Tsum Takeover variant by
JAVIER RODRIGUEZ & ALVARO LOPEZ